The Russian Pendulum

AMERICANS IN REVOLUTIONARY RUSSIA

Vol. 1
Albert Rhys Williams, *Through the Russian Revolution*,
edited by William Benton Whisenhunt (2016)

Vol. 2
Princess Julia Cantacuzène, Countess Spéransky, née Grant, *Russian People: Revolutionary Recollections*, edited by Norman E. Saul (2016)

Vol. 3
Ernest Poole, *The Village: Russian Impressions*, edited by Norman E. Saul (2017)

Vol. 4
John Reed, *Ten Days That Shook the World*,
edited by William Benton Whisenhunt (2017)

Vol. 5
Louise Bryant, *Six Red Months in Russia*, edited by Lee A. Farrow (2017)

Vol. 6
Edward Alsworth Ross, *Russia in Upheaval*, edited by Rex A. Wade (2017)

Vol. 7
Donald Thompson, *Donald Thompson in Russia*, edited by David H. Mould (2017)

Vol. 8
Arthur Bullard, *The Russian Pendulum: Autocracy—Democracy—Bolshevism*,
edited by David W. McFadden (2019)

Series General Editors: Norman E. Saul and William Benton Whisenhunt

The Russian Pendulum

Autocracy—Democracy—Bolshevism

Arthur Bullard

Edited and Introduction by
David W. McFadden

ANTHEM PRESS

Anthem Press
An imprint of Wimbledon Publishing Company
www.anthempress.com

First published by Slavica Publishers, Indiana University, USA, 2019

This edition first published in UK and USA 2026
by ANTHEM PRESS
75–76 Blackfriars Road, London SE1 8HA, UK
or PO Box 9779, London SW19 7ZG, UK
and
244 Madison Ave #116, New York, NY 10016, USA

Copyright © 2026 David W. McFadden editorial matter and selection;
individual chapters © individual contributors

The moral right of the authors has been asserted.

All rights reserved. Without limiting the rights under copyright reserved above,
no part of this publication may be reproduced, stored or introduced into
a retrieval system, or transmitted, in any form or by any means
(electronic, mechanical, photocopying, recording or otherwise),
without the prior written permission of both the copyright
owner and the above publisher of this book.

British Library Cataloguing-in-Publication Data
A catalogue record for this book is available from the British Library.

Library of Congress Cataloging-in-Publication Data
A catalog record for this book has been requested.

ISBN-13: 978-1-83999-694-8 (Hbk)
ISBN-10: 1-83999-694-3 (Hbk)

ISBN-13: 978-1-83999-695-5 (Pbk)
ISBN-10: 1-83999-695-1 (Pbk)

This title is also available as an eBook.

Contents

David W. McFadden

    Editor's Introduction ix

The Russian Pendulum

Preface 3

Book I
European Russia

I. Lenin 7

II. Workingmen—Soldiers—Poorer Peasants 12

III. War and the Old Regime 19

IV. Revolution and the Provisional Government 23

V. Zemstvo, Duma, Co-operatives 27

VI. The Soviets 32

VII. The Political Parties 39

VIII. "Land" 44

IX. "Peace" 50

X. Kerensky 55

XI. The Bolshevist Campaign 60

XII. The Question of Majority Support 63

XIII. The Bolsheviks at Work 67

XIV. "German Gold" 73

XV. Allied Diplomacy in Russia 82

XVI. Lenin's Foreign Policy 92

XVII. The Pendulum of the Revolution 98

Book II
Siberia

XVIII. The Siberian Railroads 101

XIX. The Czecho-Slovaks and the Allies 105

XX. The First Siberian Government 111

XXI. The Socialist Revolutionaries and the Directorate 114

XXII. The Cossack Conspiracy 117

XXIII. Kolchak 120

XXIV. Civil War 122

XXV. Kolchak's Regime 126

CONTENTS   vii

XXVI. Efforts to Help Russia 130

XXVII. Psychological Difficulties 135

XXVIII. Intervention 142

Book III
What's to Be Done?

XXIX. Some Elements of the Problem 146

XXX. "Hands Off" or "Stand By" 162

XXXI. Educational Cooperation 170

Index 173

Introduction
David W. McFadden

Arthur Bullard (1879–1929), the author of *The Russian Pendulum* and numerous articles and reviews, was a native of St. Joseph, Missouri and the son of Henry Bullard, a prominent Presbyterian minister. An 1899 graduate of the Blair Academy in Blairstown, New Jersey, Bullard was a student at Hamilton College in Clinton, New York. He left college after two years because of deepening concerns about the urban social crisis. Bullard immersed himself in New York City's Progressive reform community, serving as a probation officer for the New York Prison Association and a resident worker at the University Settlement House on New York's Lower East Side.

Bullard first went to Russia in 1905, at the time of the 1905 Revolution, following a brief stint as the secretary-treasurer of the Friends of Russian Freedom. Before getting to Russia, Bullard worked with William English Walling and Ernest Poole in Geneva, where he managed Walling's pro-revolution news bureau and met with prominent Russian exiles, including Lenin. Bullard next went to Moscow to report on the strike movement, and then he went to the Baltic states and the Ukraine to cover the military repression of the tsarist government. Bullard did all of his reporting under the pen name Albert Edwards, in order to avoid arrest. Numerous reports from his travels in 1905 were published in *Harper's Weekly*, *Collier's Weekly*, and other American outlets. In St. Petersburg, he joined others from the Friends of Russian Freedom, William English Walling and Ernest Poole, in forwarding the work of the Friends Bureau. From 1905 to 1907, he traveled widely in the Russian Empire and continued to write. On his return to the United States late in 1908, he began writing for the socialist daily *The New York Call* and also tried his hand at fiction, publishing two novels: *A Man's World* (1912) and *Comrade Yetta* (1913).

Bullard resumed his career as a world correspondent as World War I loomed. In 1913 he traveled to the Balkans to cover the Second Balkans War for *Outlook* magazine, returning to Europe on the outbreak of fighting in 1914. It was in 1914 that he began his most important work, as an adviser to Woodrow Wilson's chief aide, Colonel E. M. House. Bullard's analyses of the European diplomatic front were sent regularly to House. Their strong relationship, which was to last throughout Bullard's time in Russia, began at this time. Here he championed a plan for the civilian control of wartime information (in opposition to a military plan proposed by General

Douglas MacArthur), which led in 1917 to the creation of the Committee on Public Information (CPI), the official US propaganda agency. Bullard's short book *Mobilizing America* advocated a strategy of propaganda and information dissemination rather than censorship. His most notable contribution with the fledgling CPI was the compilation of documents *How the War Came to America*, of which millions were distributed.

Bullard's most important work came with the CPI in Russia. He wholeheartedly supported Wilson's prowar and pro-Russian reform policies, breaking with his former colleagues in the Socialist Party. Returning to Russia in 1917 with Ernest Poole, Bullard worked as a press aide at the American Consulate in Moscow, then became second in command when the CPI opened an office in Petrograd. He assumed the direction of CPI activities in March 1918. Bullard's efforts to mount a serious propaganda campaign to counter the German effort were at first stillborn. He was unsure how to proceed, especially in light of hostility toward Americans. Bullard recruited Malcolm Davis, a YMCA secretary, for translation. He was also full of ideas for somewhat utopian, "model" projects such as a model school, American exhibits on education and agriculture, and scholarships. But much of this was postponed since Bullard had no budget for any of it. The Russia commission headed by Root had advocated a budget of $5 million for a publicity campaign in August 1917, but this was cut back to less than $1 million, and the YMCA part of the campaign disappeared completely. By the time any money was actually available, the Bolshevik Revolution had taken place. The only really viable propaganda and publicity work was carried out by the Red Cross and YMCA missions rather than the Committee on Public Information. Bullard worked with them both, and finally developed his own publicity campaign with the help of Consul General Maddin Summers in Moscow in early 1918. The major accomplishment of this campaign was the wide distribution of Woodrow Wilson's Fourteen Points Speech in multiple copies in Moscow and St. Petersburg.

Bullard was forced by Washington to leave western Russia in 1918 lest he be taken hostage. He vigorously protested his recall but sailed from Archangel to New York on a British ship. He eventually ended up back in Russian Manchuria and then in Siberia. When the war ended, Bullard was assigned to work with Colonel House at the Peace Conference in Paris, but he fell seriously ill and never made it to the conference. Bullard wrote *The Russian Pendulum* in 1919 while convalescing from a bout of mastoiditis that nearly took his life. Toward the end of the Wilson administration, Bullard was appointed head of the Russian Division of the State Department, but he resigned upon the inauguration of Harding as president in 1921.

Following his resignation from government service, Bullard resumed his writing, editing a short-lived magazine, *Our World*, which was devoted to international affairs. His last international service was in 1925, when he went to Geneva to represent the American League of Nations Association.

Bullard's papers can be found in the Princeton University Library. They consist of the manuscripts of several of Bullard's novels and many files of miscellaneous writings in the form of articles, essays, and correspondence. Much of the collection focuses on Russia, but other papers include materials on disarmament, Anglo-American relations, the League of Nations, trade, economics, and World War I.

The Russian Pendulum is organized topically but also chronologically. It begins with the Old Regime and the February Revolution, and takes the story of European Russia through to Bolshevik control, the Civil War, and Lenin's government. It then continues with a section on Siberia and closes with its most provocative section, "What's To Be Done?"

In the preface, Bullard lays out one of his most important premises that "in the end we must judge Russian affairs by events in Russia."

Bullard begins with an analysis of Lenin, arguing that Lenin took his politics and ideology from a combination of Marx, Blanqui, and Nietzsche. He then goes on to assert that Lenin's ideas flourished in Russia because of the "slave mentality" of the Russian people. Bullard is on firmer ground, however, when he claims that factory workers, soldiers, and poor peasants were the most receptive to the Bolshevik message.

In his next chapter, Bullard goes on to argue that the only hope for a positive, i.e., democratic outcome to the revolution is to be found in the zemstvos and cooperative societies, which he believed would come to the fore ta some future stage of the revolution. He is skeptical about the soviets as an institution. While accurately portraying their development, he believes that the Bolshevik takeover of the soviets emasculated them as a potential democratic institution.

The Russian Pendulum devotes subsequent chapters to the land and peace questions, arguing that they exceed all others in importance. With regard to the land question, Bullard believed that Bolshevik encouragement of peasant land seizures was at least partially responsible for the Bolsheviks' victory. Equally important was the issue of peace. As Bullard put it, "everyone wanted peace," and it was the failure of the Provisional Government and the Allies to the revise the terms for peace that was largely responsible for their defeat. Bullard argued that "we who were in Russia representing in one capacity or another, the allied governments, waited in desperate impatience for the answer of our governments to this appeal of revolutionary Russia," and that it was Kerensky's failure to meet the demands for land and peace that was responsible for his fall.

This brings us to an analysis of the Bolshevik success. They organized around the land and peace issues, and aligned their slogans with the majority of Russians, who were in favor of the peasants taking the land, and the government advocating for an immediate peace. Thus although the Bolsheviks only briefly had the majority of support, they always had a majority of people in favor of their approach to the land and peace questions.

The next chapter in *The Russian Pendulum* is devoted to "The Bolsheviki at Work," but Bullard admits (as well he should in 1919) that "the material for such a study is not at hand. Nevertheless, he analyzes Bolshevik decrees without any evidence concerning their practical application.

More concrete is Bullard's analysis of the question of "German Gold." While insisting that there is "overwhelming" evidence that Bolshevik leaders, including Lenin, accepted German gold and help in advancing the revolution, Bullard also notes, quite rightly, that while Lenin probably made promises to Germany, he never meant to keep them. Bullard was skeptical from the beginning concerning the "Sisson Papers," which turned out to be very skillful forgeries.

Bullard's discussion of the situation in Siberia is based on his own involvement there, as well as on an analysis as of late 1918, when he left the country. This discussion is by far the weakest part of his book. He rightly points to the importance of the railroads for the political and economic health of the region, and he also criticizes the various regimes that had attempted to assert their control over various parts of the vast Siberian area region: Horvath, Vologodsky, the Omsk Government, and various local groups, including those in Irkutsk and Vladivostok. He also spends some time dissecting the failures of the Kolchak regime. Overall, his analysis agrees with most historians in pointing to the extreme conflict among all the contending parties, and the contribution of this conflict to the eventual success of the Bolsheviks.

The last part of *The Russian Pendulum* is in many ways the strongest, and certainly the most thought-provoking. Book III is entitled "What Is to Be Done?" Here, Bullard first takes pains to analyze "some elements of the problem," focusing on the need for those concerned with Russia to highlight all aspects of the current situation, not just the debate between "Hands off Russia" and "Stand by Russia." He argues that we should take pains to seek information on all sides of the conflict, and to accept the fact that an irreversivle "agrarian revolution" has occurred and that local political participation must be advanced if the revolution is to become democratic and lasting. He also cogently urges any Russian government to stress public education and commerce as the surest means of regenerating Russia. As for the debate between "hands off" and "stand by," Bullard argues that this is to some extent a false dichotomy, but that the United States should not abandon Russia but rather be involved with Russia as that nation moves on into a revolutionary future. Key to this involvement, according to Bullard, should be US assistance for the regeneration of local bodies of self-government, including the zemstvos and town councils.

Bullard ends *The Russian Pendulum* with a perhaps surprising plea for educational cooperation, arguing that "the greatest need of her [Russia's] people is for increased opportunities for education and these we can furnish free from all partisan bias." His final words constitute a wide-ranging case: "If we wish for friendly relations with the New Russia, if we wish to popularize our ideals of government there, there is no better means than the encouragement of Russian students in our institutions of learning. In no way could we do more 'to help Russia' than by the establishment of a great scholarship endowment which would attract Russian students to America to complete their technical training ... no money could be better spent."

The heart of Bullard's study is his analysis of Allied diplomacy and, most importantly, the question of the Allied governments' attitude toward the Bolshevik regime. Was it possible to keep Russia in the war, and was it possible to establish some sort of contact, de facto, between the US and the other Allies, and the Bolsehvik government?

Here it is very useful to remember that in George F. Kennan's evaluation, Bullard was "the best American mind observing on the spot the course of the Russian Revolution."[1] Bullard reported directly to Colonel House, ignoring State Department channels. Bullard's advice to House remained remarkably consistent, from the Bolshevik Revolution to his departure from Bolshevik territory in the spring of 1918: open up contact with all elements, including the Bolsheviks, promote American interests and democratic values, and do not cut the United States off from opportunities. This was essentially the advice that House wanted to hear. As Ernest Foole was to remark later, "He (Bullard) felt strongly that the work of his group should be strictly confined to the friendly publicity campaign. He was at all times strongly against taking part in any activities against the Soviet Government."[2]

In Bullard's initial 20-page missive to House on December 12, 1917, he argued strongly that informal contact with the Bolsheviks was essential to keeping open the possibility of influencing their conduct in negotiations with Germany and keeping Compub activities in Russia alive.[3] A few days earlier, in a letter to George Creel, Bullard gave his strong support to Raymond Robins, who was key in all the unofficial contacts and discussions between the Americans and the Bolsheviks:

> I suppose that you know Raymond Robins personally. I did not till I met him here... From what I see of him here, I judge that when he fights, he does it so wholeheartedly that his opponents do not quickly forget it. And I do not suppose that there is any great cordiality towards him in the camp of the Administration. But whether or not he has been on the right side before, he has been and is on the right side here. Of all the officials of our Government, whose trail I have encountered here, he has been the most important, the most intelligent, the most single-minded in his patriotism and the most sympathetic to democracy—in short, the best American. In those qualities he has been not only pre-eminent but—unfortunately—almost unique.... He

---

[1] George F. Kennan, *Russia Leaves the War* (New York: W. W. Norton, 1958), 49.

[2] Ernest Poole memorandum, Arthur Bullard Papers, Princeton University, B-1.

[3] Bullard to House, December 12, 1917, Edward M. House Papers, Yale, B-21.

has done more than any other individual here to win a little respect and trust for our country.[4]

In his January memo on the Bolshevik movement in Russia, Bullard argued that the United States needed to maintain openness and communication with the Bolshevik movement despite dislike for it and opposition to its aims and methods.

As late as March 1918, although Bullard disagreed with Raymond Robins on the question of material aid to the Bolsheviks, he still argued for contact, and cautioned against intervention.

Suggested Additional Reading

Debo, Richard K. *Revolution and Survival: The Foreign Policy of Soviet Russia, 1917–1918.* Liverpool: University of Liverpool Press, 1979.

———. *Survival and Consolidation: The Foreign Policy of Soviet Russia, 1918–1921.* Montreal: McGill-Queens University Press, 1992.

Fike, Claude E. "The Influence of the Creel Committee and the American Red Cross on Russian-American Relations, 1917–1919." *Journal of Modern History* 31, 2 (June 1959): 93–109.

Filene, Peter G. *Americans and the Soviet Experiment, 1917–1933.* Cambridge, MA: Harvard University Press, 1967.

Foglesong, David S. *America's Secret War Against Bolshevism: U.S. Intervention in the Russian Civil War, 1917–1920.* Chapel Hill: University of North Carolina Press, 1995.

Kennan, George F. *Russia Leaves the War: Soviet-American Relations, 1917–1920*, vol. 1. New York: W. W. Norton, 1958.

———. *The Decision to Intervene: Soviet American Relations, 1917–1920*, vol. 2. New York: W. W. Norton, 1962.

———. "The Sisson Documents." *Journal of Modern History* 28, 2 (June 1956): 130–54.

Lasch, Christopher. *The American Liberals and the Russian Revolution.* New York: Columbia University Press, 1962.

McFadden, David W. *Alternative Paths: Soviets and Americans, 1917–1920.* New York: Oxford University Press, 1993.

Saul, Norman E. *War and Revolution: The United States and Russia, 1914–1921.* Lawrence: University of Kansas Press, 2001.

---

[4] Arthur Bullard to George Creel, December 9, 1917, Arthur Bullard Papers, B-14.

THE RUSSIAN PENDULUM

AUTOCRACY—DEMOCRACY—BOLSHEVISM

BY
ARTHUR BULLARD
AUTHOR OF "THE DIPLOMACY OF THE GREAT WAR," ETC.

New York
THE MACMILLAN COMPANY
1919

All rights reserved

This book is dedicated to the members of the Russian division of the Committee on Public Information, with whom, under circumstances generally trying, sometimes disheartening, occasionally dangerous, but always vividly interesting, it was my privilege to work.

Preface

There is some subtle mystery about Russia which makes discussion of its affairs passionately bitter. We are able to disagree about France or Fiume without losing our temper. But difference of opinion about Russia distills a peculiar venom.

This was very noticeable to me over there. Disagreements were all passionate and personal. I attributed it to nearness to the problems and perhaps to some infectiousness in the excessive partisanship which the Russians bring to their political controversies. But since I have returned to America I find it just as noticeable here. The subject of Russia turns dinner-table discussions into brawls, turns old friendships into feuds.

Perhaps this only points to the vitality and tremendous importance of the Revolution. We cannot ignore so stupendous an event. We must take sides.

In listening to this very heated discussion, I am impressed and surprised to find so many liberal-minded persons, who are always on the side of democratic progress at home, taking up arms for the Bolsheviks. In Russia, all those who have devoted their lives to the development of democratic liberties are under the ban. They are apparently more feared and hated, certainly more ruthlessly persecuted, by the Bolsheviks than the supporters of the Old Régime.

This sympathy for Leninism is partly explained by simple misinformation, such as the play on words which translates "Bolshevism" as "the rule of the majority." Some of it is traceable to a naïve belief that Bolshevist politicians always mean exactly what it suits their convenience to say.

In a paper which always boasts of its liberalism and its well-informed correspondence, I read the other day an attack on Mr. Wilson for his "surrender to Secret Diplomacy." Why, the writer demanded, did he not insist on allowing newspaper men to attend all the Conferences "the way Trotsky did at Brest-Litovsk?" Now, anyone is quite free to regret that the President had only such moderate success in his fight for "open covenants, openly arrived at." But to anyone who was in Russia at the time of the Brest negotiations, the comparison with Trotsky was absurd. No Russian newspaper men were allowed anywhere near Brest-Litovsk. And there has been nothing in any of the countries, which are party to the Paris Conference, which can be compared to the grim rigor with which the Bolsheviks suppressed any newspaper discussion of their negotiations with the Germans. Presumably this writer, who compared the President so contemptuously to the Russian Foreign Minister, had read some speech of Trotsky's in favor of Open Diplomacy and had jumped rashly to the conclusion that he meant what he said.

It is rather amusing to hear those who protest so vehemently against our war measures which have limited free speech hold up Bolshevist Russia in comparison. When they were still in the Oppositions, the orators of the Bolsheviks made some wonderfully eloquent pleas for absolute freedom of speech and press, some of the best contributions to the literature of the subject I have ever read. But unfortunately they did not convince themselves by their own eloquence. When they won to power they changed their minds. Their methods of suppressing hostile criticism, even the mildest, make the authors and administrators of our Espionage Law seem either very timid or very tolerant.

But liberal opinion in America has been swung to sympathy with the Bolsheviks, not so much by any conception or misconception of what has been happening in Russia, as by consideration of our home politics. Senator X, who has distinguished himself by a long career of Toryism, denounces the Russians for their unholy attack on the Sacred Institution of Private Property. Ex-President Y, the apostle of strong arm methods in teaching the workingman his place, says that Bolshevism is a menace to the home. And Editor Z, who announces his intentions to stem the unthinking drift towards radical innovation, writes that "Lenin" and "Trotsky" are mere aliases—a common usage among criminals. And all the good people who are accustomed to finding their hopes of progress blocked by Messrs. X, Y, and Z immediately rally to the defense of the Bolsheviks. They do not care much what Bolshevism is. So long as their *bête-noirs* in American politics fear it, it must be good.

But however amusing it may be to these Liberals to frighten their enemies at home—Utopian defenders of things-as-they-were—by claiming to support Bolshevism, in the end we must judge Russian affairs by events in Russia.

No one knows the whole truth about these events. Those of us who happened to be in Russia saw only a few out of the myriad incidents of the titanic upheaval; we noted, and can report, only the things which seemed to us significant.

So for the reader of books about Russia it is of first importance to know what phases of the Revolution the writer could have seen. Then each reader must judge for himself from the text whether the "reporter" made a good use of his opportunities for observation and whether his "report" rings true.

After having been for some time the Secretary of the Society of Friends of Russian Freedom,[1] which brought me into close touch with many Russians prominent in the Liberal and Revolutionary Movement, I went in midsummer, 1905, to Switzerland, the center where many of the "political exiles" gathered. There I heard interminable discussions of Russian politics and made many close and enduring friendships among those who were at war with the Tsar, the most devoted crusaders for liberty it has ever been my good fortune to meet.

---

[1] The American Friends of Russian Freedom was a society founded in 1905 by American liberals, which supported the end of the tsarist autocracy and the establishment of a republic in Russia.

In October 1905 I went to St. Petersburg, and for the next three years travelled extensively in European Russia, visiting almost every large city and passing many weeks in various peasant communities. Circumstances then took me elsewhere, but my interest in Russia continued, as also my contact and correspondence with Russian friends.

Shortly after we entered the war, I returned to Russia, and was put in charge of the American propaganda work of the Committee on Public Information. I reached Petrograd on July 14, 1917, and in June 1918 sailed for home from Arkhangel and was at once sent out to Siberia to organize the work of the Committee there. I was kept in Vladivostok until after the Armistice was signed.

While this work kept me close to a desk in the larger cities, it brought me into unusually broad contact with Russian public opinion. We were clipping newspapers from all quarters, corresponding with every editor we could hear of. Every mail brought in letters by the score. Our office was a rendezvous for newspaper men from every province and of every political faction. Men from our organization, Americans and Russians, were travelling all the time and sending in reports. Our staff of translators represented all shades of political opinions. Several of them had been trained in the Foreign Office and had "gone on strike," rather than work under the Bolsheviks. We had one *ci-devant* princess, under an assumed name, folding pamphlets in our mailing room. One of our office boys was an ex-officer and monarchist. A mechanic in our motion picture laboratory had been a Bolshevist Commissaire. Our proof reader was an Anarchist. As varied an assortment of information came to my desk as could well be imagined. My work also threw me into touch with a succession of Russian officials and members of our own and friendly diplomatic missions.

My "report" on Russia follows the sequence of my experience there. The first nine chapters are based on the observations and impressions of my earlier visits to Russia and give the background for the narrative of events which I could watch after my arrival in Petrograd in the mid-summer of 1917—the fall of Kerensky and the rise of Lenin.

Book II deals with Siberia. Although closely interwoven with events in European Russia the political development of Siberia has been quite distinct.

In Book III, I have tried to throw some light on the question, so often asked, "What can we do to help Russia?"

I cannot attempt to list even the bare names of those whose information and advice has been of aid to me in this work. But I wish to mention especially my indebtedness to Maddin Summers, formerly our Consul General at Moscow,[2] whose

---

[2] Maddin Summers, US consul general in Moscow, served from 1917 until his death in 1919. He was largely responsible for contacts between the US government and the Bolsheviks from 1918 to 1919, holding numerous conversations with Foreign Minister George Chicherin. See David W. McFadden, *Alternative Paths* (New York: Oxford University Press), 125–52.

untimely death due, more than in any case I have every known of, to overwork, robbed our Consular Service of one of its ablest members and me of a valued friend.

Sugar Hill
July, 1919

Book I
European Russia

Chapter I
Lenin

My first acquaintance with Lenin dates back to the summer of 1905. I had gone to Switzerland as a journalist to try to understand the Revolutionary Movement which Father Gapon[1] had suddenly called to the attention of the Western World. Lenin was only one and far from the most impressive of the political exiles I met there.

I saw him several times in St. Petersburg during the "Forty Days of Freedom" which followed the great general strike of October of that year. And after the collapse of that revolutionary outburst, when he was again an exile, I had another long discussion with him.

Having known him in days of adversity, it was doubly surprising to watch him rise to power in 1917 and 1918. He is not an impassioned orator. Even in private conversation he talks in a monotone. He is short, rather fat, bald-headed, and unimpressive. He has none of the ordinary marks of a popular leader. He has always seemed to me the very opposite of magnetic—dreary.

Yet few leaders have ever dominated the thought of their followers as he does. Of course, the great majority of those who have called themselves Bolsheviks have never heard him speak, read his writings, nor understood his theories. But the "leaders" of the movement, the men who popularize his doctrines, accept his pronouncements with surprising docility. The editors of Bolshevist newspapers, the writers of their pamphlets, are "disciples" in the antique sense of the word. Trotsky has the erratic tendencies of an orator, but every time he has wandered from the teachings of The Master, the reprimand has been prompt and as promptly accepted. Lenin does the thinking for his cohorts. He is "the theoretician" of Bolshevism.

---

[1] Georgi Gapon, revolutionary Orthodox priest and sometime government informer who played a major role in the events of the 1905 revolution, including the march on the Winter Palace. See Walter Sablinsky, *The Road to Bloody Sunday* (Princeton, NJ: Princeton University Press, 1976).

But the magic by which he won and maintains this control over his followers is a complete mystery to me. Coming home from an all night session of the Petrograd Soviet, in the first days of 1918, where Lenin had made a long and unemotional speech to prepare the ground for the surrender to the Kaiser, I asked my interpreter, who had strong leanings towards Bolshevism, to explain the secret of Lenin's influence. He said he was fascinated by Lenin's cold logic and consistency.

Certainly no man in public life today—no one I have read of in history—has been so painfully consistent as Nicolai (sic) Lenin. He is simply doing today, now that he is in power, exactly what he said he would do, when I knew him a dozen odd years ago.

His mind, in those first discussions about politics, did not impress me as original, only as logical. If one wished to quarrel with his conclusions, it was necessary to go back and fight over his primary assumptions. His arguments are hard to combat, if you grant his first claims.

The only originality in his thought was the strange grouping of its foundation stones. There were three ideas in the philosophy which he outlined to me which he accepted as axiomatic and needing no argument. He had borrowed them from three great revolutionary thinkers: Marx, Blanqui, and Nietzsche.

In his youth Lenin was a close student of Karl Marx and today quotes from him as readily as any real Marxist I know. But he had repudiated almost all of the Socialist theories except "The Class War" and "Internationalism."

When he talks of the relation between Capital and Labor, he uses the familiar phraseology of Socialism, but with a twist not to be found in *Das Kapital*. Marx was much too human to believe that the "types" he defined were real people. He said that the man who works for wages in modern industry and the man who employs labor tend to approach the typical " propertyless Proletarian" and the "exploiting Capitalist." As they resist this trend they are likely to become eliminated in the struggle for existence.

Lenin talks and acts as if these "types" were the only real people. Many of the Russian factory workers still own a meager plot of land in the village and are peasants at heart. But Lenin speaks to them as if they were propertyless—as if they thought in the same terms as the landless proletarians of the long established industry of the West—theoretically they should. He occasionally meets an employer who thinks he is trying to be decent, but Lenin knows better. Theoretically he must be heartless. Marx described a process which he thought he saw in modern life leading towards an inevitable war of the classes. Lenin acts on the assumption that this process is completed. People and things and events in this picture puzzle of life which do not fit at once into his "theory" of the picture he impatiently throws aside, ignores and denies their existence. This habit of mind is illustrated in his attitude towards Socialist Internationalism.

Marx in a youthful outburst of emotionalism ended his Communist Manifesto with the phrase "Workers of all Nations—Unite. You have nothing to lose but your chains. You have a world to gain!" This slogan has been the rallying cry of International Labor. But very few of the leaders or members of the ranks have taken it as liberally as Lenin. To him it is an axiom—to believe the contrary would be absurd—that the laborer has no interest in his own country, that he is more closely bound in common interest to the workers of other countries than to any non-proletarian in his own land. To Lenin, the enemy, the only enemy worth discussing, is Capital. And high finance is international, traveling in search of profits from one country to another, interlocking across every frontier and dominant everywhere. Its sinister rule can be broken only by an international revolt of the exploited proletarians.

This theory was fairly common a dozen years before the war. But ocular demonstrations—that, for instance, a Belgian miner has more fellow feeling for his former boss, who commands his regiment, than for the German "Kamerad" in field gray; that a Czech peasant will postpone his quarrel with his landlord to fight Austrian peasants—has not weakened Lenin's attitude in the matter at all. "Patriotism" does not fit into his theory. He ignores it. In his letters and manifestos to the workingmen of Western countries he does not argue with them about "Patriotism," he does not warn them against being tricked by such fine phrases in the mouths of capitalist spellbinders. He assumes that they understand Internationalism just as he does and have no preference for their own country over others. He thinks that "Patriotism" is bad and so he shuts his eyes to its existence.

The second foundation stone in his thinking he has borrowed, with less alteration, from the French revolutionist, Blanqui. In common with some modern "Syndicalists," Lenin is frankly and outspokenly anti-Democratic. He cannot be interested in making "the world safe for democracy." He has no use for the idea.

In general in our discussion he was cool and passionless, but on this subject he became heated. He objects to both the theory and practice of majority rule. The mass of the people, he argues, have been too debased by capitalist oppression to know what is good for them. Bitter long hours of labor have robbed them of any chance to acquire general culture or to understand their own position and needs. And they are too ill-nourished to have the energy to struggle, too terrorized by the fear of losing their jobs to revolt. He spoke hopelessly, with marked disdain, of the "lethargic mass." The capitalists will always be able to fool the majority. He saw no hope of progress if one waited for democratic action by the masses. Towards democracy in practice he was even more bitter. What, he demanded vehemently, has it accomplished for the workers in France, Britain, or America? He was surprisingly well informed about the sore spots in our civilization. He knew many returned immigrants, who had told him all about our sweatshops and slums. He had read a translation of "The Jungle." "Democracy" is to him an empty word by means of which scheming capitalists fool the people into thinking they are free. He had heard about the corruption which has disgraced some of our elections and he held it quite natural that a half-starved workingman should sell his vote. He contrasted the great newspapers which support the interests of the upper classes and the poverty-stricken Socialist and Trade Union press. The control of Public Opinion by the rich makes "democracy" a cruel jest for the underdogs.

Lenin pins his faith on "the enlightened, militant minority," "the elite of the proletariat." He is frankly for "a minority revolution." Of course, he maintained, "the lethargic mass" would benefit by his projects and in the end rally to them. But he does not expect them to initiate anything. Revolution *for*, but not *by*, the people is his ideal. It will all work out for the welfare of the mass, and after they have been sufficiently enlightened to support the ideas of the energetic minority it may be possible to talk of democracy. But it would take too hopelessly long to out-vote the capitalists. He proposed to destroy them by the dictatorship of his enlightened friends as a short cut.

In this matter Lenin parted company with the dominant opinion of Western Socialism. Jean Jaurès, the great French leader, had said: "We need not only a majority, but an overwhelming majority." The more experienced Socialists of the West realized the great value to them of such democratic liberties as universal suffrage and freedom of discussion. Their main efforts were used in organizing their co-believers into a coherent political party which, when it had won over a majority, could take over the governing power and democratize industry as well as politics. And in this attitude most Russian Socialists concurred.

But for such slow methods, Lenin had no patience. It would take too long. He advocated minority insurrection and "the Dictatorship of the Proletariat," not of all the workers, not even of a majority of them, but of his "enlightened, militant minority." The argument over "tactics," which split the Russian Social Democrats into two factions—"Bolsheviks" and "Mensheviks"—was on this point. Plekhanov[2] and the Mensheviks were interested in the democratic liberties. Lenin was for the conspirative organization of a centralized, disciplined—desperate—group to start the minority insurrection and Proletarian Dictatorship. And he advocated this policy in Russia, where 80 percent of the people are peasants and not proletarians at all!

Lenin had borrowed his third foundation stone—also as a basic assumption—from that part of Nietzsche's teaching which is summed up in the title of his book, "Beyond Good and Evil." The ethical teachings of the day, Lenin argued, have been imposed on us like our property laws by the possessing class. The capitalist shrewdly supports the clergy to preach: "Servants, obey your masters." The university professor, who lectures about "honor," "fidelity to the pledged word," "the sacredness of contracts," is also paid by the exploiters, just as much as the corporation lawyer who defends the unjust owner in court by making the worse appear the better reason for

---

[2] Georgi Plekhanov, the "father of Russian Marxism," founded the first Marxist organization in Russia, the Emancipation of Labor Group, and influenced both Lenin and Trotsky.

a fee. The so-called Moral Law is a ruling class affair. Just as Constantine the Great bullied the Fathers of the Early Church into a theology which favored his ambitions, so the rich and powerful of our day have fostered a system of ethics which supports their graft.

Lenin repudiated all allegiance to what most people call "moral obligations." For him, the only "Good" is that which hurries on the Emancipation of the Working Class. All things which hinder this liberation are unqualifiedly "Bad," no matter what fine names may be given them by the Poets and Priests—courtesans of the Ruling Class.

I think that if Lenin should chance to read this summary of his views, the bases of his political philosophy, he would agree that it was an accurate report. And then he would boast of the consistency with which he has striven to put them in practice. Many of his actions, which seem erratic and mysterious, are quite simple to one who has heard him expound the basic ideas on which he works.

It is a difficult intellectual feat to weave a consistent policy out of doctrines so diverse. And I think I embarrassed him somewhat by one question in those discussions a dozen odd years ago. At least he showed irritability when I insisted on it.

"How," I asked, "if you repudiate the democratic verdict of the majority, are you going to determine what is 'Good,' what is helpful, in the struggle for Emancipation? There are likely to be differences of opinion within the working class. The 'lethargic majority' may want one thing and your 'enlightened minority' quite the opposite. If you are not going to consult their opinion how will you determine what is good for the masses?"

He seemed to me to dodge the issue. It was plain that the "majority" did not interest him. He used just as disdainful phraseology about it as the Anarchists and Aristocrats, who oppose democracy. He spoke contemptuously of "the fatuity of counting noses."

But it seemed to me then, years before he reached power, at a time when there was no visible chance of his doing so, that he was quite prepared to decide these momentous questions himself. He was convinced that he knew what was necessary for the welfare of the Race.

Perhaps this dazzling self-confidence, this supreme Aplomb, is the secret of his mastery over men.

Chapter II
Workingmen—Soldiers—Poorer Peasants

Theories of social regeneration are not very interesting so long as they exist only in unread books or control the conduct of a few isolated disciples. They become significant when they are accepted by great masses, who endeavor to put them into practice.

There is a "struggle for existence" among ideas just as there is in the realm of biology. The dispossessed and discontented workers of the world are faced by a score or more of bitterly competing theories of salvation. Mark Hanna invented the slogan "A Full Dinner Pail," as a substitute for "Bread and Cheese," to distract the workers' attention from their empty purses. Bismarck offered State Socialism to the discontented. The Anarchists have tried to interest the masses in Free Communism, the followers of Marx have advocated Social or Industrial Democracy. The syndicalists have pushed their theories and the Conservative Trade Unions theirs. The theories themselves are not so interesting as the question: which gets the most votes? which proves itself the fittest to survive in this competitive struggle for existence? Which most closely answers the aspirations and satisfies the needs of those to whom it appeals?

There is not a large city in the world where certain groups have not been preaching ideas very similar to Lenin's these many years. They have not been significant because few listened to their sermons. But suddenly in Russia these theories caught on. In Russia they spread like an epidemic. In Russia for more than a year now they have dominated politics. There they flourished because they fitted—were adopted to—their environment.

Typhus is a dread disease which rages today in the cities and villages of Russia. But any sanitary engineer can explain why there is small danger of such an outbreak in New York or San Francisco. Typhus needs a certain environment to flourish. It needs filth and vermin. Health also needs a fitting environment—cleanliness. In the same sense, Bolshevism or any other social theory needs a definite environment. The ideas of Lenin, which neither originated in nor have been confined to Russia, flourished there because of a certain specific social psychology, a slave mentality.

Lenin describes his government as a Republic of "Workingmen, Soldiers, and the Poorer Peasants."

The Russian working class differs profoundly from anything we know in America or Western Europe. First of all it is very small. The largest estimates give it a little above 10 percent of the population. Then the conditions of industry are so different that the habits of thought common to the workingmen of Russia are in sharp contrast to those of Western wage-earners. Some of the large industries, such as cotton spinning and mining, have existed for several generations, but most of Russia's large factories are mushroom developments, resulting from "the protection of infant industries" by Count Witte's[1] High Tariff Regime. An equally important factor in the rapid growth of Russian industry has been cheap labor.

Very few of the great mass of the peasantry have enough land to support themselves and their families. The majority supplement their meager harvest by labor on the landed estates, but Witte's Tariff Law not only fostered an artificial expansion of industry, it depressed the agriculture by which 80 percent of the population live. As the peasant communities grew, through their normal increase in population, the scarcity of work on the big estates became automatically more pressing. So a constantly growing element in villages, young men and women unable to find employment at home, drifted into the cities in search of work.

They brought with them an appallingly low standard of living and a very pressing need for a job. They had no knowledge of trade unionism as a means to protect themselves from unscrupulous employers and the police fought ruthlessly against the efforts of the Socialists to organize them. Under the stimulus of new conditions some of them were "improving their minds." The few schools, often illegal and "underground," where these peasant workers could learn to read and write were always crowded and there was a new generation growing up which had been born in industrial centers. So, little by little the working class was beginning to approach the psychology of the factory hands of Britain, Germany, and America, but the process was very far from complete. In the Moscow Basin, the oldest manufacturing district of Russia, more than three-fourths of the workers were village born, half of them went home twice a year, at seed time and harvest, to help on the family plot. Most of them loathed the city life and, when they dreamed, it was of some happy chance which would permit them to leave the wretchedness of the slum and return to the countryside. There was very little of what Western Socialists mean by "class consciousness," there was very little interchange between one trade or one factory and another. The mass of the workers, made dumb by their ignorance, were bewildered and submissive. Peasant born, these Russian workers had entered the factories to escape actual starvation. In no other modern country has the hopeless misery of the poor been more cruelly exploited by a greedy capitalism. Nowhere has the division of profit between the employer and the employed been so cryingly unfair.

During the revolutionary disturbance in 1905, I talked with the owner of a shoe factory near Warsaw. He was a German and after the High Tariff Regime had been instituted he had moved across the frontier and built factories in Russian Poland.

---

[1] Sergei Witte, finance minister from 1892 to 1903 and prime minister from 1903 to 1906, was instrumental in Russia's industrialization in the late 19th century.

His output was of poor quality because of cheap and inferior labor, but as he was protected from German competition he could charge all the traffic would bear. That year he told me had been a very bad one; there had been three strikes, closing his factories for nearly five months, one uninsured building had been burned, and he had been forced to raise wages 200 percent. He did not think his profit would be more than 20 percent. Anything less than 100 percent was a bad year for him.

Such profits from this mushroom industry have not of course been universal, but they had been very common, especially in munitions during the war. The wage schedule has always been appallingly low. Even today on the railroads, men doing work which brings $8.00 a day in America are receiving 19 roubles a month. Before the war the rouble was worth 52 cents, now it is about 10 cents.

Now there is something fundamentally wrong in the organization of industry where wages can be suddenly raised 100 percent and more and still leave the owners a profit which in the West we would call excessive. There was no effective legislation in Russia to protect the workers against such exploitation, no powerful and disciplined organization of labor, and so the most unscrupulous employer was left entirely free to set the pace. There is nothing surprising in the fact that Russian workers have proved themselves more revolutionary than those of the West. Nowhere has there been more justification for class hatred, unless perhaps among the Russian peasants who have "stayed on the land."

In almost every village in Russia there are people still living who were Serfs. There are very few peasants who have not seen some of their friends flogged. The Emancipation Edict while it legally freed the Serfs had no magic to transform them at once into full-fledged citizenship. That was not its intention. It left them "freed" rather than "free." They were economically as much dependent on the landlord as they had previously been legally on their owners. They were given a little land but it was not enough to support them and they were overburdened with the Redemption Tax with which they paid the landlords for their meager allotments. There was no allowance for increase of population, so their economic position gets worse with each baby born to them. They must supplement the income from their minute holdings by working on the landlords' estates. And it is generally "absentee landlordism" of the worst type. Taxation direct and indirect has been so heavy that great sections of the country had regularly been three, four, five years in arrears. This has prevented the accumulation of farm capital and the improvement of cultivation, for any appearance of prosperity brings the immediate visit of the tax collector.

Almost every traveller to Russia who has written of his experiences has noted the sudden contrast at the frontier where the train passes from the clean, orderly well-being of the German village to the heartbreaking squalor of Russian peasant life. That the young men and women of the village are willing to go into the horror of the industrial slums, the most atrocious housing conditions in the world, is in itself a measure of the misery of their village homes. And over the countryside hangs the pall of illiteracy. They are the "Dark People."

Standing on a favored hill, overlooking the filth and hunger and ignorance of the village, is the Great House. Its occasional inhabitants have not forgotten, any more than have the peasants, that not so very long ago they "owned the village." Their source of wealth and ease is still the travail of these men and women of the hoe. Most of the time the Great House is closed, its inhabitants off enjoying the gaiety of the capital or the pleasures of the Riviera. For a month or so in the summer, and with more conservative families at Christmas, it is filled with a light-hearted throng of merry makers, but even when "in residence," the landlords have little contact with the villagers. They do not speak the real Russian language, they use too many foreign words to be understood by the peasants, and the life they lead is too different. They read books, play queer games like tennis, change their clothes several times a day, and are happy. The peasants in their grim misery look at them hungrily and hate them as much if not more than the industrial workers hate their boss.

But above all it was the conversion of the soldiers to Bolshevism that made Lenin's coup possible. The Russian Army was conscripted, recruited from the fields and factories, and there was a deep class bitterness in the hearts of the young soldiers before they put on the uniform. Army life intensified it. The officers were drawn from the Ruling Class; the old atmosphere of Serfdom—master and man—persisted in military organization.

We have heard a great deal about the brutality of German military discipline, but at least it was regular. The German private, although his rights might be very limited, knew what they were. They were defined. He knew under what circumstances an officer had the right to strike him. He could get redress if he was mistreated irregularly. But the Russian soldier had no such protection, he had to submit to any whim of his superior.

A young invalided officer, who had seen two years of campaign before he was wounded, told me the following story of the front. Most of the officers he had met were, he declared, fine types, who did their utmost for the welfare of the men. But the colonel in one regiment in which he served was a brute. In the second Polish campaign he had been accompanied by a mistress of peculiarly vicious tastes. He used to order his soldier-servant to stand at attention and let her amuse herself by slashing the boy with a riding crop.

When my friend learned of this he was normally indignant, but he knew that it was useless for him to protest as he had been involved in some university disturbances in 1905 and was on the police black list. The captain of a neighboring company was a prince of one of the proudest families of the court. He was an Oxford graduate, a keen sportsman, and a good soldier. My friend took the evidence to him and the prince responded at once by openly accusing the colonel at the officers' mess and demanding a court martial.

All the defenders of "things as they are" immediately mobilized to hush up the scandal. To punish a colonel for brutality to a private would "undermine discipline." Such things simply were not done! The matter went all the way up to the general in command of the army group. The prince was too strong at court to be punished for disturbing the existing order, so the general got out of the impasse by transferring him to an attractive staff post on another front and the case was dropped. The colonel kept his unsavory mistress.

It was the irresponsible erraticness of the Russian Army discipline, its haphazard uncertainty, more than its brutality, which intensified the class bitterness which the soldiers had brought from fields and factories. And very little was done for their comfort. They were expected "to do their duty to the Tsar" without the encouragement of such fol-de-rols as YMCA. huts, basketball, or gramophones. All through the war, Ivan was more poorly armed, fed, sheltered, and clothed than his allies or enemies; he was more ruthlessly sacrificed by the stupidity and blunders of his officers. War to him was a grimmer misery—just as his memories of his village hut or factory tenement was grimmer—than it was to any other of the world's soldiers. He was never comforted by an ideal. Our American "Doughboys" were constantly told that they were "Crusaders," the Russian soldier was simply told the penalty for disobedience.

A point of great importance in the psychology of the Russian soldier was that he did not know what he was fighting for. Other countries spent endless efforts on fortifying the morale of their army by explaining the war to them. No such effort was made in Russia. It would have been suppressed as "politically dangerous." One day the bugles blew, mobilization was ordered, the bands played "God Save the Tsar." There was nothing in that national anthem about fighting for liberty. The Russian soldiers were not told that it was a campaign against Imperialism. The only thing they were supposed to be fighting for was the glory of the Tsar, their only incentive was fear. If they disobeyed orders, they would be shot.

It is not surprising that they showed such hatred towards their officers. In the case of the colonel with the vicious mistress, it is certain that all the soldiers of the regiment knew of the shameful brutality; very few, if any of them, knew of the vain efforts of the two young captains to right the wrong.

The same thing is true in the realm of agriculture and industry. The reputation of a cruel boss or landlord will overshadow the good deeds of the more well disposed. I have not chanced to see any factory in Russia which would be called "good" or even "fairly decent" in Western countries. But there were some model estates. Many landlords took a scientific interest in methods of agriculture, and some realized that improvement was impossible unless the peasantry were better treated. There was a great deal of effort on the part of the landlord class, which was closely similar in motives and methods to the social settlements of our great cities. But as far as the psychology of the masses is concerned such efforts were submerged in general heartlessness of the pernicious system.

WORKINGMEN—SOLDIERS—POORER PEASANTS

There was one element which affected the thought, alike of factory worker, peasant, and soldier—hopelessness! This is a matter so foreign to American life that its implications are not readily appreciated. We are all familiar with what might be called "class migration." The rail-splitter becomes President. The banker goes broke. The papers publish obituary notices of Mr. Woolworth and detailed accounts of his spectacular fortune. But these ultra-dramatic incidents are not so significant as the more ordinary cases, the grocery delivery boy who now owns a cold storage plant; the Jewish judge whose father, emerging from Ellis Island, started life again as a pushcart pedlar on the East Side; the Italian boy who was first a bootblack, then had a corner fruit stand, and now "is doing well in his new garage." In Russia there are no Correspondence Schools advertising in all the papers how John Doe and Richard Roe, who used to earn $12.00 a week, "took our course" and are now successful policemen or architects. The caste system in India is hardly more rigid.

There was one wealthy man I knew in Moscow, Suiteen, the proprietor of a large newspaper and publishing house, who was peasant born. He had made a fortune by developing an "Almanac" for the peasants. And in the south of Russia I was shown another self-made man, who had built up a combination of sugar beet factories. But the fact that this rich peasant was "shown" to me is significant. He was a curiosity. I was told that he had been nicknamed "The American."

During all the war, out of the millions of men mobilized, only a score or so were raised from the ranks to a commission. The mass of the soldiers had no such ambition—it was hopeless and this hopelessness had been with them since childhood in civilian life.

The peasant's hunger for land was passionate, but he had no reasonable hope of acquiring a self-supporting farm. With incredible drudgery, he and his family might meet the Redemption Taxes on his plot and rent a few acres more from a landlord, but, even if he had half a dozen sons, he could scarcely hope to buy land. The situation was just as hopeless for the factory workers, the chances of bettering their condition was almost nil. Besides the handicap of ignorance, the police were always on the side of the boss. Strike leaders and agitators were very quickly started on the prison trail to Siberia.

The outlook of very many workingmen in the Western democracies is dreary enough, God knows! The most pitiable, perhaps, are the men past forty, who have lost hope of bettering their condition and are looking forward tremblingly to the day when their job will go to a younger man. But how many of them are comforted—kept from despair—by hope in their children!

I once knew a grizzled old Irishman, who had worked all his life in an iron foundry. He knew that he was on the down slope and expected to lose his job at any time. His best hope was to be made night watchman of a ware—house. But his oldest daughter had gone to work in a department store and had married a floorwalker. She was the only one of his children who had not finished the common school. Her younger sister was graduating from normal college. He had three sons; one was foreman in the shop where he worked, another had gone into politics and had a comfortable city job, the youngest had gone West, working his way through an agricultural college, and was getting the best salary of them all as field advisor for a big farm loan bank in Chicago. Such a family history is commonplace in America, it would sound like a fairy tale in Russia. The old men there were hopeless for themselves and knew that their children would begin the hopeless struggle just where they did.

Smarting under oppression without end or limit, debased by humiliations and cruelties, and haggard from semi-starvation, the great majority of the Russians saw no reasonable hope of improving their conditions under the existing system. They were either desperately hopeless or they looked to some cataclysm for the complete overthrow of the society they knew. Despair or Revolt! This is the distinctive mentality of slaves. And it was to such people that Lenin successfully made his appeal. Those, whose every aspiration had not been stifled by misery, dreamed of revolutionary upheaval.

Chapter III
War and the Old Regime

The stupendous ordeal of war found Russia more unprepared than any other country. Modern war is so largely an industrial affair, it is so vitally dependent on determined public opinion.

Russia was just beginning her industrial development, machinery had not become truly nationalized; the factory system is still a bit "alien." The political leaders were not industrially minded, nor were the military men. The government still had the medieval idea that war is the affair of the army. Even at best Russian industry was not adequate for the strains of the war. A very large part of the managing brains were foreign, too often German. Russia was prepared to manufacture only a small part of the ammunition and equipment of her armies. There was no great industrial class, which could be suddenly drawn upon, for the development of mushroom war industries. And the Tsar always had fought, inevitably had to fight, against the development of an enlightened public opinion. From this point of view, even more than industrially, Russia was unprepared.

There was a strong current of Pro-Germanism in court circles, but in general the official world, especially the military caste, went into the war to win. They needed a victory to reestablish their credit, so humbled by the recent Japanese defeat. These military men wanted victory, they did not care much whom they had to fight; a triumph over the Turks or the British would have served just as well as a victory over Germany, but once the war was declared they wanted to prove their efficiency by winning. The educated Liberals were enthusiastic for the war. They knew that the German influence at court was reactionary and they hoped that the destruction of Prussian Autocracy would force the Tsar to follow the lead of his more democratic Allies. The educated revolutionists, like their Socialist comrades the world over, split. They were faced by a painful choice between loyalty to their ideals of international brotherhood and their love of country. More of the Russian Socialists took an unpatriotic attitude than elsewhere, because of the old tradition that every defeat of the Tsar brought in revolutionary reforms. The disaster of the Crimean War had forced the emancipation of the Serfs; the Japanese debacle had been followed by the creation of the Duma. "Defeatism" was based on the belief that victory would strengthen the reaction. However, many of the Russian Socialists, following the example of such well-known leaders as Kropotkin, Bourtzeff, and Breshkovskaia, took a strong pro-war stand.

As for the Dark People they did not know anything about the issues of the war. They were simply "called to the colors." They were expected to "do or die." They were not asked to fight for international justice, nor to make the world safe for democracy, least of all were they asked to fight for their liberty. Anyone who had tried to put heart into them with such ideas would have been shot at dawn.

They were ordered out by their crazy government in appalling numbers. At one time there were more than four million men in the interior camps while the High Command had no rifles with which to arm them, no officers to drill them. It was sheer waste from the economic point of view—all these hungry men withdrawn uselessly from production.

A maximum price was fixed on grain—and on nothing else. So the peasants, with all their young men mobilized, could get only prewar prices for their products, while the goods they needed—shoes, clothes, farm tools—went up in jumps of one hundred percent. The High Command took all the steel output for cannon and shells and left none for the imperative needs of industry and transportation. There was no co-ordination between the "front" and the "rear," and to add to such gross industrial inefficiency there was an even more stupid political policy. Skilled engine drivers and telegraphers were mobilized and scattered about as private soldiers because their unions were supposed to be revolutionary. So it became continually more difficult to find skilled mechanics and when an engine broke down it had to wait longer and longer to be repaired. It is a marvel that the railroad system functioned as well as it did, but it gradually became worse and worse, and this country which normally exports vast quantities of foodstuff, because of this hopeless stupidity of the Old Regime, began to starve. There was a shortage of bread in the cities and a dearth of manufactured goods for the countryside. Russia was more effectively "blockaded" than Germany.

The outside world was fed with press agent stories intended to impress one with the might and power of the great Tsar. Most of them were foundationless. We were told so much of the great popularity of the Grand Duke Nicholas, that there were grave fears of mutiny when he was summarily dismissed. Then we were told that there was even more frantic devotion to the Tsar, who had become Commander in Chief in his place. We were told how all the various nationalities that composed the Empire had forgotten their differences in a spasm of patriotic enthusiasm. In fact the outlying nationalities, such as Finns, became more bitter during the war than they had ever been before. But perhaps the most remarkable of these Tsarist fantasies, which were given to us as truth, was the picture of the mystically-minded Russian peasant praying before his favorite ikon for the time when the Orthodox Church would be able to tear down the Mohammedan Crescent from the church of Santa Sofia in Constantinople and replace it by the Cross. When at last the peasants were allowed to express their aspirations, there was no single mention of this dream of conquest at the Dardanelles. They did not know there was such a place.

The war was more miserable in Russia than elsewhere, more naked and grim and uninspiring. The winter of 1916 was more hopeless. Even the most enthusiastic friends of the Entente had begun to fear that it would be impossible to hold out longer against Germany. The dogs of war had gnawed the country to a dry bone.

The Old Regime had never enjoyed broad popular support in Russia. The Tsar and his bureaucrats did not worry about "the consent of the governed," they had worked out a system of ruling against and in spite of the majority. However a steady breeze of liberalism blew from the West. During the last century revolt had been steadily gathering momentum. At various times, the lid, on which the Autocrat and his circle of favorites sat, had been rudely shaken. It was nearly upset by popular discontent after the Japanese War. Although that storm had been weathered by a combination of reluctant reforms, the support of International Finance, and very stern repressive measures, a new and more serious outburst was threatening in 1914.

At first war was a distraction; it drew popular attention from old grievances to new problems. But this was only momentary. To the great mass of the people the war soon ceased to be interesting. The desperate and embittering old problems of how to get enough to eat reabsorbed their attention. And to the accustomed discontents was added this new misery of war. Day after day new bales of straw were piled on the already breaking back of the people's patience.

As the war dragged on a new condition developed which intensified the discontent of the more fortunate. The educated class, who were suffering least from the scourge of war, wanted victory. And rumors of treachery at court became insistent.

There is the story of the little Tsarovitch who is supposed to have expressed his bewilderment about the war by saying: "When our armies retreat Papa cries, but when they advance Mama cries." How much danger there was that the Tsar would make a separate peace with the Kaiser will probably never be known to a certainty. But beyond all doubt, a large and growing element of patriotic Russians thought the danger was serious. Politicians of every party in the Duma, congresses of lawyers and doctors and professional men generally, many of the younger officers some of the highest generals, and even a few of the Grand Dukes, thought that the "Dark Forces" at the court were betraying the country to the Germans.

The war meant to the masses, although perhaps they did not very clearly understand the causes, a deepening of their misery. To the educated classes it stripped off all the veils of the Old Regime and showed in revolting nakedness the brutality, the stupid inefficiency, the corruption and treason on which the throne rested.

The war by its super-burden of miseries, of ghastly disclosures made Revolution inevitable.

There was hardly anyone in Russia, outside the ring of bureaucrats and courtiers, who did not want a Revolution. The only question was when to start it? The miserable masses, who had little interest in the war, answered: "The sooner the better." The more fortunate classes at first said: "After the war is won." Even before the Great Upheaval people had to worry over the question which later dominated all political thought—which is more important, the war or the Revolution?

But as the rumors of treason at court gathered weight, as the prospect of a separate—and imperial—peace became more threatening, those who were most intent on victory became more and more convinced that the Revolution could not be safely postponed. To the most patriotic element of the Intelligentsia revolution seemed a means—the only means—to assure the continuation of the war, the only hope of victory.

Chapter IV
Revolution and the Provisional Government

Although almost everybody in Russia had been thinking about, if not actively planning for, the Revolution, it came suddenly and as a surprise to the nation.

There is vehement dispute today, and there will probably be dispute among future historians, as to who was responsible for the Revolution and who should claim the credit. There were two groups working independently at first and suddenly joining hands in those critical February days and each with natural egoism claims to have played the greater role. There are two theories: first, that the Intelligentsia in the Duma started a perfectly good revolution which was spoiled by the undisciplined action of the masses; second, that the masses started a revolution of their own and that control of it was momentarily snatched from them by the Duma politicians. These are the extreme positions and the truth probably lies somewhere between them. I was not there at the time, but as far as I can reconstruct those momentous days from talks with many who played an important part, I believe that what follows is substantially correct.

The revolutionary outbreaks of 1905 to 1908 had been defeated and ruthlessly punished, but after a dozen years of despair the working class in Petrograd and the other large cities were beginning to find again their revolutionary determination. There had been before the war a strike movement which increased in force from year to year and also was obviously changing from purely economic demands about wages and hours to a more revolutionary demand for political liberties. This movement was apparently reaching a crisis in the early months of 1914, but its outward manifestations were abruptly terminated by the declaration of war. Just as the Russian Government showed its industrial incompetence in such matters as the railroad administration, so it demonstrated its political inefficiency. It failed to adopt any of the programs for the protection of labor which the other belligerent nations had developed to win the loyal support of the working class. The labor conditions had become worse instead of better during the war and the discontent of the workers was again becoming a serious menace. However all their leaders, who were for the war, were preaching patience, and the existence of martial law made it more easy for the government to suppress agitation which would interfere with the conduct of the war. In January of 1917 there seems to have been very acute dissatisfaction among the working population of Petrograd but no coherent plan of action.

On the other hand, the patriotic members of the Duma were increasingly worried by the bureaucratic inefficiency and treason of the "Dark Powers" which were symbolized in the person of Rasputin. All that was needed to quiet the discontent of the Intellectuals, in the Duma and Zemstvos, was permission to co-operate in the work of the war.

But the bureaucratic ministry insultingly rejected all the offers of collaboration. They preferred to lose the war rather than give the democratic forces of the nation a chance to develop. Nearly a year before the Revolution, a delegation of Duma members made a tour of the Allied countries exchanging fraternal greetings with the Parliaments of those countries. Milyoukov was saying in Paris, at that time, that if there was not a change in the government the Tsar would be forced into a separate peace. He and his radical friends were trying to find support for a revolutionary movement among their Allies. He was met with the old proverb that it is unwise to trade horses in the middle of a stream, to which he replied impatiently, "that depends entirely on how bad your horse is." The British Government sent Lord Milner to Russia to try to combat the danger of a separate peace. He gave no encouragement to the radical Left Wing of the Duma. However, in accord with the Zemstvo organizations throughout the country and the High Command, which also dreaded treachery at court, plans took shape for a parlor revolution. The program was to send a delegation to the Tsar at the army headquarters and give him the choice between granting constitutional liberties or abdicating in favor of his son. I think that the men who proposed this hoped that the Tsar would quietly grant the parliamentary rights they wished for without any public scandal. They were planning to operate without any help from the discontented masses.

The reactionary supporters of the Tsar's policy got wind of these projects and attempted to force an issue before the Duma plans were matured. Large numbers of troops were brought to Petrograd, the police were heavily armed, and a series of measures taken to inflame the populace into a premature revolt which it was hoped could be bloodily suppressed.

But when the people came out on the streets, the troops refused to fire on them. There were a few days of uncertainty and then the army came wholly over to the side of the Revolution. The effort of the Duma conspirators to bring about a regency failed and then a long struggle began between the Duma group representing the Intelligentsia of the country and the Soviets which were the only spokesmen of the Masses.

The generation of propaganda carried on at the price of so much sacrifice and heroism by the cream of the nation's youth had achieved one result, it had popularized the word "Revolution." Few of the Dark People understood the word—in fact it is very hard to get any group of educated people to agree on a definition of the word—but no other hope had ever been held out to them. "Revolution" meant to them a mystic Open Sesame, which was to swing back the heavy doors of their misery. It would cure all their ills. To the overwhelming majority of the people it meant "land." The Dark People were not interested in politics, autocracy, limited monarchy, republic—these were foreign ideas to them. The revolution they wanted was land. The factory workers wanted land so that they could escape from the misery and squalor of the city slums. The peasant wanted land so that he could be free from landlords.

The only liberty they dreamed of was economic. The soldiers, all those who suffered from the war, wanted peace. They had been ordered to fight for the Tsar, but now there was revolution. The police had no more power, there would be no more flogging, no more executions. The whole reason for the war was gone. The soldiers wanted peace. They were tired of this hateful war, and besides they wanted to get home to their villages and share in the distribution of the land. The soldiers just as much as the factory workers and peasants thought that revolution meant "land."

But the Revolution brought no such joyous results. The Provisional Government, under Prince Lvov, was controlled by high-minded, educated, progressive liberals.

While most of them were landlords, they were all in favor of sweeping reforms in the system of land tenure. They wanted to do away with the worst abuses, but they did not want any revolutionary solution of the land problem which might be prejudicial to "good landlords." They wanted to postpone economic reorganization till it could be discussed calmly and legally in a Constitutional Assembly. They wanted to limit the Revolution to "politics" and to deal with economic reforms by "legal" action.

The Provisional Government was also in favor of cooperation with the Allies. They wished for peace, but wished to postpone it until after the defeat of Germany. For the moment they demanded an intensification of the war.

The only people in Russia to whom the Revolution immediately opened the doors of the promised land were the Orators. It was as if all the silver-tongued oratory of all the political campaigns since the foundation of our Republic, all the wild panaceas, all the dreary arguments, all the exhilarating mud-slinging and venomous personal invectives, were crowded into a few short months.

Mr. Root[1] said he was reminded of Baron Munchausen's tale of the hunter's horn which froze on a bitter winter day so that no sound came out. When the hunter returned to his cottage the frozen notes in the horn melted and poured out shrilly in the warm room. All the thoughts and hopes, the aspirations and theories and hatreds which had been frozen out of expression by the cold cruelty of the Old Regime suddenly melted into voice in the heat of the Revolution.

We can have only sympathy for the bewildered plight of the Russians in the early days of their Liberty. With no political experience to guide them, they were called upon to vote more often in a month than an American citizen votes in a lifetime. There was some kind of an election almost every week. We, of the West, in spite of our greater political maturity, find it very hard to guess how much post-election ful-

---

[1] Elihu Root, the head of the American Commission to Russia in 1917.

fillment will result from campaign promises. It is not surprising that the victory at the Russian elections always went to the "best promisers."

The old question—"Which is the more important, War or Revolution?"—became all important. In general the Intellectuals, who controlled the Provisional Government, said that the midst of a Great War was no time to attempt the complete reorganization of the economic life of the nation. They would have preferred to postpone such matters until they could have been dealt with by a Constitutional Assembly, after the conclusion of a victorious peace.

There was a middle group, whose leadership fell to Kerensky, which argued that, difficult as it was, it was necessary to attack the problems of reconstruction at once; the Constitutional Assembly could not wait on the outcome of the war, it must be convened at the earliest possible moment.

There was a third—and extreme—point of view. At first it had small support, but gradually gathered strength. It said "If war interferes with the Revolution, stop the war."

At the very first, these three points of view were evident: "Victory is the supreme interest," "Victory and Revolution are of equal importance," and "The Revolution is the only thing that matters." The history of the Revolution is the story of the struggle between these ideas.

But it is important to emphasize that at first the Revolution was almost exclusively political. In this realm its achievements were very real. It gave a death blow to Autocracy. It swept away all the old restrictions on the free expression of opinion. It at once began the political education of the people by a whole series of democratic elections.

But these were gains which primarily interested the educated classes. The great mass of the people were not interested in politics. The economic gains which they expected from this Revolution were postponed.

Chapter V
Zemstvo, Duma, Co-operatives

The fall of the Tsar suddenly threw all the burden of government of the vast empire on the people themselves. The hatred of the Old Regime was so great that all the former governing class, those who had a monopoly in experience in such matters, went into retirement. The old machinery was scrapped.

While the spirit of democracy was strong in the land, the institutions by which it could express itself were pitifully weak. Even such autocratic rulers as Wilhelm II and the Mikado have fostered the development of self-government more liberally than had the Tsar. There were two elective bodies in Russia prior to the Revolution. The local Zemstvos[1] were the older and were purely administrative. The Imperial Duma had been created as a result of the revolutionary outburst, which followed the Japanese War. It had no administrative nor executive functions, no real legislative power. It could only discuss, commend, or condemn the action of the Tsar's ministers. Both of these organizations were entirely unlike any of our government institutions.

The local government boards, called Zemstvos (the word is derived from a Slavic root, which means "the soil" and appears in such modern Russian words as "agriculture"; it might be translated "farm councils"), were instituted back in the sixties, throughout the greater part of European Russia. They were strictly limited in their scope, being confined almost entirely to "Uplift." They were empowered to raise small local taxes, and this fund, which was always pitifully inadequate, was expended in schools, agricultural improvement, and sanitation.

The election laws on which the Zemstvos were founded were medieval in the extreme. The landlords, although the peasants were allowed to go through the motions of voting, were sure to control. But no better illustration of the supremacy of spirit over form could be found. The Zemstvos were planned to be safely reactionary, but they have in fact been a great progressive force in the country. This is largely due to the fact that they have been unpopular with the reactionary class and generally ignored by them, so that only the younger and more liberal element of the gentry took an active interest. They have, of course, varied greatly from district to district. And frequently when a Zemstvo has been too progressive the reactionary landlords

---

[1] The zemstvos, local government organs in the countryside, were one of Alexander II's Great Reforms from the 1860s. The agriculturalists, teachers, and social workers hired by the zemstvos, were largely idealistic young people determined to transform the countryside.

of the district have become excited and outvoted the liberals in the next election. But in most cases the Zemstvos have represented a very undemocratic but sincere effort to uplift the peasants "from above."

The Zemstvos have also been responsible for the development of what the Russians call "the Third Element" i.e., the Zemsky employees. The Zemstvo itself is a board, composed mostly of the local nobility, who only rarely take more than an administrative interest in work. They have to employ a large number of school teachers, agricultural experts, doctors, and nurses. These employees are nearly always recent graduates from universities and technical schools and are in almost every case much more radical than the members of the board who employ them. There has been a rather amusing struggle on the part of the Zemstvos to find young people trained for this work, and at the same time sufficiently conservative to suit their tastes. But youth is always for progress and while the Zemstvo boards have been at best timorously liberal, the Zemsky employees, as a class, have been revolutionary and they are, of all the Intelligentsia, the people who come in closest contact with the peasantry.

The Zemstvos have had to fight continually against the obstruction policy of the Central Government. If they had been allowed to develop freely, they would have formed a transition link between the old autocracy and the modern democracy which was struggling to be born. For this very reason the Tsar's ministry always feared and hated them. The struggle centered over the desire on the part of the Zemstvos to organize nationally. The government always insisted that they were local bodies and should not co-operate. The fighting slogan of the Zemstvos has been "an All-Russian Congress," but such a general assembly of Zemstvo members and employees was always prohibited. When any great crisis threatened the nation, the Zemstvos tried to get together. They made an abortive effort to hold a national congress during the Japanese War. Shortly afterwards, when there was a wide-spread famine, they tried to meet informally as a relief organization. Many of them went to prison as a result.

Their opportunity finally came with this war. The inadequacy of the regular government organizations was so patent that the Zemstvos were able to take over a great part of the "Organization of the Rear"; they developed factories for producing uniforms, shoes, harness, and even munitions. Almost all the procuring and transporting of food to the armies at the front fell into their hands and they were especially helpful in the development of sanitary work. It was only reluctantly that the bureaucrats permitted them to undertake these activities, but the need and their own inefficiency was a compelling argument. Finally the obvious advantages of co-ordinating all these Zemstvo activities resulted in permission to hold an All-Russian Congress and Prince Lvov was elected to the head of the organization. The development of the Zemstvo movement had given this group of public-spirited citizens long practice, and in the great crisis of the war they had shown marked ability in organization and administrative work.

A somewhat similar development had taken place in the shorter history of the Imperial Duma. (The Russian word comes from the verb "to think." It does not imply any idea of activity nor even of the right to speak out what one thinks.) This small step towards representative and constitutional government had been granted reluctantly by the Autocrat to quiet the revolutionary movement which had grown very threatening after the disaster in Manchuria. There was never any sincere effort on the part of the governing clique to allow the Duma to develop into a real democratic institution. Its fundamental law and the policy of the bureaucratic ministry was carefully planned to make it a docile tool of the Reaction. But once more the spirit of progress, which was abroad in the land, contrived to find expression through this poor machine.

The first Duma was revolutionary and when the government found that it could not control it, it was dissolved. New elections were held and the agents of the government resorted to every trick known in the game to influence the results, but the second Duma was more radical than the first. It also was very promptly dissolved. The election law was then changed in order to assure a reactionary body and the third Duma when it assembled seemed sufficiently subservient, but as the months passed it gradually developed an esprit de corps and began to oppose the ministry. The fourth Duma was even less successful from the government's point of view. The war brought a great opportunity to it, as it had done to the Zemstvos, and a bitter fight developed between the Duma and the government.

Just as the Zemstvos struggled to achieve an All-Russian Congress, so the Dumas fought for "the responsibility of the ministry." Their ideal was a constitutional regime comparable to the British Parliament. They wanted some effective executive power. If Nicholas II had granted this reform—and all his Allies urged it upon him—the Duma element would never have joined the Revolution.

There are many comparisons between the Zemstvos and the Dumas. An enlightened government, which wished for progress, could have used either as an instrument to develop real democracy. Both constantly had to fight the ill will of the governing caste which was desperately trying to defend the last strongholds of the Dark Ages. Both organizations, in spite of their undemocratic organization, had been captured by the progressive forces of the nation and had become rallying centers for all the friends of democracy. However, there was one sharp contrast. The Zemstvo group had had experience in administrative work, but no training in parliamentary activity. It was exactly the opposite with Duma members; they had had great opportunities to discuss all sorts of political theories and legislative projects, but they had had no experience in the carrying out of their programs.

There was another organization in which the democratic aspirations of the nation were finding some expression, but which had no governmental functions—the Co-operative Movement. It is impossible to give any adequate description of this development in short space. It was immensely diversified, going way back in the history of Russia. Before the abolition of Serfdom, the peasantry had had experience in various forms of co-operative enterprise. After the Emancipation, the development of free co-operatives became more noticeable—or at least was more carefully studied and recorded. There was one general distinction between "producers'" and "consumers'" co-operative societies. Sometimes a group would organize itself to make wagons, to build a boat for fishing, to rent a tract of land for a joint farming enterprise. More recently, especially in Siberia, the dairy farmers have organized co-operatives to erect cold storage plants and in the Ukraine a number of large co-operative beet sugar enterprises have started. Side by side with these producers' co-operatives, there have developed groups who bought at wholesale to eliminate the profits of the retail middleman. Sometimes they co-operated on only one item. A village might send one of its men into the nearest large city to buy plow irons or horseshoes for the community. Co-operative seed buying groups were common. Gradually the Co-operative General Store made its appearance.

One cannot emphasize too strongly the spontaneity and diversity of this development. It grew up out of concrete problems and varied with local needs. The fishermen of Arkhangel might combine in order to buy more cheaply the fishing tackle they needed from England and the fishermen of Astrakhan would combine to market more effectively the season's output of caviar. The sparse population of Siberia were faced by the problems inherently different from those of the congested Jewish pale.

It was only in relatively recent years that a group of the Intellectuals have realized the significance of this spontaneous movement and have begun to work for its unification. The best instance of this phase is the Moscow Popular Bank, which has been organized to handle all financial transactions of the Co-operative Societies. It has succeeded in bringing most of them together and the size of the movement may be judged by the reports of the last All-Russian Congress of Co-operative Societies which was held in Moscow in 1918. They recorded nearly twenty million members of their various societies and estimated that sixty million out of the hundred odd million population were directly or indirectly interested in the Co-operative Movement.

To a certain extent the development of the Co-operatives has been obstructed by the government, but its leaders in the past have very carefully avoided any political action and so have come less in conflict with the government than the Zemstvos or Dumas. Occasionally they have been fostered by the government in the hope that it would distract public opinion from political questions.

In their organization they are completely democratic. They stand out in sharp contrast to the Zemstvos and Dumas in that their idea of progress is from the bottom up. As the scattered local societies have been co-ordinated and their finances—now running up into many millions—are concentrated in the Central Moscow Bank, a great overhead organization has of course grown up. And the higher officials, as they get more and more power through the growth of the movement, tend to become somewhat separated in thought from the rank and file. But this is inevitable. We see it in our own political life. There is a great deal of difference between a session of the Cabinet and a town meeting or ward caucus.

The bases of the Russian Co-operative Movement are soundly democratic and they are rather more successful in choosing for high posts representatives who really represent the aspirations of the members, than our American political parties.

I find that most American observers share my opinion that this great co-operative organization is the foundation stone on which the regeneration of Russia must be built. The men who have spent their lives in this movement are, in the best American sense of the word, "practical." As one man expressed it to me: "They are the idealists who have had to make their books balance every night." No man could work up in the organization unless first of all he had met successfully the practical problems of some small local co-operative. While many of the most heroic and devoted of the revolutionary and liberal elements have spent all their energy on political theories and have never encountered the disciplining control of practical achievement, the workers in the Co-operative Societies have daily had to check their aspirations by the test of hard reality.

In such a social turmoil as Russia is going through no group nor organization can be unaffected and certainly the co-operatives have been sadly disorganized by the whirlwind of revolution. They have been seriously tempted to abandon their safe policy of sticking to economic problems and ignoring politics. They came into inevitable conflict with the Bolshevist regime. But the organization is too widely spread and has too completely proven its utility to be permanently overthrown. The Co-operative Movement is there and it will develop into a powerful ally to any force seeking to develop democratic institutions in Russia.

Chapter VI
The Soviets

There was another political tool at hand, when the old organization of government was scrapped. While it lacked the traditions and experience of the Zemstvo, Duma, and Co-operative Societies, it was destined to play a more important role than any of them—the Soviet.

The word can be translated literally as "council." It was used traditionally just as we use that word. The "Upper House," under the Old Regime, corresponding to our Senate or the House of Lords, was called the Imperial Soviet. There were religious and medical "Soviets." The Society of Bee Keepers and the Vegetarians had their "Soviets." It is only recently that the word has been used in Russia primarily in the sense of a council of workingmen or to denote a system of government.

At the time of the great general strike in October 1905, the formal government was paralyzed and the strike committee was the real power in St. Petersburg. It was composed of delegates from most of the large factories and took the name of "the Council of Workingmen's Deputies." This was the first Soviet in the sense that the word now has. I was in St. Petersburg at the time and had a good opportunity to observe how it worked.

One problem which was under continual discussion was the working out of a form for the organization, which would make it at once representative and workable. It started most informally. Any factory could appoint some of its men to go to the Council and small factories often had more delegates than the largest. In the midst of very hectic events, the Soviet tried to organize itself on a fair basis of numerical representation.

Another difficulty which it had to face was that various factories frequently changed their delegation, so that it was common to have the Soviet pass some resolution one night and a few days later, having completely changed its personnel, pass a new resolution in direct conflict with its previous action. Also there was no accepted tradition as to the power of the deputies. In some cases the factory insisted on reviewing the votes of its representatives and it happened not infrequently that a delegate would arise and explain that while the night before he had voted "no" on some resolution, that that morning his factory had held a meeting to discuss the matter and had instructed him to change his vote to "yes."

The point I wish to emphasize is that the first Soviet was an emergency body without any tradition and without any clear-cut policy. The deputies chosen from the various factories had no experience in the kind of work before them and so, to a greater extent than in our labor organizations in America, they were ready to follow leaders. Many of the men, whose names have become familiar in the last year, had their apprenticeship in such work in this first Soviet. The real struggle within the Soviet, as I saw it then, was rivalry between the various Socialist factions as to which should exercise this intellectual guidance.

In Russian assemblies the parliamentary procedure differs from our customs. Instead of a single presiding officer they elect a "Presidium" of anywhere from three to a score of members. They hold the chair in rotation and are really an executive committee. They arrange the order of the day, they appoint or at least nominate the sub-committees.

The Presidium is generally chosen by some method of proportional representation. Minority factions are supposed to have a voice according to their strength. Of course, the assembly is always free to revolt against the Presidium and elect a new one, but barring such occasional contretemps, the Presidium generally runs the show. The faction which has won control of this presiding body can railroad through almost anything.

The executive committee of our American Federation of Labor does not have nearly as strong a hold on that body as the Presidium of the Russian Soviet. But on the other hand Mr. Gompers is not so much exposed to sudden waves of passion. American Labor, with a long tradition of organization behind it, knows what it wants. It is not so easy to stampede it.

While the organization of this first Workingmen's Soviet in 1905 made "control" by a party machine peculiarly easy, there was less continuity of policy than one would expect. The workers had not settled down to any coherent program.

I had supper one evening with Martov, a leader of the Menshevist faction. He said, with great satisfaction, that, after a long struggle, his crowd had won control of the Presidium and he told me in some detail just the order of business they were getting put through that night. I went with him to the Soviet meeting and as soon as it had been called to order, an unknown and brand-new delegate began to speak, without being recognized by the chair, and he swept the assembly into a stampede against the leadership they had the day before decided on.

This first "Soviet of Workingmen's Deputies" was suppressed when the reaction gained once more the upper hand. If it had been allowed to persist it undoubtedly would have developed a definite form and its discussions would have gradually produced some uniformity of policy among the workers.

When the Revolution broke out in February, 1917, a new Soviet sprang almost spontaneously into existence. As the garrison had sided with the revolutionists, its name was expanded to the "Council of Workingmen's and Soldiers' Deputies." In the first days of the Revolution there was a strong sentiment for union in the face of a possible reaction and the various Socialist elements buried their differences for the moment. The first Presidium was a coalition of all the Socialist factions. An appeal was issued calling on all the workers of Russia to organize local Soviets and they sprang up in every industrial center. The nearest analogy which we can find in our American life to these organizations would be the local trade union federations in our big cities. All the workers, irrespective of their trades, were grouped in the same Soviets and, in general, delegates were elected from each factory. But any analogy with our labor organizations is misleading. It is necessary to emphasize the extemporaneous character of the Soviet. None of the Russian cities had been thoroughly unionized. This was the first organization which the great mass of the workers had joined. There was a complete lack of tradition. Most American trade union members have a pretty definite program; they have been members of a union for years, have seen its struggles and have reached an estimate of what is desirable and what is possible. In the discussions of the American Federation of Labor, delegates are always referring to past experiences and one convention after another follows a definite policy. The Russian workingman has all this yet to learn. This, which might be called a corporate ideal of our working class, changes and evolves constantly but rarely abruptly. The decisions of the Russian Soviets quite naturally have often been fantastically contradictory.

Very shortly after the Revolution, the Petrograd Soviet called a National Congress of all the local Soviets and, besides delegates from the workingmen, there were many soldier deputies from the interior garrisons and from the armies on the front. This congress, and all those that have succeeded it, also spent a large part of its time in discussing the form of their organization. There were many obvious anomalies, some districts and some trades being immensely over-represented, and there was constant and heated discussion between the soldiers and workers as to the division of power.

Very shortly the first beautiful spirit of unity among the Socialist parties evaporated and the Soviet became a scene of bitter party intrigue. There was no doubt on the part of the rank and file that they did not want leadership from the Bourgeois parties. The Soviets wanted Socialism, but what kind of Socialism was uncertain. The mass of the workers had never had any opportunity to hear free discussion of the merits of the rival parties, only a very small percentage had ever adhered to any of the organizations. The mass of delegates in the local Soviets were unused to the problems they were asked to solve; they were deeply impressed with their own ignorance and illiteracy and were searching for leaders whom they could trust with the great responsibility they had assumed. This was a very favorable field for the development of party machinery and Tammany Hall politics. It was amusing as well as depressing to us, Americans, to see how thoroughly some of the immigrants, returned from our shores, had learned the lessons of gang politics in New York. When the chairman put across some particularly "raw deal" in the way of refusing to recognize a would-be orator, it would not be uncommon to hear indignant cries from some deputies, who had been in America, of "Charlie Murphy"![1]

The intellectual leaders of the Soviet contrived the form of the organization and it was very easy for the Presidium to control. Lenin and the Bolsheviks only differed from other Socialist leaders by the frankness with which they expressed their contempt for the majority rule. None of the leaders of the Soviet, as far as I could see, tried to find out the will of the delegates and assist them in achieving it. They all felt they knew what was best for the masses and tried to manipulate the Soviet machine. As our old guard politicians would have told them, they quickly discovered for themselves that the strategic point in the organization was the "Credential Committee" and when one faction after another succeeded in capturing the Presidium, they always appointed their most expert driver of the "steam roller" to the chairmanship of this committee. When the Bolsheviks won the control, the other Socialist factions protested loudly against the ruthless manner in which Kamenev[2] threw out their regularly elected delegates, but there was as much envy as righteous indignation in their protest. When they had been in power they had also tried—only a little less successfully—to control the Soviet in this manner.

Hardly a week had passed after the deposition of the Tsar, when a bitter conflict arose between the Soviets and the Provisional Government. I have spoken before of the underlying cause of this conflict. The Duma and Zemstvo group had formed the Provisional Government under the premiership of Prince Lvov.[3] They felt that they had originated the Revolution and could carry it on satisfactorily, if these illiterate workingmen in the Soviets would not interfere. The Soviets on the other hand claimed that it was their Revolution and that it was necessary to fight the Provisional Government to keep the "Bourgeoisie" from robbing the working class of its victory.

At first the Soviets did not desire to assume all the power and at the same time all responsibility. They were only gradually organizing themselves and for the first months of the Revolution preferred to let the Provisional Government carry the responsibilities. They were content to keep a close watch on the Ministry, spur them into more radical action and, when they did not like a minister, they were able to throw him out. This anomalous situation of the responsibility in the hands of one group and the power in the hands of another was clearly shown in "the Milyoukov incident." He was Foreign Minister under the Provisional Government and his policy, which among other things included insistence that Constantinople should be annexed by Russia, did not meet the approval of the Soviet. There was a sharp crisis and Milyoukov resigned.

---

[1] Charlie Murphy, American socialist labor activist.

[2] Lev Kamenev, early Bolshevik leader and colleague of Lenin.

[3] Prince Lvov, the first head of the Provisional Government, 1917.

The question of the relative power of the Soviets and the Provisional Government was rather intricate. The Revolution meant first of all the disintegration of the old police power of the State. The Provisional Government inherited all the problems of the Tsar, though none of his coercive power. But there is no doubt that in the early months of the Revolution they had the good wishes of the great mass of the people. They were trying to hold the country together until a Constitutional Assembly could be convened to organize a legal government.

On the other hand the Soviets in the early days of the Revolution had a very limited support in general public opinion, but they had immense power through their control of the strategic industries. The two strongest, oldest, and best organized trade unions were the railroad and telegraph employees. They had proportionately very large representation in the Soviet and came nearer to the Socialist ideal of a "class conscious proletariat" than the other Russian workingmen. And the group which controls railroads and telegraphs, when a nation is at war, is supreme.

The power of the Central Committee of the Soviets over its local branches was always limited and varied greatly. But in general it could call a strike in these organizations and also in ammunition plants. It could not always get the men to go back to work, it was much easier to pull them out. The general democracy of the country was too poorly organized to counterbalance the power of these more disciplined, industrial minorities. There were a whole series of elections in the months before the Bolsheviks won to power and in all cases they showed that the majority of the nation was opposed to government by the Soviet. But these votes were mere expressions of opinion and did not alter the fact that the only power was in the Soviet organization.

This was so clearly realized by the Russians that the principal subject of discussion in their newspapers, both Bourgeois and Socialist, centered around the demand of the Bolsheviks that the Soviets should assume all power. When I reached Petrograd in July, 1917, this question was already to the fore; the Bolsheviks had taken for their slogan, "All Power to the Soviet." They had failed to get the support of the Soviets themselves for this idea. Not only in the Central Executive Committee, but in local Soviets throughout the country, there was still confidence in the sincerity of the Provisional Government and faith in the Constitutional Assembly which was soon to be convened. Impatient at the slowness with which the working class rallied to their ideals, the Bolsheviks attempted an insurrection in the middle of July. It failed from lack of support. The army almost unanimously reasserted its allegiance to the Provisional Government and there was very little response, even from the working class councils, to the idea of government by the Soviets. There was no question at this time, nor had there been for several months, that the Soviets, if they wished it, could paralyze the country, overthrow the entire Provisional Government, as they had occasionally thrown out individual members, and organize a government of their own. But the idea of the dictatorship of a minority class found no broad support even among the industrial workers. The country wanted a democratic government. All classes looked hopefully to the Constitutional Assembly.

The political importance of the Workingmen's Soviet lay in the fact that, while the old State Power had crumbled suddenly, the new government had not yet organized. The policy of the Old Regime had been to prevent the organization of any groups which might supersede it. Neither the Zemstvos nor the Duma had a broad enough popular support to take up the business of government at once. The Co-operatives were not politically minded. And certainly the war made the task of organizing power more difficult. Russia was like a tremendous snake, which had just shed its old skin—the new skin had not yet hardened.

Russia was in a state of solution. The new form had not yet begun to crystallize. The Workingmen's Soviet, in spite of all its imperfections, was a form. It was a new organization, without traditions, still rather undefined, still in the process of finding itself, but the best organization there was. And, through its control of a few vital industries, very much more powerful than anything else.

But at first the Bolsheviks made very little progress. The Soviets themselves were reluctant to use this power. It is very much easier to stop a machine than to make it go. In vote after vote, in the Central Executive Committee and in the local Soviets, the workingmen showed their reluctance to assuming the responsibilities of government.

The Soviet which sprang up simultaneously with the Revolution was primarily a "Strike Committee" an organization of factory workers.

Almost all the agitation which had been carried on among the Petrograd workers, practically all their "organization," was the work of the two Social Democratic factions—Mensheviks and Bolsheviks. Their leaders, who were well known to the workers, at once "captured" the Soviet.

The Socialist Revolutionary Party, which had spent its main efforts among the peasantry, was scarcely represented. There had always been bitter rivalry between them and the Social Democrats. So the Socialist Revolutionaries, in order to give themselves the foundation for a bid for power, at once called an All-Russian Peasant Congress and organized a parallel "Soviet of Peasant Deputies." For several months the Central Executive Committees of the two organizations met in different buildings and a struggle for power between them—really a struggle between the Social Democrats and Socialist Revolutionaries—went on. But from the first, in spite of the relative numerical importance of the city workers and the agricultural population—roughly 10 percent as against 80 percent—the proletarian organization was much the more powerful.

The reason for this anomaly was that the smaller group of industrial workers was very much better organized. The peasant Soviet was a hand-picked affair. It was an artificial—almost fictitious—assembly. The Socialist Revolutionary Party saw the obvious fact that the city workingmen were exercising a vast deal more power than their numbers warranted. They wanted to give the overwhelming peasant majority of the nation a machine for political expression. But in the rural districts there were no pre-existing organizations to build on. The peasant deputies were inevitably chosen from above rather than elected from below. It was inherent in the facts of Russian life that it would take a long time for the peasant masses to become articulate. The first peasant congress was convened in a hurry.

On the other hand, while the workers of no Russian city were "well organized" in our Western sense, there was at least the beginning of a Labor Union Movement. In every factory center there were some organized groups of workers. Their unions were weak and unstable, their ideals were inchoate, but still they could take the initiative in creating local Soviets.

In the general political chaos which followed the collapse of the Tsar, the factory workers, although very weakly organized, were better organized than any other group—very much better than the peasantry.

Tchernov,[4] the leader of the Socialist Revolutionaries, when he became Minister of Agriculture under Kerensky, created "Land Committees" all over Russia. Nominally they were to collect statistics in regard to landholdings, but quite as much they were intended to create local rural organizations which could elect deputies to the All-Russian Peasant Soviet and give it some representative force and vitality.

The obvious struggle which stared every newcomer in the face was that between the Provisional Government and the Soviet of Workingmen's and Soldiers' Deputies, but all the while somewhat deeper below the surface was preparing a conflict of power between the ten million factory workmen and the eighty million peasants. The city proletariat—already somewhat organized—had everything their own way at the start. The peasants, with no pre-existing organization, were inevitably inarticulate and the work of organizing them into a coherent political force was necessarily slow.

---

[4] Victor Chernov, Socialist Revolutionary leader and minister of agriculture in the Provisional Government under Kerensky.

Chapter VII
The Political Parties

No concise definitions of political parties can ever be adequate. Every group is divided and subdivided and there is a certain amount of overlapping and interlocking between parties. But as reference must be made to the various Russian parties, I will attempt a very brief survey of them.

It must be always borne in mind that the Russian parties, so recently organized, so recently emerging from underground conspiracy to legal organization, differ in almost every detail from the political parties we know in Western Europe and America. Until the revolutionary outbreak following the Japanese War forced the Tsar to convoke the Duma, all political party action was illegal. It is only within recent years that it has been possible to attempt such organizations as those we know. Until the Revolution of 1917 there was no opportunity for public discussion of political theory in the press or in meetings. In the Duma, the elected delegates of the people had a certain immunity and could talk freely about their party platforms. But only a small part of this discussion found its way into the press of the country. Only the literate upper classes of the nation had had any opportunity to form political affiliations.

In the old days I have, for instance, visited secret meetings of the various Socialist parties, but they had no resemblance to Socialist party meetings in America. Generally some university graduate, who had joined one or the other of the conspirative organizations, had a "class" of workmen or peasants and was teaching them to read, using as a textbook the propaganda tracts of his group. There was almost no opportunity for an illiterate adherent of one party to know the thought and program of the others. In the old conspirative days, it was inevitable that the loyalty of the rank and file was to personalities rather than to principles. Into the bleak misery of some factory or village there would come—in disguise—a young man or woman from the schools with a message of hope—the first word of hope that had ever been heard. In some corner, safely hidden from the police, the newcomer would read aloud a strange book about the Revolution and the happy days beyond. He would explain, sentence by sentence, all the unfamiliar words. "Do you want the Revolution?" The newcomer would ask at last. "Land for the peasants, bread for the worker, and liberty for all?"

"Of course."

"Well, then you belong to my party."

If by any chance one of the audience had heard of some other party and asked about it, he would surely be told that that was all foolishness. If he really wanted the Revolution he must stick to the speaker's party.

The elaborations of the various party programs—and such discussions were marked by extremely bitter partisanship—were confined almost entirely to the Intelligentsia. The rank and file took no interest in, had no understanding of, these arid discussions of principle. They gave their loyalty to the person who had first stirred them from their miserable hopelessness by a promise of better things.

One main line of cleavage is encountered in almost every Russian discussion. It goes back to the days when Peter the Great tried to Europeanize his subjects. An opposition party at once sprang up, which later was called "Slavophile." On one side of this line of cleavage were those who wished to introduce into Russia innovations from the West, on the other side those who believed that the Russians were a peculiar people and that their own institutions, properly developed, would suit them best. This struggle has been very evident in the Russian literature, more recently it has appeared in the realm of practical politics. Among the liberals, for instance, you will encounter some who always use the foreign word "Parliament," and others who express almost the same idea by the Russian word "Duma." This matter of vocabulary is a fairly accurate indication of the political opinions of those who use them.

Within the Socialist ranks the cleavage had been more sharp. On the side of Peter the Great are the "Marxists." They wish to Europeanize the Revolution. They have taken their ideas from the political philosophy of the West and try to impose them, in spite of reluctant facts, on Russia. They draw their inspiration from the thoughts and words of Karl Marx, rather than from the realities of the social structure they are trying to remodel.

On the Slavophile side are the Socialist Revolutionaries, who believe that the Russian Revolution must be Russian, that the better future they dream of can be achieved by the development of distinctly Slavic institutions.

This theoretical distinction works out in very real practical differences. The Social Democrats—both the Mensheviks and Bolsheviks—have confined their activity almost entirely to the city populations, where they find factory workers, more or less resembling the industrial proletarians of Marx's philosophy. They believe as he did that the agricultural workers are fated to become industrialized and until this evolution is completed are unfit for real revolutionary activity. The Socialist Revolutionaries, on the contrary, have to an equal extent confined their work to the peasantry. Eighty percent or more of the Russian people live and work on the farm. They have institutions of their own—unknown in the West—which offer a basis for the new order. To the taunt of the Marxists that the village commune, the Mir, the Co-operatives are not pure Socialism, this party replies complacently that they are better.

In general the Social Democrats are influential among the city workers and the Socialist Revolutionaries among the peasants.

It is necessary to emphasize once more that these party distinctions are clearly understood only by the educated. The mass of the people have only the vaguest ideas of the differences in theory which make such bitter conflicts among their leaders.

The Duma in 1917, on the eve of the Revolution, was divided from Right to Left in the following groups:

1. The Reactionaries. They were opposed to the very existence of the Duma and wanted the Tsar to abolish it and go back to the fine old days of the last century.
2. Next to them sat the "Octobrists." They accepted the Tsar's manifesto of October 1905, which created the Duma, as their platform. They did not wish to see parliamentarism develop beyond that point.
3. The Constitutional Democrats—Kadets. They were the most progressive element of the Intelligentsia. Their leader, Professor Paul Milyoukov, was a fearless orator and one of the most severe critics of the reactionary and inefficient government. This party stood for "constitutional progress." They had for their avowed ideal a limited monarchy on the pattern of England. Many of their prominent members, however, in private went further and desired a republic. They constituted the center of the Duma but were more radical in the economic reforms they demanded than either of our great American parties.
4. Next to them was a combination group, sometimes called Popular Socialists, sometimes "Trudoviks" or Laborites. They had been much more powerful in the first Duma, but had now dwindled to a small intellectual group, who were Socialist in their conceptions, but were avoiding any program which the government would prohibit as illegal. One of their leading members was Kerensky. He was really a Socialist Revolutionary, but camouflaged as a Trudovik, so that he could stand for election to the Duma.
5. On the extreme Left were the Social Democrats divided into their two factions, Bolsheviks and Mensheviks.

The Socialist Revolutionary Party was not formally represented in the Duma as it was illegal. It had always stood for conspirative terrorism, and the famous assassinations of Von Plehve and the Grand Duke Sergius had been acknowledged by them. It was a crime to belong to their party and they could not openly nominate candidates for the Duma. But some of their members, like Kerensky, had been elected under different labels.

When the Revolution broke out in the spring of 1917, the two parties of the Right, the Reactionaries and the Octobrists, disappeared and from then on the Constitutional

Democrats, under the leadership of Milyoukov, constituted the extreme Right. The Socialist Revolutionaries, now able to come out in the open, became the strongest of all the political parties. In the numerous elections which marked the first months of the Revolution, this party nearly always won by a large majority. They polled nearly three-quarters of the votes in the municipal elections of Moscow and well over two-thirds of the votes for members of the Constitutional Assembly, the last general election which has been held in Russia.

One very striking phenomenon of Russian politics was the important role played by the Political Exile. The mass of the people knew very little about the fine distinctions in theory between the parties, but they all instinctively revered the men and women who had suffered for their political opposition to the Tsar. The Revolution opened all the prisons, and a flood of those who had suffered in the cause of liberty came back from Siberian or foreign exile to Petrograd and Moscow. The "Comrade" who had gone to jail on behalf of the people was sure of an attentive audience. His devotion to the Revolution was proven, he did not need arguments.

But it was equally evident that the career of the revolutionary conspirator had not been a good training for the work of practical politics in a free country. The predominance in politics of these returned exiles was a misfortune for Russia. Most of these men and women were exceptionally high-minded, but their previous life had naturally unfitted them for the task before them.

It had been above all a "hectic" life. There had been periods when it was necessary for them to meet calmly a great danger, not the easier task of the soldier in taking risks in common, but isolated bravery, the greatest strain of all. After a time, generally brief, of agitation among the masses, constantly hunted by the Tsar's police, there would come arrest and a long spell of bitter monotony with nothing to do but pace the cell and think. Then perhaps there would be another tense moment of escape, followed by the dreary life of the political exile—idleness, cigarettes, and interminable cups of tea—endless, futile, hair-splitting discussions—in the poor cafes of Paris, Zurich, or the East Side of New York. There was admirable devotion to the cause of liberty among these returned exiles, but very little practical experience in the work of government.

I have known many of these exiles, in New York, Paris, and Switzerland. There was an infinite pathos in their thwarted nobility of spirit. All they had wanted was to serve. And this generous impulse had landed them in prison. The very strength of the idealism which had made it impossible for them to tolerate in silence the infamy of the Old Regime had made them intolerant fanatics. They were so desperately sincere, so passionate in their devotion, that their partisanship was bitter and often petty. Their vices were high-hearted virtues distorted by a crazy tyranny.

I recall one gentle girl, whose whole soul had been wrapped up in music. With never a thought of politics she had gone out into the villages to gather and record folksongs. A provincial governor, of almost unimaginable stupidity, took fright at her wanderings and sent her to Siberia as a dangerous political agitator, on an administrative order, without even the form of a trial. It was from her cellmate in prison that she had had her first lessons in revolution. After some years in prison she escaped and returned not to her music, but to preach revolt.

She was hanged in 1906. But at least her life, after she joined the Revolution, was full of activity.

More pitiful in a way was the case of those who dragged out an empty existence in exile. No manner of life could be contrived less fitted for training people in the work of politics. These people who turned the Soviets and Assemblies of Russia into debating societies, bitter and barren, while the real work of reorganizing the country was neglected, had never been allowed the chance to earn experience in the problems they discussed. If they were first, last, and all the time impractical, inexperienced theoreticians, the blame lies with the Old Regime, which had intentionally, stubbornly, ruthlessly thwarted all their generous aspirations. The Tsar had not wanted them to learn the business of government.

But although it is impossible to blame them for their peculiar mentality, it was very obvious that their prestige in the days after the Revolution was disastrous to the country and also to the very ideals to which they had devoted their lives.

The old traditions of conspiracy were a tragic handicap in the attempt to organize a free government. The doctrinaire self-certainty which comes from solitary confinement made co-operation difficult. Discussion of fine points in theory, which seem worth arguing about in the idleness of exile, were heartbreakingly out of place when action was needed. The mass of the people looked to these "Heroes of the Revolution" for leadership. They received instead of the healing bread they hungered for a cold and cruel stone of Byzantine disputations, which they could not understand.

Chapter VIII
"Land"

The main issue, which would face any revolution in Russia, was sure to be the land problem.

The catastrophic world war might distract some people's attention, the desperate insistence of the city workers that their demands should be met first might complicate and obscure the basic conflict. But such things could be only momentary diversions. 80 percent or more of the population were peasants, whose only idea of "Revolution" was freedom from the oppression of the landlords. The same proportion, of course, held for the army.

It was no new problem. Many heavy tomes had been written on the agrarian question. They are highly controversial. But there would be general agreement among the disputants, I believe, on the following outline of the situation.

When the Serfs were emancipated, a little more than fifty years ago, the edict required the former master to turn over to the "freed" peasant a fixed acreage per capita. The peasantry entered into immediate possession and the landlords were immediately paid a compensation by the government. The peasants became debtors to the State for this amount.

The law was typical of the evils of governmental centralization. It looked uniform on paper but worked out very diversely in practice. Soil conditions, of course, varied greatly in different provinces. The peasant allotments, while barely sufficient to support life in the richest districts, were utterly inadequate in the less favored regions. The landlords were allowed to select the portion of their estates to be allotted to the peasants and, while perhaps some of the landlords good-naturedly gave their best farms to the peasants, the temptation was strong to unload on them the least profitable land. The redemption tax, by which the peasants paid the state for their lands, was also uniform on paper, but it was exceedingly heavy even on the communities which by a combination of lucky chances had drawn fairly good land and absurdly impossible for the great mass of the peasants who had been allotted poor land. In 1906 I was shown an official tax chart of European Russia. There were only a few white spots indicating districts where the full taxes had been paid up to date; there were various degrees of shading and great black blotches—territories bigger than New England—where the peasants were more than five years in arrears on their taxes.

The methods of the tax gatherers were not gentle. They seized farm animals and farm implements if the taxes were not paid. This forced the peasantry to use the very lowest forms of farm culture. If by a miracle of thrift one peasant accumulated a small capital, he did not dare to invest it in any tangible thing which the tax gatherer could see and grasp. There is small reason to accuse the Russian peasant of stupidity because of his inadequate methods of agriculture. He had no incentive and no possible methods of improving them.

While there were very few peasants who could be called "prosperous," there was great inequality in the degree of their misery. I saw some statistics gathered by the Zemstvo organization to show how the lot of the peasants about the beginning of the century varied from district to district. In almost all parts of Great Russia the communal holdings were so small that the peasants had to work some of the time as laborers on the big estates. In some provinces the average number of days which the peasants worked for the landlords was five a month. In the worst districts the average ran up to five days a week. The average for all Russia was, as I remember, ten days a month. It was very rare that their own allotment sufficed for their support and absorbed all their labor.

In the old days of serfdom a form of communism had developed in the villages. When the master wished to have three men plow one of his fields on a certain day, he did not go to the trouble of picking the individuals to do it; his bailiff called on the village elder and said three men were needed. The Serfs, through their own organization, divided the work demanded among themselves and when they were freed, the land allotments were not given to them individually but to their communities. They were not individually liable for the taxes, the state dealt directly with their communal organizations. This further discouraged individual thrift, as the property of any individual could be attached for communal debts, and as the communities were chronically in arrears on their taxes, there was little chance for any improvement in the condition of the peasants.

The importance of this village community—"the Mir"—has been one of the subjects of keenest controversy, but after all an exaggerated importance had been given to the discussion. The Mir system is not universal even in European Russian and is practically unknown in Siberia. My own impression is that the peasants feel this communal organization is a protection against government oppression and the more miserable their condition the more loyal they are to it. But where there is any possibility of prosperity, the individual peasants are inclined to leave the Mir.

After the collapse of the revolutionary movement in 1906 and 1907, a series of land reforms was instituted by the reactionary Premier, Stolypin.[1] His policy was stern repression for the rebellious factory workers and an attempt to break up the communal unity of the village by allowing the development of class differences among

---

[1] Petr Stolypin, prime minister from 1906–12.

the peasants. He struck off the greatest part of the back taxes and issued laws making it possible for members of the Mir to sell out their share in the communal holdings. In the decade that has passed since these reforms went into force, there have been very considerable changes in the status of the peasant, but it is too short a period to determine what the results would have been. There does not seem to have been any general agreement among the peasants as to their policy towards these reforms. In some cases they have rallied to the defense of the Mir and resisted Stolypin's project, in other districts they seemed to have welcomed the change. There has probably been, although statistics are lacking, a considerable increase in the number of small holdings, and many peasants, who had found it impossible to support their families in the village, have sold out and gone into the cities to find work in the factories.

From all sides one receives evidence that it is an almost universal belief of the peasants that "the land belongs to the tiller." They do not seem particularly interested in the legal aspects of land tenure, but they have this profound conviction that the land *ought*—in an almost religious sense—to belong to the peasant who works it. It was certain that the relaxation of state terrorism, which would be implied by any revolution, would be accompanied by an effort on the part of the peasantry to put this vague faith into practice.

There was almost an equal unanimity among the more fortunate classes on the need of sweeping reforms in the system of land tenure. Even in the third Duma, the most reactionary of the four, there was no organized group which dared to defend things as they were. There was, of course, violent difference of opinion as to what reforms should be undertaken and how far they should go.

Roughly the Russian land system may be divided into four categories:

1. Immense estates. They include the monastery lands, the royal appanages and hereditary estates which go back to court favorites of Catherine the Great. In general these immense estates are obviously inexpedient from the point of view of general welfare, they are nearly always mismanaged and the culture is very low. Those who enjoy the immense income from them give no compensating service to the community.
2. Moderate estates. Some of these go back a long way in history, but they are more likely to be modern in origin. Some of them are merely pleasure places for people whose main source of income is lucrative court posts or city industry. A number of them, however, are successful agricultural projects being managed by experts and models of good farming.
3. Small holdings. Small holdings are the normal condition in Siberia, in some of the Ukrainian and Caucasus Provinces. Due to the Stolypin laws they are becoming more numerous in the central provinces of Great Russia.

4. Communal plots. The largest part of cultivated farm land in Great Russia, which is in the hands of those who work it, is held by the village communities. The degree of culture is very low and they are from the economic point of view very poorly developed and in general inadequate to support the communities which own them.

Practically all of the political parties have favored the expropriation of the immense estates and their redistribution among the peasantry. The Kadets are divided in regard to the moderate estates. Some would break them up into small holdings, but others are impressed by the idea that agriculture can be carried on more profitably in large units. This is a very dubious argument, as countries where small holdings prevail, Belgium and France, are more productive than countries of large estates like England and Hungary. All the Socialist parties are in favor of some form of nationalization of all the land.

Of the various agrarian programs, that of the Popular Socialist Party seems to me the best thought out. It is one of the weakest of all the parties numerically and its influence is small, but it has some very intelligent members. They have recognized first of all the dangers of any centralized solution of the problems. Conditions of soil and climate and custom vary so greatly in Russia, that any uniform system is certain to be intensely unpopular in some districts. They have worked out what they call "The Labor Norm," i.e., the amount of land which can be cultivated under any given conditions by one family without help of hired laborers. They propose that careful investigation in each province shall establish a "Labor Norm" for that district, the actual inhabitants of the territory to be given land up to this "Norm." As the density of population varies, some districts would be overcrowded and some underpopulated and they propose an elaborate system of cross-migration to meet this problem.

There is also a burning discussion on two details of the general question. First of all there is a controversy between those who believe in individual ownership by small holders and those who favor nationalization. This seems to be largely a local dispute. People coming from districts where individual ownership is long established realize that any nationalization of the land would be resisted. On the other hand, representatives of provinces where the old communal ownership system is prevalent and popular, wish to generalize the customs of their home communities. In this matter also the Popular Socialists have very wisely emphasized the need of decentralization. They would allow the actual workers on the land in each district to determine for themselves the principle of land tenure.

Another great subject of discussion is that of "Compensation." To what extent should the landlords be repaid for the land which is to be distributed among the peasantry? Here again there is general unanimity that royal appanages and church lands and most of the immense estates owned by the descendants of old court favorites should be taken over without compensation. The Kadets and Popular Socialists are in favor of compensating the owners of estates above the Labor Norm who have acquired land as a result of their own efforts and thrift. But this matter is wholly an academic dispute among the politicians of the Intelligentsia. The real problem is what the peasants, who would have to pay a compensation, think. There is little doubt that they are unanimous against any compensation to the old landlords. They have suffered so heavily from the crushing redemption taxes, which they had to pay in exchange for their starveling allotments, they are so convinced that they have already been immensely rack-rented by the landlords, that they are reluctant to discuss any compensation whatever.

There was every reason to expect that the agrarian program of the Socialist Revolutionists, which differed only in detail from that of the Popular Socialists, would be the one finally decided upon. They carried almost every election by a large majority and the Constitutional Assembly, which was supposed to deal with the matter, was theirs by two-thirds. Kerensky, himself a Socialist Revolutionary, had appointed Tchernov Minister of Agriculture. Tchernov was the author of their agrarian program. He had created peasant Land Committees throughout the entire country, partly to collect statistics about the conditions and partly to prepare for the enforcement of his party program. It is uncertain business speculating on what would have happened in politics if something else had not happened, but there is every reason to believe that, if the Bolshevist Insurrection had not overthrown the Constitutional Assembly, a serious attempt would have been made to solve the Russian land question according to the program of this party.

However there was another element in the situation, of which the Bolsheviks, although they were not responsible for it, took advantage. The peasants were becoming impatient. When the first news of the fall of the Tsar reached the country almost all the landlords fled in terror to the cities. They expected an immediate outbreak of peasant disorder. They knew the discontent of the peasantry and there had been very serious "jacqueries" during the disturbances of 1906 and '07. When I reached Russia in July 1917, almost all of the landlords had gone back to their estates. To everyone's surprise the peasants had not started "to take the land." There was here, I think, a very definite feeling on the part of the peasants that an orderly and legal redistribution would be preferable to haphazard disturbance. However, the Revolution meant nothing to them, unless it meant land. Throughout the summer there came increasing evidence that the peasants were losing their patience. Month after month they were told that the Revolution had succeeded, but it did not in any way meet their problems. In July I heard of two or three cases where the peasants had sacked a manor house and driven off or killed the landlords. By the fall such news items were common in the papers; they were too widely scattered over the country to indicate anything but a very general and growing discontent.

Shortly before his fall, Kerensky summoned in Petrograd "the Democratic Conference." It was not an elected body in our sense, but various organizations—

Trade Unions, Co-operative Societies, Zemstvos, Town Councils, etc.—were asked to send delegates. It was sometimes referred to as the "Pre-Parliament" and it was hoped that it would hold the country together under Kerensky's lead until the Constitutional Assembly could convene and take over the power of the state.

The opening address was made by Madame Katherine Breshkovskaia,[2] the oldest delegate. She spoke, I think, some of the wisest political words that I heard in Russia. She pointed to this rapidly rising wave of peasant discontent. At first the peasantry had had complete confidence that the revolutionary leaders would show them a peaceful way to the solution of their difficulties. But gradually month by month, as the consideration of the peasant's needs was postponed, this confidence was waning. Here and there, more frequently every week that passed, peasant communities lost faith in the revolutionary government and tried to solve their difficulties locally. Madame Breshkovskaia told the government that in this question of the land they would have to hurry.

The realization of the land program of the Socialist Revolutionists, or of any thought-out, planned solution of the problem was threatened by delay. The peasants were getting to the limit of their patience.

---

[2] Ekaterina Breshko-Breshkovskaia, Populist and Socialist-Revolutionary, often called the "grandmother of the revolution."

Chapter IX
"Peace"

In sharp distinction to the perennial "land question" the peace issue was temporary, but it was no less burning. Everyone in Russia wanted peace, but almost everybody wanted an honest, democratic, and general peace. In midsummer of 1917 no one, not even the Bolsheviks, wanted a separate peace. The argument raged over the question: How to get a general peace?

Even in 1914 it was only the more enlightened classes who were enthusiastic about the war. The great mass of the Dark People did not understand it. They were simply driven into it. By the first of 1917 even the officers were tired of it. Russia was exhausted, the flimsy industrial structure of the country was about to collapse. Russian soldiers had fought with clubbed rifles from lack of ammunition. The Zemstvo workers, who knew most about it, were pessimistic, there was no possible chance of getting the necessary supplies to the army. Unless peace came quickly it would be impossible to keep the troops in trenches much longer. Already by midsummer, 1917, there had been sectors of the front where there had been no food distributed to the soldiers for three days on end. When the transport was further dislocated by the winter snow, whole regiments would die of starvation. Back of all the theoretic discussion of "war and peace" was the specter of "Force Majeure."

Moreover, after the Revolution the progressive democratic elements in Russia needed peace, so that they could turn their energy to the rebuilding of the nation. This desire on the part of all the Russians to have peace was not popular with the censors of the Allies, very little news of it got out to the Western world, but the desire was there. "How to get a good peace?" One extreme—ignoring all unpleasant facts—said: "Crush Germany. Intensify the war. Win!" At the other extreme were those who—also avoiding all unpleasant facts—said: "Let's go on strike against war. If Russia sets the example of throwing down its arms, all the world will follow suit."

But thoughtful people, carrying the great mass with them, took a middle position, and in this the Petrograd Soviet and the Provisional Government at first were in complete accord. They lined up with President Wilson. They believed that if the nations of the Entente offered a just and democratic peace, one of two things would happen; either the liberal elements in Germany—the famous "Reichstag Majority"—would be able to win control and force the Kaiser to give up his imperialistic dreams, or the issue between democracy and autocracy would be so clear that every

Russian soldier would see that it was necessary to continue the war in order to protect the Revolution. They set the fashion by publicly announcing that Russia abandoned all aggressive claims and they asked their allies to join them in offering a peace on the threefold base of "no annexation, no indemnities, the self-determination of nations." They were not so naive as to believe that the Kaiser and the Pan-German maniacs would accept this formula. They believed that the unity of the German nation was maintained only by the theory that they were fighting in self-defense and they believed that if this bugaboo of threatening dismemberment were dispelled there would be a political turnover in Germany.

It is necessary to clarify this point. It was misunderstood by the allied statesmen. In one of President Wilson's speeches he exhorted the Russians not to trust in the sincerity of the Imperial Government of Germany. It was arguing against a straw man. They never had.

The new government of Russia was revolutionary. They knew the secret treaties—which later Trotsky made public. They knew how viciously imperialistic the war aims of their predecessors had been. They knew that, whoever had been responsible for the outbreak of the war, the Germans were, in 1917, defending their Fatherland from dismemberment. They renounced, as far as Russia was concerned, all the evil projects of the Tsar.

Their own Revolution had succeeded so easily that they probably exaggerated the intensity of popular discontent in Germany. They hoped that, if their allies followed their example in giving up all schemes of conquest, publicly announcing "purified" war aims, the enemy countries would also follow their example and establish democratic governments in place of the war lords. In this they were only taking a new step along the road clearly indicated in so many of President Wilson's speeches as his own and the American policy.

It is necessary to emphasize one other point in this revolutionary peace program. The Provisional Government and later Kerensky never pretended to be sure it would work. It might fail. Perhaps the German people, even if assured of a generous democratic peace, would not revolt against the Kaiser, perhaps they all were infected with this mania of military grandeur. But, they said in that case Russia can continue to fight. Then we could go to our discontented, discouraged, war-weary soldiers and inspire them to a new enthusiasm, a new ardor. If only we can put the issue to them clearly. If we can say, the war would stop tomorrow, if the Germans wanted a just peace, they have been offered a democratic, revolutionary peace, but they will not revolt against their Tsar, as you have done; if only we can make our people see that the Germans have refused a frank offer of democratic justice, that they continue the war because they wish to enslave the world, our soldiers will go on with the war, they will go without food, they will fight with sticks and stones to protect the Revolution.

This was the general attitude I found in Russia in the midsummer of 1917. Everyone wanted peace. Especially all the leaders of democracy. They could not attend at the same time to the reconstruction of the country and the prosecution of the war. But what they needed and yearned for was a general peace. They begged their allies to appreciate their desperate position and help them.

"We have renounced all the Tsar's dreams of conquest. Purify your own war aims. Join us in offering a peace on the bases of 'no annexations, no indemnities, self-determination of nations.' Then one of two things will happen. Either we will make a general peace—not with the Kaiser—but with his revolutionary people. Or, if this offer is refused by the Central Empires, our people will forget their weariness in the ardor of a revolutionary war."

We who were in Russia representing, in one capacity or another, the allied governments, waited in desperate impatience for the answer of our governments to this appeal of revolutionary Russia. There was not a ghost of a chance that Russia would stay effectively in the war if her allies refused to co-operate in her hope for a general peace. We had no way of knowing what was going on in the diplomatic councils of London, Paris, Rome, and Washington; we were like "Sister Ann" in her tower looking out in agonized suspense for the coming rescuer. We could see only our little corner of the chessboard and the move which was obviously necessary there, but the strategists of the game were watching moves and determining their policy on conditions beyond our vision. There was a fighting chance of stabilizing Russia—the cause was not yet hopelessly lost—a chance of kindling renewed ardor in the army. If the Central Empires had refused—as I believe they would—to accept a democratic peace, then it would have been possible to make the Kaiser appear the one great counter-revolutionist.

We will not know until men still young write memoirs in their old age why the Allies refused to define their war aims. If Mr. Wilson could have formulated his fourteen terms in July instead of January there would have been some hope. But the refusal of the Allies to even discuss the Russian proposals was fatal as far as Russia was concerned; it dampened the ardor of all our friends and it gave a new and tremendous weapon to our enemies.

It was not till this refusal had become clear that the Bolsheviks dared to advocate a separate peace with Germany and they could not have won large adherence to this idea except for their assertion that separate negotiations would force the Allies to consent to general negotiations. There were three themes in all their arguments. First, they vastly overestimated the importance of Russia in the crisis. They asserted that if they struck against war the Allies would lose all hope of victory and be forced to "purify their aims." I think they were sincerely surprised and rather peevish that their forecasts were disproved, that the Allies carried on the war against Germany to a successful conclusion without them. They were very sure in those summer months of 1917 that, if they withdrew from the war, their former allies would lack the courage and resources to continue the fight.

Their second theme was that the refusal of the Allies to discuss openly the terms on which they would agree to peace was a direct admission at once of villainous schemes of conquest and fear of revolt by their own working class, if these schemes were known. "Why," said the Bolsheviks, "should revolutionary Russia go on fighting for the hidden aims of foreign governments, the allies of our former Tsar, war aims which they are ashamed to admit to their own people?"

Their third and favorite theme was the impending revolution in Germany. It was only delayed by fear of the imperialist projects of the Entente. The Bolsheviks asserted that if the Russians repudiated their allies and threw down their arms, that the German working class would be so impressed by their *beau geste* that they would at once revolt against the Kaiser. Revolutions would become epidemic. The capitalist governments of the Entente and America would be overthrown. The era of brotherhood among nations would begin.

I have never heard anyone state the proposition that two plus two is four with more conviction than the Bolsheviks argued on the above lines.

Lenin's prophecies of what would happen were perhaps no more inaccurate than those of other politicians, but he was willing to gamble everything on his guess. The ordinary statesman tries to plan some reserve in case his guesses fail.

If Kerensky had been convinced that Lenin's forecasts of what would happen were correct, he would have sided with him in this matter. He also wanted the earliest possible peace. All the discussion on the subject in Russia, from the Revolution in February up to the signing of the treaty at Brest-Litovsk, was on this point of method. Everybody wanted a general, democratic peace. The question was how to get it?

Lenin and his friends said: "All we have to do is to lay down our arms and we will get a just revolutionary peace." Trotsky was not going to treat with the governments of the enemies and allies, but directly with the people. Those who argued, and later fought, against the Bolsheviks said that this method would not give them peace. "Having renounced all the imperialistic designs of the Tsar—annexation and indemnities—we must hold our line, protect the Revolution until the democratic elements among our allies force their governments to a democratic definition of war aims. Then if there is a revolution in Germany we will get the peace we want. But, if the Germans do not accept a just peace, we will have to fight on. Then it would be a clear issue between democracy and autocracy and we could get up enthusiasm for war. But we cannot throw down our arms now on the strength of Lenin's promise that there will be an immediate revolution in Germany."

More and more clearly as the summer dragged on this became the issue between the Bolsheviks and the Provisional Government on the peace question. Lenin insisted that if Russia threw down her arms, both the enemy and allied nations would be forced to follow suit. It is easy to be wise after the fact and show how utterly wrong Lenin was in his forecasts. But the politicians of the parties opposed to the Bolsheviks were wise before the fact. They foresaw very clearly that Lenin's proposals would not work.

Chapter X
Kerensky

The first year after the fall of the Tsar can be summarized as the gradual break-up of the revolutionary majority. All reports concur that the first days of the New Regime were marked by a wonderful unity of spirit, all the nation united in common rejoicing that the tragedy of the Tsar was ended, in a common aspiration to make freedom succeed. There was no fear of reaction in those first days because the majority in favor of the Revolution was so overwhelming.

When I reached Petrograd in July this revolutionary unity was already shattered. The Russians talk a great deal about "co-operation," but more often they act on the opposed principle of "No Compromise." In general a Russian, if he is outvoted—whether on the board of directors of a symphony orchestra or in councils of state—resigns. When the liberal landlord element under Prince Lvov found that they could not have their own way with the Revolution, they withdrew. When Professor Milyoukov discovered that he could not impose his pet ideas of foreign policy on the nation, he resigned in a huff. And this incident instead of being laughable was tragic, for he was the dictator of the Constitutional Democratic Party and carried them with him into the opposition.

The extreme radical parties, who wanted immediate peace, immediate socialization of industry, immediate solution of the land problem, following the example of the conservatives, refused to give any support to a government which did not accept their entire program.

So by midsummer, Kerensky was left almost alone to face the reaction on one side and the rising tide of popular disillusionment and impatience on the other. Even his own friends—the Socialist Revolutionary Party—did not support him solidly. It was divided into a Right, Center, and Left faction. And the "Left," because they could not have everything their own way, resigned and went over to the Bolsheviks.

It is doubtful if the Archangel Gabriel could have succeeded in the task before Kerensky. He was faced by a vicious dilemma, he believed in the necessity of continuing the war until a general and democratic peace could be secured. This of course implied the maintenance of national unity in the face of the enemy. He continually struggled for a coalition ministry, "uniting all the vital forces of the Revolution." But this meant certain concessions to the landed liberals, some compromise with the industrial magnates who controlled the output of munitions, and a conciliatory attitude towards the corps of officers, the indefinite postponement of some of the social and economic reforms to which he was pledged, in which he sincerely believed, and for which the people clamored more threateningly every day.

Most of Kerensky's critics blamed him for not having had the "strength of character" to suppress seditious propaganda. But this is simply condemning the sincerity of his democratic ideals. Hanging Trotsky would not have solved the land problem, nor have made the population long for peace less passionately. Kerensky was a lawyer and all his life he had dedicated himself to the defense of political prisoners caught under the Juggernaut of the Tsar's tyranny. He really believed in this liberty he had so long defended. He did not want to rule as the Tsar had ruled. He was a true democrat. Besides he was a shrewder politician than most of his critics. He knew the limitations of his power. The illusion that the situation might be restored by an appeal to violence was deep-seated and persistent among the educated classes of Russia. It was shared by many of the allied officials, who were advising the government. Of course, the illiterate had their illusions too, but the upper class had a fixed idea that what was needed was a little flogging, a few court-martials.

"If the first time the peasants sacked an estate, the Provisional Government had sent troops and made a real example—"

"If they had enforced the death penalty in the first case of mutiny at the front—"

It was so easy to say! But the troops which supported the Provisional Government would not march against the peasants, and soldiers who mutiny against their officers are as useless for execution squads as for assault.

Kornilov[1] tried to reestablish discipline in the Army on these lines. The strangest mixture of liberal college professors, ex-favorites of the Tsar, and former revolutionists persuaded this simple-minded Cossack that he was an incipient Napoleon. When he gave orders to march against the Revolution nobody marched but his staff of officers. It was an attempt at strong arm work, but the arm was withered.

After Kornilov, another Cossack, Kaledin,[2] tried it. But even the Cossack troops were so tired of war that they pretended to be Bolsheviks in order to avoid a new campaign.

Napoleon was the popular commander of a victorious, glory-hungry, enthusiastic army when he made his bid for power.

It was very striking to watch how slowly a comprehension of what the Revolution meant in this matter spread in Russia. Everyone among the Intelligentsia seemed to think at first that the Revolution meant the triumph of his own ideas. They were sadly disillusioned, and wrote out their resignations as soon as they found they could not have their own way. Very few realized at first that the real import of the Revolu-

---

[1] Lavr Kornilov, general of the army under Kerensky, led an attempt to overthrow Kerensky in August 1917, which was turned back with the help of Red Guards.

[2] Dmitrii Kaledin, leader of anti-Bolshevik faction during the Civil War of 1918–21.

tion was that force had evaporated from the state. The policeman and his club had vanished.

For months after the necessity had passed, the peasants continued to bow low before the landlords and pay rent. The old ruling class pushed humble people into the gutter, as though there still was a police force to protect them if their arrogance was questioned.

Very gradually the Dark People awoke to the new situation. The peasants learned that there was no one to protect the Great House on the hill, the workers learned that they could not be imprisoned for demanding a living wage, the soldiers and sailors discovered that they could square their grudges against their hated officers without fear of punishment.

I remember a very harassed paper manufacturer from whom I was trying to buy stock for our "American Bulletin." The Revolution was summed up for him vividly in one incident. The newly formed "Shop Commitee" in his works invaded his luxuriously furnished private office one morning and told him to get out. They wanted to hold a meeting there. They made themselves at ease in his sanctum they trampled with their heavy boots on his choice Bokhara rug—they even spat on it. The thing which impressed him most was that they had lost fear of him. Just so Louis the Dense and his proud Queen Marie must have felt when the Great Unwashed of Paris invaded the Tuileries. It was the end of the world—their world.

Now I do not think the Shop Committee had any important business to discuss that morning. If so, they would have sought more familiar and congenial surroundings. I imagine that the incident was just as symbolic to them as it was to him. They had to convince themselves, just as they had to make him realize, that they were no longer afraid of the boss. I do not think that you could have interested them that day in a discussion of the practicability of their theories of social reorganization. Anyone who had argued that they might be killing the goose which laid the golden egg would have been ignored. First of all, the goose had never laid any golden eggs for them and then—of much more importance—they were insulting their boss with impunity. It must have given them a glorious thrill of independence, of freedom.

No one but a hide-bound doctrinaire of "economic determinism" would believe that they would have been willing to exchange this sense of power and freedom for any mere raise in wages or improvement of working conditions. They were enjoying for the first time the feeling that they could not be compelled.

Kerensky understood this. He knew that orders could no longer be enforced, the people could not be driven, and he tried desperately to hold the nation together by explanation and persuasion. Very few others had as sound an understanding of the situation. The criticism that he was "weak" was merely uncomprehending stupidity. A "strong government," for which so many wished, was an utter impossibility.

There is a chance, probably a small one, that Kerensky might have held the army together if he had given up his idea of "coalition," freed himself from restraints of the landlords, and emancipated the land, on the ground of military necessity, as Lincoln emancipated the slaves.

At the opening of the "Pre-Parliament," a few weeks before the Bolsheviks won to power, this plan was on Kerensky's desk. It was proposed to issue an edict confiscating all the large estates and the allotments of "Deserters." The thorny question of compensation was to be settled by the eventual Constitutional Assembly, and the priority in the distribution of the land so acquired was to be given to soldiers with honorable discharges.

If Kerensky had proposed this measure to his Cabinet, several of his Ministers would have resigned. A few perhaps would have done so from selfish economic interests, but more of them from a real conviction that such grave matters of national reconstruction ought to be dealt with by the Constitutional Assembly, duly elected by democratic vote and not by edicts, issued on its own initiative, by the Provisional—and irresponsible—Government.

But if Kerensky, making up his mind to lose the support of these legalistically minded politicians of the Intelligentsia, had gone direct to the people with this revolutionary measure, if from the forum of the Pre-Parliament he had put the issue squarely before the nation on the ground of military necessity, he might have regained the popular support which he was losing by the postponement of the economic reforms for which the people were clamoring.

On one side was the desire of all the educated classes to devote much time to the study and discussion of the various proposals for land reform, so as to arrive at an ideally perfect solution. This desire was by no means confined to the landlords, who stood to lose by the reforms. There were no end of Socialists of all factions, who had already written out the orations on the agrarian problem, which they were going to deliver in the Constitutional Assembly. All these would-be debaters would have been exceedingly peevish if their orations were rendered useless by a sudden—and to them, premature—revolutionary solution of the problems. All who had sincere reverence for the idea of democratic action were opposed to "anticipating the work of the Constitutional Assembly." Kerensky himself was pledged to the theory that the Provisional Government should take no action of a permanent character which could be left to the regularly elected assembly of the nation.

On the other hand were the Dark People with their hope for relief so long deferred. They could not comprehend these subtle legal arguments for delay, they did not want to listen to interminable discussions. They were losing patience. The army was rapidly disintegrating through the desertion of the peasant soldiers, who wanted to get home to share in the distribution of the land. The "ideally perfect" solution was of all things the most impractical. It would take time and there was need to hurry. The patience of the Dark People was exhausted. And there was no power in the state to force them to wait.

Such a revolutionary and admittedly imperfect solution of the land problem as this which was proposed to Kerensky might have stopped desertion. It might have given the peasants an ideal to fight for. It might have awakened a national enthusiasm which would have made the continuation of the war possible and have held the country together till the organization of a permanent government by the Constitutional Assembly. It was a bold proposal, a gambling proposition, with at best a small chance of success. If it was hopeless, as Kerensky evidently believed, his situation was hopeless.

But hopeless or not, it was Kerensky's only chance. The two burning issues of the day were "Peace" and "Land." If he had met either issue squarely, he might have postponed the other. It was political suicide to allow the opposition to appropriate both of the popular slogans. The Bolsheviks, quick to seize the opportunity offered them, took for their war cry: "Immediate Peace—Immediate Distribution of the Land." And so, becoming the "best promisers," their success was assured.

Chapter XI
The Bolshevist Campaign

All through the summer of 1917 the propaganda of the Bolsheviks had been intense, their presses—and they had a surprising number of them—never stopped. They developed a very much more efficient organization for the distribution of their papers and tracts than the rival parties. They obviously had more money. Their various newspapers, "Pravda" (Truth), "Pravda of the Trenches," the "Peasants Pravda," had immense circulation.

A student of "mob psychology" would find interest in a collection of the Bolshevist propaganda papers. They were not hampered by any effort to live up to their titles. Truth? That was the least of their interest. They were looking for results.

Their propaganda was intended to undermine all popular confidence in the government, to make the continuation of the war impossible by destroying the morale of the troops. They wanted the soldiers to believe that the German working class desired a democratic peace more than the proletariat of the Entente. They wanted the workers to believe that nothing stood between them and the promised land but the traitorous obstructionists, like Kerensky. They needed a conviction on the part of the peasantry that the Socialist Revolutionary Party was keeping them from the land. The means they used to produce these results were indifferent to them. For facts, they used assertion; for argument, reiteration.

Rumors about the revolutionary plans of the German Socialists were compared favorably with rumors about the plots of the Entente Imperialists and both were stated as facts. There was no uncertainty about it at all. There would be a proletarian uprising in Germany the minute the Russian workers offered a democratic peace. It was equally certain that the capitalists of the Entente were more afraid of the Russian Revolution than of German Imperialism. They were already getting together on the famous plan for "Peace at the Expense of Russia." The Germans were class-conscious workingmen, full of sympathy for their Russian brothers; the British, French, and Americans were all greedy, profit-mad capitalists. There was no doubt about it. The Entente was more to be feared than the Central Empires. Russian soldiers were asked to fight for French and British Imperialists. Mr. Root had bribed Kerensky. "No war, no loan." American capitalists were paying him so much for every Russian soldier killed. They circulated a bitter cartoon in the trenches, which showed a simple-minded Ivan, asked to attack a kindly Fritz, while a sinister John Bull was stealing

Arkhangel and Uncle Sam was walking off with the Trans-Siberian Railroad. No partisan of the Old Regime attacked Kerensky as scurrilously and unscrupulously as the Bolsheviks. He had sold out. He was cheating the workers of the fruits of their revolutionary victory. He had moved into the Winter Palace and was sleeping in the bed of the Tsar. "Kerensky the First" they called him.

There was to us, Americans, one note of humor in the campaign. They wanted to tie up our ambassador with Sir George Buchanan, "the envoy of British Imperialism." And so they knighted him; they always spoke of "Sir George and Sir Francis."[1] How indignant Missouri democracy must have been if it heard of this insult to its favorite son!

Sometimes this campaign of lies overreached itself. I was in Petrograd at the time of the first unsuccessful attempt to cause a revolution against Kerensky, in mid-July. The government tottered for a few days and was finally saved as much by rain as anything else. It was rotten weather for an insurrection—a solid week of merciless downpour. Out on the street one day with my interpreter, I encountered a very bedraggled and very angry group of sailors from the naval base at Kronstadt. The night before a delegation, claiming to be Bolsheviks, had come to their barracks and urged them to hurry to the city to save the Revolution. The Kadets were besieging the Soviet. After marching all night in the rain, with fine revolutionary ardor, they had arrived at the Soviet headquarters to learn that it was all a hoax. The Kadets, instead of attacking the Soviets, had ordered all their members to resign from the Ministry. But it was only rarely that the lies by which the Bolsheviks attempted "to get results" were so quickly and completely proven false. They were generally clever enough to be plausible.

Perhaps the most unscrupulous—while at the same time the most effective—phase of the Bolshevist propaganda was the new sense they gave the word "Counter-Revolutionist." To the editors of the various "Pravdas," anyone who did not bow the knee to Lenin was counter-revolutionary and an enemy of the people. In fact they were much more bitter in their attacks on the rival Socialist parties than on advocates of the old regime. The veteran revolutionist, men and women who had spent long lives in the fight against the Tsar, if they did not accept the new dispensation of Lenin, were put under the ban. With uncanny precision they caught at every hatred and suspicion and impatience of the Dark People and fanned it to flame.

It is a serious charge to accuse a political party of deliberate falsehood in their propaganda and it will be indignantly denied by their sympathizers in this country. But files of their newspapers are available. And any of their friends, who read Russian, can easily satisfy themselves on this matter. They will find there not only deliberate lies, but carefully prepared articles by Bolshevist leaders elaborating Lenin's theory that "truth" is a bourgeois prejudice, which should be scoffed at if it stands

---

[1] David Francis, American ambassador to Russia, 1916–18.

in the way of proletarian emancipation. "Truth" was the least of their interests, they were after results.

Such a campaign of cheap demagoguery, of deliberate falsehood, of cynical "promises" may seem incredibly dangerous to politicians, who are used to democratic institutions. Even if totally indifferent to moral considerations, our candidates are somewhat restrained by caution. But this policy was admirably suited to the ends of the Bolsheviks. They were not planning to win and hold the support of a majority. That would have taken altogether too long and they were impatient. All they needed was to fool enough of the people enough of the time to allow their "enlightened militant minority" to capture power. Once they won control they did not intend to worry about what the majority thought of them. Lenin has been very explicit on this point. They did not even pretend to be interested in democracy.

The original unity of the Revolution was hopelessly shattered. Too many people had "resigned." There was no organized majority, the nation was split up into innumerable little factions. There was an ideal opportunity for an energetic minority to capture the government.

As I have said, the Bolsheviks became the "best promisers." They were reckless and unscrupulous about it. They had no worry about fulfilling their promises. To the shattered and war-weary army they promised "peace," to the city workers "The Dictatorship" of their class, and in the fall of 1917 they stampeded the Congress of Peasant Deputies by the promise of the immediate distribution of the land. When Lenin gave the signal for insurrection, Kerensky's ministry—deserted by all those he had tried to conciliate—fell like a house of cards.

Chapter XII
The Question of Majority Support

There has been much vague discussion, much assertion and counter-assertion in the American press, on the question of how much popular support there is back of Lenin's regime. This would seem a very futile discussion to him. He does not believe in the democratic rule of the majority. He says quite frankly that the majority is ignorant, unenterprising, lethargic.

I have no doubt that in the fall of 1917, when Lenin succeeded Kerensky, that a very large majority of the Russians wanted peace. Lenin told them that Kerensky was insincere in his efforts and had failed dismally to get the general people's peace they all wanted. Lenin and Trotsky said they were in earnest about it and could succeed. Before they won to power and for months afterwards, Lenin and Trotsky frequently said that they would not sign a "shameful," "separate" peace, that they would never deal with the German Imperial Government. They promised to start revolutions everywhere. It was a revolutionary "People's Peace." They said they could end the World War, not only the Russo-German War, immediately. It would be easy. All that was necessary was to overthrow the counter-revolutionist, Kerensky, and give them a chance. They probably believed themselves when they said that they could do this.

Also the great majority of the nation were in favor of immediate action on the land problem. They wanted the old system of land tenure destroyed and the land divided among those who tilled it. The Socialist Revolutionary Party, which had given the most thought to the agrarian problem, wanted not only to abolish the old system but to work out an orderly and equitable redistribution; they had also, in the interest of democracy and of national unity in the face of the enemy, agreed to leave the solution of this problem to the Constitutional Assembly. However there had been too much delay, the patience of the peasantry had worn out and there was no power to hold them back. They had already in scattered districts, to an extent variously estimated from 25 percent to more than 50 percent driven away the landlords and proceeded with much inequality and considerable fighting to divide the old estates.

Lenin said: "Kerensky and his gang of traitors is only fooling you with this talk of legal delays. The Socialist Revolutionaries have sold out to the landlords. They are the most dangerous counter-revolutionists of all. We, Bolsheviks will settle land problems for you at once, overnight."

And also there was only a very small minority who were averse to making the "bourgeoisie"—the former master class—uncomfortable. Very few Russians have been as shocked as, for instance, the British Foreign Office at the execution of the royal family. The great mass of the people have suffered too much and too long under the Old Regime to be seriously disturbed by the Red Terror against the former aristocracy.

The majority—in Lenin's frequent phrase—is "lethargic," more so in Russia than in our Western countries. They are not used to taking the initiative in political affairs. They had been and still were very miserable, and they hoped vaguely for better things. They hated the landlords, they hated the industrial bosses, above all they hated the war. So far the Revolution had disappointed them. They were ready for a new experiment. Perhaps Lenin would succeed where Kerensky had failed.

But this does not mean that there was any widespread comprehension or support of Lenin's political theories. If he had had any respect for the voice of the majority he would have waited till the votes for the Constitutional Assembly were counted. The elections were already in progress. But he knew that the vote would go overwhelmingly against him. He made his stroke in time.

Certainly the great majority of the nation took no active part in the final Bolshevist uprising. Even in the cities only a small number did any fighting.

I was in Petrograd when the affair started. It was all over in a few hours. Kerensky dashed off to the headquarters in a vain effort to rally the army. So there was no one to lead the resistance. A few hundred students from the military schools were the only ones who risked their skins in defense of the government. I left that night, after the Winter Palace had "fallen," for Moscow where the only serious fight took place. The Bolsheviks had considerable but not unanimous support from the working class. The General Strike was far from complete. They had at least a promise of neutrality from the garrison troops. A few regiments are said to have paraded in their behalf. I only saw a couple of companies in formation.

I happened to be marooned, during the week of fighting, in the Consulate, which was in the middle of "No Man's Land," just about halfway between the Soviet Building and the Military School which was the headquarters of the "White Guard." Our point of observation was uncomfortably near the center of things.

The actual fighting was carried on by the White Guard, defending the interests of the City Council. It was composed of a few university students, a number of army officers, and the corps of cadets from the Military Academy. The Red Guards were mostly workingmen with a scattering of individual soldiers. In no case near the Consulate did I see any organized unit from the garrison.

Street fighting, which always does more damage to buildings and innocent bystanders than to the combatants, went on for several days in an indecisive way. I doubt whether there were ever more than a thousand men actually fighting on either side. Out of a city of two million inhabitants, it is doubtful if ten thousand people took any active part in the fighting. Some fought for a day or two and then went home; the actual combatants were changing continually throughout the week, but ten thousand would be a very large estimate of those who in the entire time pulled a trigger. The most impressive memory of that week was the listless inaction of people, who in their talk took a most violent partisanship for one side or the other. Towards the end of the week, some Bolshevist sailors arrived from Petrograd. Their presence proved that the Bolsheviks had won in the capital, that Kerensky's effort to rally the army had failed, and that they could spare some of their best troops to help their comrades in Moscow. Continued resistance to the New Regime seemed hopeless and the White Guard laid down its arms.

There were two instances of that period which are indicative of the way in which the Bolsheviks went about their work. When I arrived in Moscow, having come direct from Petrograd, I found that strikes had tied up all the newspapers except the Bolshevist organ. It was issuing frequent bulletins, handbills printed on one side of the paper and headed "Radiograms from Petrograd." This was the only "news" service in Moscow in the days when the Bolsheviks were trying to bring about an insurrection. These alleged wireless dispatches from Petrograd were absolutely false, obviously so to one who had just come from the capital. They had been composed—fabricated out of whole cloth—in the office of the Bolshevist newspaper in Moscow. One of the Bolshevist leaders afterwards boasted to me of the clever foresight with which this hoax had been prepared. It was not the truth but what the Bolshevist leaders thought would help to "get results." It was what they wanted the people of Moscow to think was true.

The week following the insurrection was the date set for elections in Moscow for the Constitutional Assembly. The Bolsheviks suppressed all the opposition papers and in their own were naturally jubilant over their victory. They discussed the advisability of a St. Bartholomew Eve and a general massacre of the bourgeoisie. Their papers had a good deal to say for and against this idea. Now, I do not believe that the Bolshevist leaders had any idea of starting a general massacre and they probably would have done their best to prevent it, if it had started, but they wanted to scare the bourgeoisie away from the elections and they succeeded. There were Red Guards at all the voting booths and two-thirds of the registered voters, who had cast ballots in a municipal election a few weeks previous, stayed away from the polls. Only one-third of the population voted and the Bolsheviks, who counted the ballots, won by a narrow majority.

At the time of the insurrection the majority of the city population sat back in passive inactivity—in a spirit half way between dull indifference and vague hope—and watched Lenin oust Kerensky. Of course most of the villagers did not hear of the new Revolution until days or weeks after it had occurred and they heard of it only through "Official" and highly colored Bolshevist dispatches.

A statement that Lenin had—or had not—the support of the majority after his advent to power is pure guesswork. The council of the People's Commissaires has never consulted the people. It has not asked for a popular verdict of approval. If Lenin had wanted it, if he had felt that it would strengthen him, he could probably have rigged up a plebiscite to endorse his regime, just as Napoleon III did. There is no more striking proof of his contempt for democracy than that he has never tried it. He simply is not interested in the opinions of the "lethargic majority."

Chapter XIII
The Bolsheviks At Work

There is no possibility as yet for any exhaustive account of the attempts of the Bolsheviks to put their social and economic theories into practice. The material for such a study is not at hand. Many of their projects, some good, some bad, have never progressed beyond paper. Some of their edicts have been enforced in one locality and not in others. This is the cause of hopeless confusion to those who follow closely the reports coming from Soviet Russia.

There has, for instance, been circulated in America the text of a "Land Law" approved by the Soviet Government. Irrespective of the merits or demerits of the proposal, one is entirely uncertain as to the attempts made to apply it. I have not been in European Russia since this decree is said to have been promulgated, but in Siberia I could not find any evidence that the Bolsheviks, while they were in power there, had tried to enforce it. No satisfactory information on this subject has come from Soviet sources. What news we have indicates that new legislation, intended to break up the village unity and to create class war between the poor and the "poorer" peasants, has superseded this widely advertised Land Law.

This difficulty is at present insurmountable in any effort to evaluate the social and industrial innovations of the Bolshevist regime. From the files of their official newspapers we could collect an appalling number of decrees, but very little information about their application. After they won to power, the Bolsheviks gave up their policy of "No Compromise" and became frankly opportunistic. If one decree did not produce the results they desired, they at once issued a new one.

I was forced to watch closely the series of decrees in regard to the "Strike of the Bourgeoisie." Few if any of the Bolshevist rules work both ways. While they were out of power they had been ardent supporters of the right to strike. But immediately after the success of their insurrection, they were seriously embarrassed by the fact that many employees of the former government did not care to work for them. A couple of the translators in our office had come from the Foreign Office. They did not like Trotsky and preferred to work for someone else. But the Bolsheviks declared them counter-revolutionists and rained decrees against these "bourgeois strikers." One day the morning's edict on the subject would say that if the strikers did not return to work at once, they would be discharged and lose their pensions. The next morning a raise in salary would be offered to all who returned to their jobs within twenty-four hours. Neither of these decrees "got results." Then the saving banks were prohibited from paying out money from the accounts of the "strikers." It was declared "reactionary" and illegal to lend them money or for a merchant to give them credit. I could not discover that any effort was made to enforce these decrees. They were intended to bluff the strikers back to work.

The point I wish to emphasize is that, quite aside from the wisdom or unwisdom of any decree, it was next to impossible to discover whether any serious attempt was made to enforce it, or even whether there was any intention to enforce it. Some of their edicts they applied rigorously, some could always be gotten around by small bribery and seemed to have been issued with this intention, some were still-born. The mere text of a decree is not very enlightening unless it is accompanied by evidence of what happened to it, after it was issued.

While there is heavy obscurity over most of their social and economic legislation, it is much easier to follow the steps by which they sought to consolidate their political power. And this, as with their predecessors, seems to have been their principal interest. One of the first of their decrees dealt with the land problem. Lenin said that he thought it was "unscientific" and objectionable, but it would win them support among the peasants. And very many of their decrees were frankly intended to get political support, rather than to solve the economic problems with which they dealt.

Lenin's "active, militant minority" had succeeded easily in upsetting the tottering regime of Kerensky. He set to work at once, according to his theories in a professedly undemocratic way, to consolidate and perpetuate his control of power. The first necessity was a Pretorian Guard. This problem faces any government not certain of widespread popular support. It must have a dependable military force. Much of the best brains of the Bolsheviks has gone to the organization of the new militarism. They have made many experiments and have only gradually worked out their present organization. At first their main reliance was upon the sailors of the Baltic Fleet, but gradually these were superseded by the famous Old Corps of Lettish Sharpshooters. In the months that have followed, the distinctive nationalistic character of the corps has been lost by the incorporation of new recruits, who are not necessarily Letts. It seems at present to be the principal internal police force. It is kept contented with high wages, good food, and a large license in the matter of spoils, and it is rarely if ever called upon to fight anybody but unarmed bourgeois. The Red Guard is a sort of local militia, recruited from factories. It has proved difficult to get these forces to leave their home districts, they are not considered very "dependable" and are relied on principally for preserving "Bolshevist order" in the factory districts and for demonstrations and parades. The "Red Army" has been more recently organized for large scale operations against "The Foreign Aggressors." It is impossible to get anything more than unreliable guesses as to the number of soldiers under Trotsky's command or of their degree of discipline.

What I saw of the Red Army during the early months of the Bolshevist regime was far from impressive. The Czechs and the new Siberian Army have very little respect for its fighting quality. On the other hand a report from Arkhangel says that our American officers there consider them formidable opponents. But if Trotsky has a million men under arms as he claims, it is certain that most of them are kept idle in interior garrisons. Kolchak's Siberian Army is in the neighborhood of 100,000 men, the anti-Bolshevist forces in North and South Russia, including the few Allied troops, are probably less than 50,000. If Trotsky has a million soldiers, he has his enemies very much outnumbered.

Even if all the Bolshevist forces were recruited because of intense loyalty to the cause of humanity as defined in Lenin's dogma—which is emphatically not the case—it would not prove any democratic sanction behind the regime. At the very highest estimate only a small portion of Russia's hundreds of millions are in these ranks. But an overwhelming majority of the rifles, machine guns, and hand grenades are in their hands.

The nation is faced by starvation—not a vague threat for the future but a present reality—and the Bolsheviks control the "food cards." They do not have to worry about the will of the majority.

While this force was being organized, as fast as the Bolsheviks gained confidence in their power they proceeded to the suppression of all outspoken opposition. The development of their press control is typical. At first they contented themselves with the old-fashioned censorship system of the Tsar, but Russian editors are expert in eluding such control. The Bolsheviks then nationalized advertising and made it a state monopoly. If you wanted to advertise, you sent your copy to the Commissaire of the Press and he awarded it to "a well-intentioned newspaper." This robbed the independent press of the largest part of its financial support. A few of the richer papers continued in spite of this, so the Bolsheviks at last requisitioned all print paper. No editor could get paper for his presses unless they decided that it would be "socially useful." This wiped out all chance of opposition publications.

There was one move in this campaign to control the press which promised to be amusing, but like many Bolshevist reforms it looked better on paper than it proved in practice. An edict was issued making it illegal to publish a lie. If anyone saw a statement in the press which seemed false, he could complain to the Soviet and the editor was to be locked up until he proved it true. But nothing much came of this promising edict. I only heard of one or two editors—not Bolsheviks—being arrested for falsehood. This however was the only element in the Bolshevist campaign against the freedom of the press which was laughable. It was probably the work of one of his subordinates, for Lenin is not a joker. In the days of Stolypin of evil memory, the press had more freedom than under Bolshevist rule. And with the same rigor with which they prevented the free circulation of the printed word, they tried to prevent the chances for public speaking on the part of their opponents. In this of course they could not hope for so complete control. It is possible to locate and control printing presses, to requisition paper and ink and type. But no tyrant has yet discovered how to control the raw material of speech.

Nobody knows what a majority of the Russians want. There has not been any opportunity for them to express their wishes. The only elections since Lenin came into power have been Soviet elections, in which no one but the supporters of the Soviet may vote. Theoretically, although the Soviet rule eliminates all class opposition, the great majority of the people should be free to vote within the Soviets. In practice this has rarely worked out. The Soviet system is peculiarly adapted to gang rule and the electorate is more easily flimflammed than any experienced democracies.

But even within the circle of the Soviets, Lenin does not believe in bowing to the will of the majority. In the early summer of 1918, the elections in the Soviet of Yaroslav, a large industrial city north of Moscow, were unfavorable to the Bolsheviks. The Council of the People's Commissaires in Moscow claimed fraud and sent a detachment of Lettish sharpshooters to Yaroslav to dissolve the refractory Soviet and oversee the new elections. But this high-handed interference in local politics angered the population and resulted for the Bolsheviks in an even more crushing defeat at the polls. The Council of the People's Commissaires issued a decree, stating that as the working class of Yaroslav had twice proven their unfitness for self-government, their inability to recognize their own, obvious, best interests, their insane preference for a slightly different brand of Socialism, they could not be allowed to have a Soviet at all. Yaroslav was pronounced a "nest of counter-revolutionists." Every attempt of the people there to organize self-government—and there have been several such attempts—has been bloodily suppressed. Very similar events have taken place elsewhere. In such ways does the "theory of minority revolution" work out in practice.

The "Constitution" of the Soviet Republic, which has been widely circulated here by the friends of Lenin, would lead one to think that if the workers of any community tired of Bolshivism, it would be easy for them to elect another party to office. But such is not the idea of Lenin and his friends in Russia. The experiment has been tried a number of times. Whenever a local Soviet has the bad judgment to vote against the Bolsheviks, it proves itself counter-revolutionary and must be suppressed. There are exceptions, of course. No human system is perfect. Insignificant little local Soviets have been allowed some leeway. But whenever an important Soviet—as in Yaroslav or Krasnoyarsk to mention only two examples—has gone Menshevik or Socialist Revolutionary it has been forced to "reconsider."

The consistency with which the Bolsheviks have put into practice Lenin's "Theory of Minority Revolution" has been impressive. With equal consistency they have carried on "The Class War" according to his precepts. And the ideas he has been preaching on this subject for many years differ profoundly from the interpretation put on the phrase by most Socialists in Russia and the Western world.

Lenin puts into the capitalist class all those who do not acknowledge his leadership, irrespective of whether they possess capital or not. His hatred for them has not been tempered by the responsibilities of power. He has organized their persecution on a wholesale scale, not as a punishment of individual malefactors, but as the proscription—the extermination—of a class. He teaches that the principal function of the proletarian dictatorship is to wreck the whole system of capitalist production by the violent destruction of the capitalist—only after this has been accomplished can the workers hope to enter into their own. He is holding with remarkable consistency to this theory, doing today just what he said he would years ago, when there was no reason to believe that he would ever have the power to execute his threats.

Circumstances which he apparently did not foresee have forced him to modify some details of this program. He has, it is reported, decided to spare some of those he calls "Capitalist," especially those with technical training, on condition that they co-operate in the extermination of their class. But this is a mere opportunist compromise in detail. The whole series of banking decrees illustrates the main theory, which he has so often expressed and on which he does not compromise. It is necessary to uproot capitalism completely, destroy all possibility of credit operations, before proletarian production can be organized.

"The Class War" has become for the Bolshevist Premier a new phrase for the old Latin maxim about dividing your subjects in order to rule them more easily. There was complete unity among the peasants in their civil war against the landlords. It was an asset for the Bolsheviks as long as there were any landlords left to drive away. But it was soon evident that such unity among the vast rural population was a serious menace to the dictatorship of the very small class of industrial workers in the cities. I have written in the chapter on the Land Question, of how the reactionary Premier Stolypin adopted the motto "Divide and Rule," and tried to break up the solidarity of the peasants. The Bolsheviks followed his example and carried "The Class War" into the villages. They developed a distinction between "poor peasants" and "the poorer peasants." To be a little less poor than the poorest became a serious crime against the Revolution. It was rather like starting a civil war between orphans and half orphans. But from the point of view of the Bolsheviks it was good politics. The tragedy of it did not matter to them. Civil war in the villages kept the peasants from uniting against the dictatorship of the cities. It "got results."

Lenin has been forced to modify still another detail of his theory of proletarian dictatorship. One morning in May, 1918, almost the entire issue of the Bolshevist newspapers was taken up by a long dissertation from his pen. It was divided like the treatise of a medieval scholastic philosopher into a number of "theses." One of these had to do with the organization of political machinery. He restated his old arguments for the dictatorship of the proletariat at length, but he pointed out that in the present dismal state of illiteracy in Russia, the proletariat was too backward to exercise power wisely and it was obviously necessary to have, temporarily, a personal dictatorship in their behalf. Circumstances, over which he acknowledges no control, have forced this position on him. The dictatorship by the minority has become a dictatorship by an individual.

The Bolshevist campaign for the suppression of all opposition has not been limited to the hated capitalists. They believe that even greater danger threatens the proletariat- or at least themselves—from the propaganda of other Socialist parties. They have been more venomous and violent in their attacks on the Socialist opposition than on the supporters of the Old Regime. When, if ever, the lists are published of the victims of Bolshevist execution squads, there will be the names of more Socialists on them than of aristocrats. The other revolutionary factions, which differed primarily from the Bolsheviks in their loyalty to the ideas of democracy, really believe in fighting for freedom and have therefore been most energetic in their opposition to the new tyranny and so have suffered the most.

Lenin and his followers have been desperately consistent to his dogmas of "class war" and "minority revolutions." They have been just as consistent in their contempt for the moral concepts, which bind together the life of ordinary communities. They have made no "fetish" of truthfulness. No "reptile press" in the world has been so subservient to power, so consciously and cynically false, as the official organs of the Bolsheviks. In their theory a thing is true if it helps in the emancipation of the proletariat—false if it hinders. Inevitably in their practice, "the maintenance of themselves in power" takes the place of the "emancipation of the proletariat."

"Honesty" is another bourgeois conception for which they have no patience. Some of Lenin's associates have been very crude grafters. As he needed their help, he has winked at their graft. While there is no serious charge that he himself has been tainted by such corruption, he has certainly "let his friends get theirs."

The Bolsheviks have not even felt bound by the concept of loyalty to their own comrades. Perhaps the most shocking dishonor of their regime has been the cynical betrayal of those who trusted them. When they thought it paid to have class war in Finland and the Ukraine, they encouraged it. When they found it embarrassing to keep their pledges to these other revolutionists, they coldly abandoned them to their fate.

There was something bitterly amusing in the way they proposed dishonorable deals to others. According to their theory, the capitalists of the various countries were supporting the war for what they could get out of it and were ready to commit any turpitude if it paid. They thought for instance that the French capitalists would stop their quarrel with the German capitalists rather than lose their immense investments in Russia. And, of course, we Americans were the capitalists par excellence—the shrewdest and crookedest of the gang. They were naively perplexed when we did not fit into the place they had made for us in their theory. For a while they thought they could bluff the nations of the Entente by threatening to repudiate the national debt. One day it would be announced that a definite decision to repudiate the debt had been arrived at. The next day there would be news that the matter was being reconsidered. The unsettling of values so caused allowed some on the inside to turn a number of dishonest pennies, but it did not bring any of the former Allies to their knees.

Losing patience at last with French stubbornness, they turned to us. One of their plenipotentiaries laid before some representatives of the United States the proposal that, if Washington would recognize the Soviet Government and grant a loan in rolling stock for railways and rifles for the civil war, the Council of the People's Commissaires would make an exception in our favor in the general repudiation of the debt. In short, if we would sell out our allies and lend the Bolsheviks some more money, they would give us their word of honor to pay what they owed us. None of us Americans there would have claimed to be extraordinarily honest, but none of us had the nerve to transmit this proposal to our government in the terms in which it was offered. And the Bolsheviks' envoy did not seem able to comprehend why, out of loyalty to our allies, we would reject such a promising deal.

Of course Lenin's contempt for "Morals" laid him wide open to German intrigue.

Chapter XIV
"German Gold"

If it is sometimes difficult for Westerners to understand what the Bolsheviks are aiming at in internal affairs, the basis of their system of international relations is even harder to grasp.

There is for instance overwhelming evidence—circumstantial and direct—that some of their prominent leaders accepted German money. But the situation is much more complex and bizarre than this simple statement implies. One of the worst counts against them, to my mind, is that they justify this action on the grounds that they did it "dishonestly" with every intention of violating their agreement.

There is a certain type of mind which maintains that it is no disgrace to accept a bribe, provided you have no intention of living up to the guilty contract. But there is one very practical objection to this quaint ethical idea. People who are loyal to the old-fashioned ideas of honesty are reluctant to enter into credit relations with those who profess this new dispensation.

Every few days now a ballon d'essai is sent up from Moscow—a vague hint that the Soviet Republic is prepared to do business with the former allies of Russia. But as they boast virtuously of having broken their pledges with Germany, the statesmen of the Entente are naturally skeptical.

To make this bizarre situation more clear it is necessary to go into some detail.

First of all, there was an a priori expectation that the Bolsheviks would turn to the Germans for help. In the insurrectional period from 1904 to 1907, most of the revolutionary parties in Russia accepted Japanese assistance. Some took it directly, others insisted on a degree of camouflage. Milyoukov's party, the Constitutional Democrats or "Kadets," made the patriotic boast that they did not accept "Japanese gold," but they raised a good deal of money in England, the ally of Japan. The Socialist Revolutionary Party, with the connivance of the British, organized a filibuster in an English port, and loaded a ship with arms to land in Finland. With the direct assistance of the Japanese, they carried on an intense propaganda among the Russian soldiers who had become prisoners of war.

Now these revolutionists, who accepted Japanese help in 1905, were not partisans of the Mikado. They were just as much opposed to his autocracy as they were to the Tsar's. They were simply so intent on their own struggle for liberty that they were willing to accept help from anyone. The agents of Imperial Japan had no sympathy with such revolutionary ideas, but—all's fair in love and war—their country was at war with Russia and the more revolution in the Tsar's domain the better.

In 1914 the German General Staff—in the same frame of mind—was enthusiastic for any revolutions which would embarrass their enemies. They subsidized trouble in South Africa, India, Egypt, Ireland, and Morocco. We may be sure they were eager to finance revolutionary agitation in Russia.

Now that the war is over we can afford to be "objective" once more. Such tactics were universal. Future historians will see very little difference between President Masaryk and Sir Roger Casement—except that Sir Roger was caught and executed before the "Cause," in which he believed just as passionately as the Czech leader believed in his, won. The governments of the Entente gave aid and comfort to the technical "traitors" among the subject races of their enemies, just as the Germans and Austrians attempted to foment disturbances behind the fronts of our allies. Russia offered an especially fertile field for such intrigues.

At the outbreak of the war in 1914, many Russian revolutionists of all shades of opinion hoped that the Tsar would be defeated. They believed that a victory would strengthen his sinister grip but that his regime would crumble with a new disaster. The Russian political exiles in Switzerland, who took this view, could—by asking—get all the money they needed for their propaganda from Germany. And we know that many of them although utterly opposed to the idea of Kaiserism, felt they would be justified in doing so. There is every probability that some of them—not only the Bolsheviks—did.

But with the fall of the Tsar in the spring of 1917, almost all the Revolutionists, with the exception of the Bolsheviks, rallied to the defense of the New Regime. All the exiles in Switzerland, who now took a strong patriotic attitude, were allowed by the French and British authorities to travel through their territory and return to Russia. But Lenin continued to denounce the war as an affair of capitalists. The French and British refused to grant him passports.

The Germans, who had as much reason to hope from his anti-war propaganda in Russia as the Allies had to fear, put a special train at his disposal and allowed him and his closest disciples to cross Germany to Sweden. To be sure, they sealed the train and guarded it closely to make certain that no Leninism spilled out during the transit. It was in Russia, not in the Fatherland, that they liked his ideas.

It is highly probable that Lenin had to make some definite pledges to the German authorities to secure this privilege. But it does not necessarily follow that he ever meant to keep them.

The most astute politicians could not foretell what would happen in Russia after the Revolution. If the world had been at peace, foreigners might have watched the developments without attempting to interfere. But the tragedy of the war was too poignant. Would Russia throw new and revolutionary ardor into the struggle against German Imperialism? Or would internal chaos overwhelm her? Both belligerent groups were too keenly interested in this question to remain indifferent—or inactive. Each side tried to sort out from the muddle the elements which would help them to win. From the first, although it was not at once apparent, the dice were loaded against us. What we needed was constructive, orderly upbuilding. All the Germans needed was disorder. We had to try to weld together great masses whose interests conflicted, to harmonize a chaos of divergent forces. The goal of the Germans was infinitely easier to attain. It was child's play to make trouble. Even if we had been able to work in unison on a united program, it is doubtful if we could have held things together.

More often than not the Allied Embassies in Petrograd were supporting conflicting programs. Some were trying to keep Russia together as a unit. Others, losing faith as a whole, supported the separatist movements of the Ukraine and the Caucasus. The largest amount of American assistance went to the Kerensky regime. But any group of Russians, who professed to be for the continuation of the war against Germany, could get financial assistance from one or another of the Allied Embassies. Of course those who advocated an immediate and separate peace could get help from the Germans.[1]

There is a great deal of circumstantial evidence to bear out this inference. Lenin's special train through Germany is an example. The intensity of the Bolshevist propaganda indicated a suspiciously large financial backing. None of the Allied Governments supported the pro-war factions generously enough to allow them to compete in expenditure with the Bolsheviks. Some of the Anti-Entente cartoons circulated by the Bolsheviks were examined by experts in Petrograd, the paper and ink were analyzed, the drawings studied. They could not have been produced in Russia. They had been "Made in Germany." A long list of such circumstantial evidence could be cited, but it is unnecessary, for direct, documentary evidence exists.

Much controversy has raged about the documents published by the Committee of Public Information. However, the statement that Bolshevist leaders received large sums from Germany does not rest solely on these documents. While disagreeing with some of the conclusions Mr. Sisson draws from these papers, which he secured while in Russia as my chief and which I have never had an opportunity to study closely, I believe that with possibly one or two exceptions they are authentic.[2] They fit in so closely with the course of events, they dovetail so accurately with the many other records obtained by other governments through entirely different channels. I have seen some of the evidence obtained by the Czecho-Slovaks in Siberia; I am told that Bourtzeff, the Russian historian, is now engaged in a critical analysis and comparison of all this diverse evidence and will shortly publish a definitive report.

---

[1] For a full and detailed analysis of this situation, see Michael J. Carley, *Silent Conflict* (Lanham, MD: Rowman and Littlefield, 2014).

[2] The so-called "Sisson Papers" have definitively been shown to be skillful forgeries. See George F. Kennan, "The Sisson Documents," *Journal of Modern History* 28, 2 (1956): 130–54.

It was inherently probable that the advocates of immediate peace in Russia would be offered support by Germany. The Bolshevist leaders frequently acted as though they were receiving such aid. And there is overwhelming evidence that they did.

However it is a far cry from that to the conclusions that they were friendly to the Kaiser or that they were advocating the ideas they did solely for the pay they were receiving. If you were pushing a Prohibition Campaign, you would not go to a drunkard and bribe him to reform and pretend to share your ideas. If you were starting an anti-Prohibition drive, you would not seek out a confirmed teetotaler and pay him to compose orations in favor of John Barleycorn. A bribed hypocrite is never a convincing advocate. The Germans wanted to disorganize the Russian resistance and they were shrewd enough to know that Lenin, who had been agitating against any kind of war for a dozen years or more and was very anxious to continue this agitation in Russia, would be more effective than any fake pacifist they could find. They did everything they could to facilitate his "mission." They undoubtedly expected that he, having accepted their help, would take their advice. But this was assuming an honesty on his part which he did not profess.

The Bolsheviks accepted money from the German Government, whom they hated, to support their own propaganda, but with the full intention of betraying their benefactors at the first—and every—opportunity. If an attack had been made on them with the proof that they were taking German gold, they would probably have replied laughingly: "Two kinds of people have given us funds—honest sympathizers and fools. If there are any more kings as foolish as the Kaiser who would like to subscribe to our International Revolution, they can mail their checks to our treasurer."

There is a story I was told by one of the Bolsheviks. It is almost too pat to be plausible, but whether it is literally true or an invention it is wonderfully illustrative of Bolshevist ethics. The Council of the People's Commissaires was discussing what manner of observance they should authorize for the anniversary of "Bloody Sunday," January 2, the day when the followers of Father Gapon had been massacred before the Winter Palace in 1905.

This was an immensely important date in the history of the Russian Revolution. There had been all sorts of individual acts of revolt before. There had been riots among the university students. But this was the first time that the people had participated. It was the beginning of the mass movement, the opening scene in the Revolution.

But Father Gapon himself was a traitor to the Cause. He had first of all been in the pay of the police. For a few months in 1905, he seems to have thought that the Revolution was the winning side. And then in the days of discouragement which followed the triumph of the reaction, he went back to his old paymasters—the secret police. In the end, he was hanged by some of the workingmen, who had learned of his treason.

Three currents developed among the People's Commissaires, as they discussed this matter. One element said that, as Father Gapon was undoubtedly a crook who had betrayed the people, his "day" should be ignored. Another element proposed to banish his name from the celebration, but to make it a great funeral fête in honor of those who died that day the first victims of the Revolution. But a third element accused these other two of being enslaved to the bourgeois conception of morals. "Let us be realists, "they said. "What does it matter whether—according to capitalist ethics—Gapon was honest or a crook? He lit the torch of Revolution. He started the mass movement. Let us honor him as a hero of the proletariat—our hero. We are all grateful for what he did. Let us be frank and fearless about it and drop this bourgeois hypocrisy."

In all probability the attitude of the Bolshevist leaders towards "German gold" was very similar. Some of them would have been shocked at the idea of taking the Kaiser's pay. If they asked embarrassing questions, they would be told that the money was donated by the German Socialists. Some of them would say: "We need the money for our work, but don't let anyone know." Others would say: "What matter? Why be hypocritical about it? Our object is so important, the means we use cannot be anything but right. It is a case of 'spoiling the Philistines.' Don't be bluffed by the outcry of these capitalist patriots. Anything we do to liberate those they so shamefully oppress will seem wrong to them."

And undoubtedly the matter was further complicated by the presence in their midst of bona-fide secret agents of Germany. The current political trials in Paris seem to prove that the German Secret Service succeeded in introducing its agents into the very center of French politics. It was a much simpler affair for them in Petrograd.

The Bolsheviks, who knew where their money was coming from, did not worry. They were quite sure that they were cleverer and stronger than the Kaiser. They would take his money, but in the end they would overthrow him. They naïvely overestimated their own power. In the end, the man who pays the piper calls the tune. The sincere ones among them were quite as anxious to cause a revolution in Germany as in any of the Entente countries—and believed they could do it. But all of them were not sincere, and besides it was more difficult to strike at Germany than elsewhere. They were not strong enough to be as impartial as they claimed. Nothing they could accomplish against Imperial Germany was to be compared in seriousness with the blow they gave the Democratic Alliance by the separate peace into which contrary to their avowed expectations, they were forced.

They overestimated their strength in regard to the "fraternization" at the front, which they encouraged from the first and made "official" as soon as they reached power. They hoped that they could demoralize the German troops as easily as their own. They claimed to us—and perhaps half-believed—that they had succeeded. They asserted that the German High Command would never dare to transfer these troops to the Western Front.

Of all their efforts to produce a revolution in Germany, the one which impressed me as most earnest was the paper they published in German; at first it was called "The Torch" and later "The People's Peace." Any German official, who had had a hand in supplying them with funds, must have writhed and raged if he saw a copy. It contained a mixture of sound socialism and the familiar vituperation of the "Pravda." They could print a few hundred thousand copies and get them down to the front. But the German discipline still maintained the death penalty. No one could do more than guess how many of them were read. It was a sincere effort, but compared to the bulk of revolutionary propaganda being sent across by our army on the Western Front it was a mere drop in the bucket.

However, at one moment it almost seemed that the Bolshevist leaders would escape from their paymasters. Their one chance lay in an immediate revolution in Germany. During the first period of negotiations at Brest-Litovsk, they made their great play. Trotsky, to the indignation of General Hoffmann and the German delegation, continually talked over their heads directly to the popular masses of the Central Empires.

Strikes broke out in Vienna and Berlin. We did not know anything about them in Petrograd, except what the Bolshevist papers published. But they seemed to have a revolutionary, stop-the-war character. Trotsky broke off the negotiations at Brest and returned to Petrograd in triumph. There was jubilation in Bolshevist circles. I attended a meeting where Trotsky reported and Lenin spoke. I had conversations with a number of their immediate associates. They were beyond doubt immensely pleased by the thought that their revolution was spreading, that they had succeeded in ending the war. Not content with the meager telegrams they received from abroad, they invented wild stories of outbreaks in Scotland, insurrections in France, mutinies in American training camps.

I think this was the turning point in Bolshevist history. It was the top of their wave. All the sincerity they had went into rejoicing over this revolution in Germany which did not happen. After these hopes were disappointed, they were more disillusioned, more cynical, more cruel. They were more dependent on those they had failed to betray.

If they had succeeded, Lenin and Trotsky might have gone down in history as saviors of society. If a revolution in Germany had ended the war in those early spring days of 1918, there would have been very much less mourning in America, and all the world.

They were within one step of the sublime. Unfortunately they had vastly overestimated their influence. The revolution in Germany did not come off. The famous statement that "it is only one step from the sublime to the ridiculous" hardly applies to Lenin and Trotsky; it was not a laughing matter. In falling that one step short of the sublime, they were worse than ridiculous, they were tragic, and brought infinite tragedy on all those who had trusted them.

Disappointed in this matter, they found one last crooked arrow in their quiver. They tried an eleventh hour—an eleven fifty-five—conversion to Tolstoyism. Trotsky ordered the demobilization of what was left of the army and made a "moral" appeal to the German Army not to march against the defenseless Russian workingmen! There was nothing approaching the sublime about this. No more insincere and sardonic bluff has ever been attempted in international affairs. Trotsky and Lenin posing as advocates of non-resistance! Not even General Hoffmann and the Pan-German Junkers are more ready to shed blood to gain their ends.

In spite of the "Fraternization," from which the Bolsheviks had hoped so much, this last pitiful bluff of a "moral" appeal to the shades of Tolstoi was promptly called. The German Army obeyed its officers without hesitation and advanced towards Petrograd.

The only really dignified thing left for Lenin and Trotsky after this fiasco was suicide. They had made a stupendous gamble. The stakes were not their own, they had put up the nation on the chance. They had lost. And all the millions of people, with whose interests they had played, had to bear the loss.

The deceit which they had practiced had been gross. They had not said they would try to get a universal, just peace. They had not said that they hoped their method would result in the revolutionary People's Peace, which they had said was the only peace they would consider. They had not made any saving conditions. There had never been any doubt in their assurances. They had been very certain about it. They had won to power on definite promises. And now they could not fulfill them.

At least they should have abdicated. Ludendorff, when he lost his big game, resigned. A certain dignity would have followed them into their retirement, if they had resigned. At least one could have believed that they had been sincere in their mistake. They could not hope to stay in power unless they made abject terms with the winners of the toss.

"Abdication," I am told, is the most distasteful word in the vocabulary of politicians and probably the most sincere thing about Lenin is his conviction that the welfare of the human race is dependent on his maintenance in office. He preferred to hold his position, no matter how humiliating the terms demanded by the Germans might be, and the Germans, knowing how he had tried to play false with them, were not inclined to be tender to him.

With the arrival in Moscow of Count von Mirbach, the German Ambassador, a new era began. "What can we do?" One Bolshevist leader, who had formerly advocated a rapprochement with America, said to me: "The Germans are only a day's march from Petrograd. What could the Entente do for us, if we resisted? They could give us nothing but kind words such as they gave Belgium and Serbia."

All chance of "impartiality" in their hostility to foreign imperialism came to an end. But if they could not carry on their revolutionary propaganda very successfully in Germany, they could continue it in the Entente countries. The Germans were ready to help them by financing and securing false neutral passports for their agitators in England, France, and America.

The period from the signing of the peace to the arrival of the German Ambassador was the most critical in their early history. On one side they were afraid that Mirbach would kick them out and throw the German influence to the reactionary parties. This had been the German policy in the Ukraine. They had forced a separate peace out of the revolutionary government at Kiev. As soon as the treaty was signed the Germans turned against the Ukrainian revolutionists and tried to put the landed aristocrats back on their estates. It was possible, even probable, that the Germans would turn against the Bolsheviks. No one knew what Mirbach would do on his arrival. On the other side the Bolsheviks were faced by a dangerous revulsion from the ignominious peace they had signed. Trotsky's love of Open Diplomacy had not lasted long. The press control was now well established and everything was done to keep the terms of the treaty from general knowledge. However, the mere fact of having signed a treaty with the Kaiser, so absolutely contrary to repeated pledges, had stirred up a great deal more patriotic feeling than I had thought existed.

One of the most able men supporting the Bolshevist regime was the manager of the plant where we had all our printing done. It was there also that the German propaganda paper was produced. He had been long an exile in Paris, where he had accepted the doctrines of the Anarchist Syndicalists. While he had many theoretical disputes with the Bolsheviks, he was prepared to support any form of Proletarian Dictatorship. It was the one big plant which I happened to see which worked well under the Bolshevist regime. There were several others I heard of, but all seemed to depend on an outstanding character, who was able to get the confidence and affection of all the employees. If the Bolshevist industrial scheme in general could work even fifty percent as well as this shop, it would be an irresistible success. Certainly a very large part of its success here was due to the passionate sincerity and amazing energy of this man. I think he worked on an average more than eighteen hours a day. He was getting out morning and evening papers and supervising both.

He had been absolutely convinced that Trotsky's tactics would succeed. First, he expected a revolution in Germany. Then he was sure that there would be a mutiny, if General Hoffmann ordered an advance, after Trotsky's theatrical appeal to Tolstoy. I saw him nearly every day during this period. When the Germans did begin to advance he organized his entire shop, several hundred men, in a Red Guard unit. They were ready to follow him to a man. "We'll die in the barricades, if necessary, but we'll never sign a peace with the Kaiser," he said to me a hundred times.

I saw him a few hours after he got the news that Lenin had sent out the famous wireless message saying he would sign a peace on any terms. I have never heard the Bolshevist leader denounced more violently by any "capitalist" than by this honest workingman who had trusted him. And there were very many like this printer, who were utterly disillusioned at this time. There had been many who believed that

Kerensky had not been sufficiently energetic and that more vehement action such as the Bolsheviks proposed would precipitate a crisis which would result in a general democratic peace, without annexations or indemnities and assuring all peoples the right to choose their own government. They had supported Lenin, or at least had sat back passively, in this faith. But now they were confronted by an utter deception—a separate peace the most imperialistic the world had ever known.

It was at this time that the Russian Bolsheviks sold out their "Comrades" in Finland and the Ukraine and broke their agreement with the Czecho-Slovaks. It is Lenin's professed theory that "Loyalty to Pledges," "Moral Obligations," etc., are merely bourgeois phrases to trick and subjugate the Proletariat. He acts up to this theory not only in his relations with the hated "capitalist Imperialist" but also, when it suits his convenience, in dealings with his revolutionary friends. The Germans wanted a "free hand" in the Ukraine, the granary of Russia; they did not want their puppet landlord government disturbed by Bolshevist agitators and for political reasons they were tired of the civil war in Finland. They did not want to have the Czecho-Slovaks and other allied troops leave Russia to fight on the Western Front.

When Von Mirbach explained this to the Bolshevist government, he undoubtedly rattled his sabre. Resistance to his demands meant abdication. Lenin withdrew from his "alliance" with the Reds of Finland and the Ukraine just as cynically as he had repudiated engagements with Britain and France. He entered into an agreement with the Czecho-Slovaks, by which they disarmed to prove their good faith. And then, thinking they were helpless, he ordered the attack on them. The treaties with the former allies had been signed by the Tsar. But the pledges with these revolutionists, which he repudiated, were of his own making. And the working class in Helsingfors and Kiev—deserted by Moscow Bolshevism—was treated to a bloodletting more ruthless than Thiers's vengeance on the Communards of Paris in '71.

Chapter XV
Allied Diplomacy in Russia

It is doubtful whether the diplomats of the allied nations could have done anything to help Russia in this stupendous revolutionary upheaval. Perhaps the kindest thing of all would have been for them to go home and to leave the Russians to their own resources. But the war was too vital and passionate a reality to allow anyone to take this philosophical attitude of indifference. However it is certain that any chance of the representatives of the Allies doing good by staying in Russia was ruined by their lack of unity. It was the same problem on the diplomatic field, which it took us so long to solve on the military terrain. If the Entente had wished to accomplish anything in Russia, they should have sent some diplomatic Foch to unify action.

It was not only that the various embassies were often at loggerheads. No one of the ambassadors was of strong enough character to dominate and control his own flock. Grouped, about each embassy, there were military missions, secret services, publicity agents, commercial attaches, all busily engaged in trying to serve their country, but with no one to co-ordinate their actions. They were continually getting in each other's way.[1]

One day General Nieselle, the head of the French Military Mission, summoned a publicity conference. It met in my room at the Hotel Europe. He brought with him another French general, there were a couple of British officers, General Judson, our military attaché, and myself.

When we sat down General Nieselle announced that at last, after repeatedly refusing his requests, the French Government had put funds at his disposal for propaganda purposes. It was, he said, rather like locking the door after the horse was stolen, for the Bolsheviks were already in power and peace negotiations had commenced at Brest-Litovsk, but he said he had the money and must do something with it. He believed that our cause was lost in Great Russia, he could see no chance of bringing it back into the war. He felt there was still a fighting possibility of keeping the Ukraine lined up on our side and he had decided to spend the bulk of this money in that hope.

---

[1] The best account of Allied diplomacy in Russia during this period is Michael J. Carley, *Silent Conflict*. See also David W. McFadden, *Alternative Paths: Soviets and Americans, 1917–1920* (Oxford: Oxford University Press, 1993); and David Fogelsong, *America's Secret War Against Bolshevism: U.S. Intervention in the Russian Civil War, 1917–1920* (Chapel Hill: University of North Carolina Press, 1995).

The Ukraine was not Bolshevist; it was breaking away from Russia because of fear of Bolshevism and, if their movement for independence was cordially supported by us, we might hope to keep them on our side.

It was a hazardous project at best. German influence was already active in the Ukraine, but the military argument for attempt was strong. It was the only possible hope of protecting Romania and of connecting up with the pro-allied forces in the Don and Caucasus. He wanted the co-operation of the British and American missions.

One of the very few definite instructions we received from the State Department had arrived a few days before, stating that our government was flatly opposed to the encouragement of separatist movements in Russia.

I started to say that I could not discuss the merits of his argument as my hands were definitely tied by these precise instructions. But I was interrupted by General Nieselle's subordinate. He jumped up to protest against his chief's proposal. It was one of those emotional outbreaks where you cannot help sympathizing with the man's obvious pain, but cannot at all sympathize with the delirious proposals which result from his pain.

He had spent many months in the Ukraine, had helped them organize their National Army, and he had no confidence in them. To spend money on them he thought was to waste it. They were no better than the Great Russians. "Traitors" he called them all. He launched into bitter tirades against Russia. France would never have been in this war except for loyalty to her alliance with Russia and now the Russians had betrayed them.

"*J'ai déja perdu deux fils dans cette maudite guerre,*" he said, but he had given them willingly. France he thought would profit; "never did I lose faith, I was assured of victory, but now—*J'ai peur*—we may be defeated—not by Germany but by these Russian traitors. Do not spend any more money here. Send it back home to buy more bullets for the Boche." Tears streamed down his face, he turned to General Nieselle. "*Mon Général*—I ask you—beg of you—I pray you let me go home so that I can fight. Am I not a soldier of France? Why send me back to Kiev? That nest of traitors! Why give them good French gold to spend on their mistresses? *Votre projet est absurd—idiot! Ill ne vaut rien—rien—rien!*"

General Nieselle had to bang on the table and call his subordinate to order. He saluted sullenly, sat down, wiped the tears from his face, and did not open his mouth again.

This incident was typical of the contradictory opinions which made unity of action, even among the representatives of one nation, impossible. The other Allies were just as badly divided.

The British Embassy was officially against the Bolsheviks, but the government at London had sent out a former Consul General, named Lockmart, with the instructions to flirt with Lenin and Trotsky and report on their intentions. I frequently met representatives of these two British factions and what they said about each other was far from diplomatic.

Our own representatives—embassy, military mission, Red Cross, and consulates—were just as bitterly divided.

In general the French point of view was purely military. They felt that France had been drawn into the war through loyalty to the alliance and now that the Russians had repudiated this alliance they had small patience with any talk of Russia's rights or wishes. Their one object was the defeat of Germany. They had been taught to believe that this could be accomplished only by simultaneous attacks on her Eastern and Western Fronts. America had not yet developed her power and there was no certainty that we would be able to compensate for the Russian deflection. The French saw clearly the aid which Bolshevist propaganda was giving Germany and thought of the Bolsheviks as open enemies. Of course some of the French representatives took other attitudes, but in general this "military" point of view dominated their councils.

The British on the whole—although here, too, there were pleasant exceptions—seemed to take the social point of view. Those who had been there any length of time had made friendships with the old aristocracy. None of the Bolsheviks were on their calling lists. They were not so bent as the French on making war on the Soviet leaders. They were contented to cut them dead. Then a large number of British subjects, who had been for many years in business in Russia, had been taken into official service, because of their knowledge of the language. Most of them had seen their businesses, the work of many years, ruined by Bolshevist decrees and so brought a personal animus into their anti-Soviet policy.

The various American representatives brought fewer prejudices, military, social, or business, to the problem, but very few of them had been long enough in Russia to know the language and were very much at the mercy of their interpreters.

Despite my best efforts I have never been able to get an interpreter in Russia who was not partisan. If he were a Constitutional Democrat, he never found anything worth reading to me in the papers except the news of his party and his interpretation of events would always have a Constitutional Democratic slant. If I discharged him because his views were too obviously biased, the man I got in his place would always have as intense a partisanship in some other direction. So the prejudices of our non-Russian speaking representatives were largely second-hand—derived from their interpreters.

But even one who was fluent in the language was confronted by a mass of conflicting testimony and a dearth of verifiable evidence. In one district there was plenty of food and in another none at all. In all probability you would get reports from both districts on the same morning, both true but flatly contradictory.

I recall especially the effort we made to determine what the troops of the garrison in Petrograd were going to do. Every day I would get reports from several barracks and about half of them would pass a resolution in favor of the Bolsheviks and the other half against them.

In John Reed's *Ten Days that Shook the World* there is a very vivid description of a meeting on the eve of Lenin's coup, where an armored motor car regiment was swung to the Bolshevist side. I was not there that night, but I had attended a number of similar meetings. His description rings true in detail; it is wonderfully well written.

He was impressed by the Bolshevist success. My impression of those "ten days" was that most of the garrison wanted to be neutral in the ruction between Lenin and Kerensky. I could see no large enthusiasm among the soldiers for either side. We both were watching the same events but drew quite different conclusions. How to determine what items out of the news were significant? How to determine which interpretation of events was correct? Inevitably every one chose what was congenial to his own temperament.

I suppose the worst way to determine between two proposed courses of action is to pitch a penny. But it would have been better to roll dice to decide on which policy the Allies should follow and have accepted loyally the results, than to continue, as we did, at cross-purposes. The very worst proposal which I heard from any of the allied representatives would have been better than no policy at all. Some at least of the Russians would have rallied to us on any clear-cut program we might have united upon.

When the Russians wanted to know what to expect from the Central Empires, they did not have to waste time going to Constantinople, Sophia, and Vienna. They could get a direct answer from Berlin. But if they wanted to co-operate with their former allies, they had to consult Rome, Paris, London, and Washington, and I do not think they ever received a similar answer from any three out of the four.

There was one very interesting—and at times comical—controversy which arose over the lack of diplomatic relations with the Soviet Republic. All the allied governments had refused to recognize the Council of the People's Commissaires, but their representative claimed all the customary "diplomatic immunities." There is a very delicate point of international law involved. What right has an ambassador to ask for ambassadorial privileges from a government to which he is not accredited and whose existence he is supposed to ignore? But more fundamental than this legalistic quibble is the question of how far a diplomat has the right to claim immunities when he violates the implied contract by mixing in local politics, conspiring against the de facto government? All the Entente embassies were more or less involved in anti-Bolshevik conspiracies—some timidly and discreetly, others blatantly and indiscreetly.

The Bolshevist newspapers fulminated against the machinations of the representatives of foreign Imperialism—"Sir George and Sir Francis"—but at first the Council of the People's Commissaires, although they knew that the allied embassies were definitely hostile and were using what courage and ability they had to plot the overthrow of this New Regime, allowed them all the privileges they would have had a right to expect, if they had been duly accredited and really friendly.

When the Bolsheviks arrested the Romanian Minister in Petrograd, the diplomatic corps called formally on Lenin—it was the nearest they ever came to recognizing him—and gave him a lecture on diplomatic immunities. He surprised them by accepting their arguments and ordering the release of the Romanian Minister.

The explanation of this surprisingly docile attitude was not far to seek. Lenin was trying to secure "diplomatic immunities" for his agents abroad. He thought he would be able to pick men more clever at conspiracy than the representatives of the Allies in Petrograd. He did succeed in having his missions received in some neutral countries. But when at last he discovered that there was no use hoping to open conspirative centers under the disguise of embassies in the capitals of the Entente, he began to put the screws on their representatives in Russia and finally drove them out of Bolshevist territory.

That Lenin had no right to take a "holier-than-thou" attitude in regard to the misuse of diplomatic immunities to cover conspiracies is proved by the history of his mission to Switzerland. It was finally expelled for having violated all its pledges and its chief, Bersin, when he returned to Petrograd made a public report admitting—and boasting of—the perfidy with which the Swiss Government charged him.

It is difficult, in regard to Russia, to be wise even after the fact. There was so much conflicting evidence, so much honest and passionate difference of opinion. But I believe now and believed at the time that the air might have been cleared—to the great relief of both sides—if one man could have been sent to Russia as a High Commissioner of the Allies.

In the midsummer of 1918, we had naval forces at Murmansk including an American warship. The Japanese and English had landed small forces of marines in Vladivostok. Officials of one or another of the Allies were implicated in almost every effort to overthrow the Bolsheviks. Yet the governments of the Allies were professing neutrality in the internal affairs of Russia. The Bolsheviks had ample justification for sarcastic comments on the incoherence of our policy. On the other hand the Soviet Republic claimed to be neutral in the World War but it was fighting beside the Central Empires against our ally, Romania. It was carrying on, or at least permitting, many acts of unneutral assistance to Germany. We had plenty of justification for returning its taunts about incoherence of policy.

It would not have been difficult for a High Commissioner of the Allies to have drafted a note which would have forced Lenin into a public discussion and have brought about a definition of purpose on both sides. The air would have been wholesomely cleared by an ultimatum—in the more formal language of diplomacy—along such lines as these:

I am instructed by the governments I represent, your former allies and friends, to open discussions with the de facto government of Russia.

The older democracies of the West have no desire to interfere with the internal, social, and economic readjustments resulting from the Revolution in Russia. We watch with interest, if with some skepticism, the hurried experiments in socialization you are now attempting. If they develop as you hope into demonstrable short cuts to happiness, our people—enjoying political freedom in such matters—will doubtlessly follow your example. In this age-long struggle to ameliorate the lot of man there may be friendly rivalry between nations, but no jealousy. Even though we doubt the wisdom of some of your proposals, we can only hope that you will succeed in blazing new trails, in surpassing that measure of happiness which our people have already attained and which we are to-day defending against the armed aggression of the reaction in Central Europe.

You have demanded that we should define our attitude. That is simple enough. We are at war. The danger to our treasured—if imperfect—liberties, to the democratic institutions which are synonymous for us with our national existence, has forced us to concentrate all our strength, all our thought, on the one aim of victory. And until victory is attained this fact of war will dominate all our decisions.

While we deeply regret, and question the wisdom, of your decision to withdraw from this war, we do not question your right to do so. However, it is of vital importance to us that you also should now define your intentions.

The governments which I represent have repeatedly affirmed their desire to re-establish friendly relations with the German people. But they are at war with the government which now controls in Germany, and with all its allies. We desire to maintain truly friendly relations with the people of Russia. They have fought heroically beside us in the past and we count confidently on their future co-operation in the eternal upward struggle of civilization. But if any government which may arise in Russia allies itself with our enemies, by open agreement or covert aid, we will be compelled to wage war against it.

The reports of our various representations here on the intentions and acts of the Council of the People's Commissaires are diverse and contradictory. Some claim that your attitude is friendly, some believe that they have found evidence of unfriendly dealings with German Imperialism. Whatever policy you may have determined upon has not been made clear. The Supreme War Council of the Allies at Versailles has sent me directly to you to seek a frank discussion of these problems, and a definition of your intentions.

While we concede your legal right to withdraw from the war at your discretion, you must now definitely adopt and loyally observe an attitude of neutrality or expect us to regard you as an enemy. You have, in somewhat uncertain and unfriendly terms, declared for neutrality. But certain of your acts are in direct contravention of this declaration. I am instructed to inform you that if you desire us to recognize your neutrality you must at once agree to the following conditions. The only alternative is a state of open war. Refusal to agree to these terms can only be interpreted by us as an open avowal of intentions to aid our enemies.

I. Continued occupation by our forces of the Murmansk Coast until the signing of a general peace. This territory—of vital importance to our naval strategy—is at present threatened by a German expedition. The Soviet Republic has no forces there to prevent it from falling into the hands of our enemies. The population has never given you its allegiance. It is friendly to us and desires us to remain. We intend to maintain in this naval base, which we created at the request of Russia, while you were still belligerent, a sufficient force to protect it from our enemies.

II. Temporary occupation of the ports of Arkhangel and Vladivostok. We have no intention of permanent control in these places but we desire and demand the tranquil opportunity to destroy or remove the war stores there. They are our property, as you have announced that you will not pay for them. They are of no value to you as a neutral and are desperately needed by our enemies. We are reliably informed that large quantities have already been transferred to them.

We also expect your pledge to ship into the interior as rapidly as possible and to prevent the sale to Germany of other munitions and war supplies, which we furnished to you while you were our co-belligerent.

III. Free and unimpeded passage to ports of exit for all allied troops now in Russia—including all war prisoners of Armenian, Czecho-Slovak, Italian, Polish, Romanian, or Serb nationality, who have expressed their desire to join, or have already been incorporated in irredentist regiments and who would be executed as traitors if they fell into the hands of their former oppressors. We pledge ourselves to remove these soldiers from Russian territory as soon as shipping conditions permit and to prevent their taking part in the internal dissensions of Russia during their transit.

IV. The immediate cessation on the part of the Soviet Republic of all military operations or hostile propaganda against our ally, the Kingdom of Romania.

If the Council of the People's Commissaires agree to these terms within ten days from date, the associated governments which I represent will on their part pledge to withdraw as quickly as possible all their armed forces from Russia to the ports mentioned in paragraphs I and II, and transport them as ships are available to the Western Front, leaving in these ports only sufficient troops to fulfill the objects stated in the agreements; they will scrupulously respect the neutral rights of Russia and refrain from any interference in her political life.

What would Lenin have replied to such an ultimatum? He might have decided on a loyal neutrality. My personal guess is that, no matter how much he might have liked to, he could not have done so. If faced by a definite decision, I believe, he would have had to throw in his lot with Germany. I do not think they would have permitted him to be honestly neutral and he had no power to resist their demands. The result would very likely have been war with the Soviet Republic. But the uncertainty would have ended, many false issues brushed aside. The Russians as well as the Allies would have benefited by an incident which forced Lenin to show his hand. Many Russians would have sided with us in a war against his government in those days before they had lost patience with our indecision, lost confidence in our ability to help our friends.

Such an incident would have been a general signal for all the anti-Bolshevist groups in Russia to revolt at once. Instead, they frittered away their forces in isolated outbreaks—in the Caucasus, the Don, Crimea, Yaroslav. Now it was the reaction which started a local uprising, then the extremely revolutionary followers of Marie Spirodonova, who had at one time sided with the Bolsheviks. Our own disunity and inaction was largely responsible for allowing Lenin to crush the opposition bit by bit.

Of course we, in Russia, had only the sketchiest idea of what our governments were doing and planning at home. Reports and recommendations were sent home but no one ever knew if they arrived. It is possible that some project similar to that outlined above was discussed in the chancelleries and wrecked on the familiar reef of "Disunity." We cried "Union, Union," and there was no union. The allied representatives in Russia would certainly not have agreed on any such proposal. The French would not agree that Russia had a right to repudiate her alliance. In general the British did not believe that a "government of blighters" could last very long, so why should we withdraw our troops? Some few wanted to use the soldiers we already had there in the Civil War—throw out the Bolsheviks ourselves.

Disorder was the only word for allied diplomacy in Russia. Were we at war with the Bolsheviks? Apparently not. But there was no dodging the fact that they were at war with our ally, Romania. Did this constitute war against us? If so, how much?

I will never forget the desperate uncertainty of those days when our governments were trying to decide whether to desert Romania, in the hope of maintaining friendship with Lenin, or to stick by our sorely pressed ally even if it meant war against the Bolsheviks. While we were all discussing this hectically, expecting every minute a cable committing us to a definite policy, poor Romania—unable to fight off the Hapsburgs and the Bolsheviks simultaneously—surrendered, ceased to be our ally, and so settled this peculiar question for us.

Then came a period of utter despair for all our friends in Russia. We seemed to have decided to abandon them also to the Bolsheviks in spiked helmets. All the allied troops in Russia were ordered to entrain for some port of exit—Murmansk, Arkhangel, or Vladivostok. Hardly a day passed when some Russians, prominent in the revolutionary movement, did not come to my office and argue desperately for allied intervention. It was useless for me to tell them that I had nothing to do with such matters, that all questions of political affairs should be dealt with through the regular diplomatic channels. They were so desperate about it they insisted on having their say. There seems to be a common impression in America that it was only the reactionary elements which wanted allied intervention. My own experience was quite the opposite. Mr. Wilson's idea of making the world safe for democracy had already alienated from America any friendship of the Old Régime. His overtures to the Bolsheviks, when he still hoped that they could be appealed to on democratic grounds, had enraged the reactionaries. America was anathema to them. Once some Constitutional Democrats of the Republican Left Wing called on me in this connection, but most of the pleas for allied intervention were from Socialists of long revolutionary tradition.

Always the argument took the same form. "You Americans say you do not want to interfere in our internal politics. But you see how the Germans are interfering! You say we ought to settle our own disputes. We ought to and we could, if they were our own disputes. We could and would throw out the Bolsheviks, if they stood alone. But we aren't strong enough to fight them—and the Germans. All we ask is a counterpoise for the outside help they are getting. Help us—the democratic forces of Russia—as much as the Germans are helping them."

I was not convinced by such arguments. We did not have any too many rifles on the Western Front. It would take a long time to send a rifle to Russia and then the chances were at least even that it would be used in civil war against Russians. We could send our rifles much more quickly to France and then we could be sure that they would be fired at the Germans.

If the Bolsheviks had of their own volition declared war on us, or if they could have been jockeyed diplomatically into doing so, the situation would have been different. But unless there was a formal state of war, I was opposed to "Intervention."

But the Bolsheviks decided the question for us. In a moment of madness, probably prodded to it by the Germans, they upset the plan of transporting our troops to the Western Front by attacking the Czecho-Slovaks and trying to prevent their withdrawal.

If the allied diplomacy in Russia was uncertain about whether the attack of the Soviet Republic on one of our small allies constituted war on us, it was even more at sea on this question of "Intervention." Large numbers of allied troops, principally technical units, had come to Russia in the days of the Tsar. After the Revolution, the Provisional Government had encouraged the formation of Irredentist regiments from the camps of war prisoners. These former subjects of Austria, Germany, and Turkey had mostly surrendered voluntarily to escape from service under their hated masters. They hoped, as passionately as any citizen of Paris, for the victory of the Entente. The "Kerensky Offensive," in 1917, which started so brilliantly, had been led by Czecho-Slovak shock troops. When the Bolsheviks won to power there were considerably over 100,000 allied troops in Russia. And these soldiers, even if the Russians stopped, wanted to continue the war. When the armistice was signed, they started home. Some of them had the luck to get ships and were in at the death in the triumphal advance on the French and Italian fronts. All of them were on their way to the ports and, if the Bolsheviks had left them alone, would have been out of Russia by early in 1918.

Naturally the Germans and Austrians did not like to see this procession of valuable recruits get to France. The question of intervention was decided by the Bolsheviks. They certainly did not want any effective intervention, but neither would they permit a withdrawal. They claimed to be afraid of the counter revolutionary designs of the Czecho-Slovaki. In order to show their good faith the Czechs disarmed, down to one rifle for every ten men. Then the Bolsheviks attacked them. Scattered all over Russia and Siberia there were units of homesick allied troops, who had to fight to prevent being handed over to the Germans. The smaller units were wiped out. The stronger groups were able to fight their way through and join in with their comrades. The Bolsheviks called this unwarranted intervention.

But if you wanted to drive an allied diplomat into a rage all you had to do was to ask: "Has your government intervened in Russia? If so, when?"

The situation of the representatives of the Allies in Russia was hard on the temper, but no matter how mad we sometimes got at each other, we all, except a few hot heads, realized that the important moves of the great game were being played by the Supreme War Council at Versailles beyond our vision. Nothing we could have hoped to gain by carrying out any of our policies in Russia could have compensated for a break—or even the risk of one—in the alliance which was still fighting Germany. We were often disheartened when our various governments failed to back up our pet schemes. It was especially disheartening that they could not agree among themselves and tell us definitely which oar they wanted us to pull on together. But I presume that the governments at home were just as much puzzled by our inability to agree as we were by theirs.

The signing of peace cannot but have a hopeful effect in Russia. One of two things will happen. Either there will be an effective League of Nations, which can unify diplomatic action, or each government will feel free to follow a policy of its own without fear of offending its allies. In the first case there will be the united front we all hoped for. In the second case, while there may be conflict between the policies of the different nations, we can at least hope that each government will work out a consistent policy of its own and have union in its own diplomatic representation.

Chapter XVI
Lenin's Foreign Policy

The Bolsheviks explained their treaty with the Kaiser as a "strategic retreat," "a mere disloyal truce," "a breathing space," to allow the revolutionary proletariat of Russia to consolidate their organization, "to gather strength for a new and decisive attack on International Capitalism." Bolshevism cannot stand alone in Russia. Lenin has never had any illusions on this subject. He has always told his followers that their victory in Russia would be sterile unless their Revolution spread to other countries. Foreign propaganda is the base of his foreign policy.

He was forced to promise Germany to stop all agitations there. But he boasted—discreetly, while Imperial Germany was still strong, more openly now—that he did not feel bound by such a pledge. To live up to such a promise would be suicide for him, acknowledgment of failure. The imperial police kept a rigid check on Bolshevist propaganda in the Fatherland, but in underground ways, at which long experience had made them expert, they gave considerable aid to the Liebknecht faction. And after the signing of the treaty at Brest-Litovsk, the Bolshevist agitation in allied countries was—with German aid—intensified.

The spreading of their revolution, the export of their ideas, is and must be their principal preoccupation. The "government" they are running in Moscow is a side issue compared to the importance of internationalizing their doctrines. They may make—and keep—any bargains in other matters, they may make any promises in regard to this, but their main effort, no matter what pledges they sign, more important to them than any internal problems, must be to win the world for Bolshevism.

This campaign of the Bolsheviks to evangelize the democratic and capitalistic heathen of other lands cannot be treated like the armed gospel of Islam and held in check by force. Lenin, from this view point, is more like Luther in his attack on Rome than like Mohammed in his assault on Christendom. The emissaries of this new dispensation do not wear distinctive turbans which betray them to the sight. Just as the secret presses of the Reformation spread the Bible in the vernacular across every frontier, in spite of the sword of temporal power and the auto-da-fés of the Inquisition, so the missionaries of this new creed will contrive to pass any barrier of force. The armies of Tchaikovsky, Denikin, and Kolchak may enter Moscow and hang a few hundred of the Bolsheviks, but that will not kill the idea. History is overloaded with evidence that no dynamic idea has ever been suppressed by force. Any attempt to put an "embargo" on Bolshevism is predestined to failure. Execution, imprisonments, deportations will not save the world from such propaganda. The doctrine was born under the Tsar—the worst tyranny the modern world has known. It grew up in hiding. It festered—and prospered—in prisons. Persecutions will not stop it.

The determination of the Bolsheviks to spread their evangel is desperate. This is not only implicit in their doctrines; it has been explicitly stated by Lenin time after time. Few graver questions face the world today than this: how much success will the Bolsheviks have in their foreign policy?

Prophecy, as has often been remarked, is the least excusable of human errors. But repetitions in history depend on reproduction of conditions. A study of conditions allows us to make some forecasts. It is possible to isolate some of the elements on which the development of Bolshevism in Russia has depended.

One undoubtedly is a "theory," preached with fanatic energy by a forceful group of agitators. There is nothing startlingly new in these ideas, they have been always with us, but they will be preached with new passion as the result of their sudden conquest of power in Russia and behind them will be the desperately energetic propulsion of Lenin's organization.

However no amount of "agitation" will make Bolshevism spread where another condition does not exist—a fertile soil. In Russia, to a greater extent than anywhere else in the world, with possible exception of Romania and parts of Hungary—the soil was fertile. There you had a country overwhelmingly agricultural. And the misery of the great mass of the people was beyond exaggeration. Even more important than the misery of the peasants was their abject hopelessness about it. They had no share in the prosperity of their country and no tangible hope of acquiring any.

There is not much choice for the Russian factory worker between the Tsarist frying pan and the Bolshevist fire. One tyranny is not so much worse than another. The collapse of industry, the closing of so many factories and mines, is not so serious to the Russian as it sounds. Only about 10 percent of the population was interested in industry. Many of the unemployed went back to idleness on the farms, where they were hardly more miserable than when employed in the factories. Many of them enlisted in the Red Army, and drew much better wages for drilling than they ever dreamed of while "at work."

But German labor leaders are more afraid of unemployment than of anything else. They would like to nationalize the factories, but only on conditions that they can make them work. The situation is even less promising—from Lenin's point of view—in the democratic countries. We do not know much about the actual conditions of the German working class, the horrible burdens of the war may have driven them to desperation. But in France, England, and America, Organized Labor instead of growing hopeless has waxed confident. A Labor Ministry is said to be a near possibility in England. The men who are inspired by this expectation are likely to turn a deaf ear to Lenin's appeal to despair.

Organized Labor has played a patriotic and very helpful role in the conduct of the war. Certain definite reforms have been promised to it in all countries. Labor believes that it has the power to get them. Four years of war has not tended to make men gentle.

In 1916, at a session of the Prussian Landtag, a Socialist member, arguing in favor of immediate reform of the suffrage, warned the Chamber that Junker resistance to this democratic reform was causing ominous discontent among the workers. A reactionary deputy interrupted him, saying that, if the Socialists became threatening, the government would revive the exceptional laws of Bismarck against labor organizations. The Socialist laughed at him. "Do you think," he jeered, "that the German workingmen—after two years of this hellish war—will be afraid of a policeman's club?"

It was a significant retort and it applies to all the world as well as to Germany. We have been spending our best energies in teaching our youths—most of them workingmen—not to be afraid of 42 centimeter shells, of hand grenades or mustard gas. When they get home they will not be awed by the policeman's *club*.

The most universally important political fact of our day is that the world has taught its young men to settle disputes with bayonets. It is supremely necessary to get them once more into the habit of ballots.

A few months before we entered the war, at a table in a Washington club, the inevitable subject of "Preparedness" came up for discussion. One of our generals, who had evidently read Von der Goltz's "A Nation in Arms," presented the usual arguments for universal military service. A senator, who had never read anything on the subject and "viewed with alarm" any development of militarism, said that he preferred something like the Swiss system.

"That would be impossible," the general said. "In Switzerland every citizen is armed and takes care of his own equipment. We could not afford to let every man have a rifle in his home in a country like this where there is so much social unrest."

"On the other hand," I put in, "if we did adopt the Swiss system and allowed every citizen to keep a rifle over his radiator, we could not afford to have so much social unrest."

This suggestion of mine was ruled out as flippant. But it is just what the war has done to us—and to all the world. The actual possession of a weapon is not so important as familiarity with its use. If society wants to avoid Bolshevism it simply cannot afford to have widespread and justified social unrest.

We must arrange things so that no great number of our people are desperate, so that our young men will have enough faith in our political institutions to get back into the habit of balloting. We must give them some better reasons for respecting the policeman—the symbol of orderly government—than mere fear of his club. It is up to the rest of us who did not fight to see that they like the policeman, that they think of him as a defender of human rights—not simply of somebody else's property. This,

I take it, is what Lloyd George meant by saying that he feared reaction more than revolution.

A reactionary policy today will meet a more violently inclined opposition than formerly. We have taught our young men that it is right to fight for Liberty and Democracy. The world has become "quick on the trigger."

We can expect revolutions in all backward countries, where the mass of the people have been oppressed and have had no adequate representation in government, no hope for progress. We have planned to bring them about in Central Europe. They will be violent and destructive, just in proportion as the reaction is bitter and stubborn. They will be supported, as Labor will be everywhere in every minor dispute with Capital, by Lenin to the extent of his power. He recognizes very clearly that Russia cannot stand long alone, the success of his adventure depends entirely on the spread of his doctrines.

His government can never make a real peace with Democracy. He has only scorn for the idea. He does not believe in majority rule. He believes in the Dictatorship of the proletariat—a minority dictatorship. If a majority of the people are so foolish as not to be proletarians—so much the worse for them. Just as he boasts that his treaty with the Kaiser was a sham, that he violated it whenever he dared, so any engagement he might make with us would be hollow. This is inevitable from his own logic. He denounces our form of government as much as the Prussian regime. And—as the Finnish revolutionists know to their sorrow—he does not feel bound even by the pledges he makes to his revolutionary "Comrades."

Lenin will and always must do everything in his power to swing every revolutionary movement to Bolshevism. To keep up the confidence of his own following he will always claim success. And the reactionaries of Western countries are playing his game whenever they allow justified discontent to fester to the point of open revolt. They are playing his game whenever they call an honest demand of labor for improved conditions, an effort of progressives for improved democracy in politics and industry, "Bolshevism."

It is a manifest error, ignorant or ill-intentioned, to pretend that every revolutionary movement is a step toward Bolshevism. This is nowhere more clearly shown than in Lenin's own words. He is not at all satisfied with the march of events in Germany. As is their custom, the Bolshevist newspapers gloss over all unpleasant facts. They ignored the military campaign, the "unlimited force" which finally crushed the German military machine. When the Armistice was signed, they claimed all the credit for it. It was Revolution—their Revolution—which had caused the surrender, not the surrender which had caused the Revolution. And then they had to clamp on the censorship to protect their followers from knowing that the revolutionary Government in Germany was fighting against Bolshevism—sending Joffre, their ambassador, home, locking up their emissary, Radek; using machine guns on the extremists like Liebknecht.

Lenin's denunciations of Ebert and the leaders of the German and Austrian workingmen indicate very clearly that he does not consider their revolution the "right kind." He is as bitter against them as he was against the Kaiser or Kerensky. Dissatisfied with the way things went in Germany, the Russian Bolsheviks are now hoping for a "Second Revolution." They stake their faith on "The Spartacus Group."

There is a very real significance in the name which these extremists—the Bolsheviks of Germany—have chosen for their party. Spartacus led a revolt of slaves. They are calling to the slaves of modern Germany and are unlikely to get followers except among such as consider themselves "slaves." Assuming that they succeed in getting those they call upon to follow them, the question is: How many of the German people of to-day think of themselves as slaves?

It is hard to know what changes the war has brought to the national psychology of Germany. But certainly the number of Germans who, before the war, could have been drawn into a slave revolt was very few. The thoughtful, intelligent workers, those most likely to dominate the thought of their class, had won some degree of well-being. The intricate threads of the co-operative societies and various forms of industrial insurance—all fostered by the State—had given them a stake in the community.

The German workers had numerous acute dissatisfactions, but they were the opposite of hopeless about them. They realized that the medieval election laws of Prussia were the greatest obstacles to the progress of their class. But they were expecting to win universal suffrage, not in a dim and remote future, but soon. The typical pre-war workman of Germany, with great confidence and pride in the steady advance of his party—already the strongest single party in the Reichstag-with an effective, growing labor organization, convinced that he was on the eve of sweeping democratic reforms, was in every sense a citizen. And the psychology of the citizen is the very antithesis to the mentality of the slave.

The danger of a slave revolt in any community is dependent on the number of slaves. No Roman citizens joined Spartacus. And slavery is not wholly a matter of legal definition. In this connection it is more a matter of subjective psychology. We may be sure, many who were legally "slaves" did not join the revolt of Spartacus. Some had soft jobs, some felt they were at least "upper class" slaves and had no "solidarity" with mere gladiators. And most important of all, some hoped to buy their freedom. No one who has a tangible hope of improving his condition is ever quite a slave.

Of course a few slaves, if driven to desperation, can start a revolt. But they cannot upset a society in which most people are fairly contented. Leninism depends for success on the widespread existence of slave mentality.

The American Socialist Party has never succeeded in rallying to its membership the majority of our working class. An important element in their failure has been their insistence on "orthodox phraseology," borrowed from the Europe of 1850. "Wage slavery" has never been a popular phrase with American workingmen. However miserable their condition—even in the worst sweated trade—few Americans like to think of themselves as "slaves." They may be deeply and justly discontented; they may be ready to strike and even to riot to improve their conditions, but they go at it in the frame of mind of free men. The more doctrinaire socialists often antagonize and lose their audiences by calling them "wage slaves."

The American Federation of Labor has won much more support than the Socialist Party. It has encouraged the men to demand and defend their "rights" as citizens.

In Russia, Lenin found an appalling number of people—in the army, in the slums of the industrial cities, in the squalid villages of the peasants- who had all the misery and hopelessness of slaves. In every material way the gladiators of ancient Rome, who revolted under Spartacus, were better off than the recently freed serfs of Russia. And it was not only in a material sense that their position was better. The gladiator had to face hardships and brutality, but at least there was an element of adventure in his life—great risks, no doubt, but also great prizes. The misery of the Russians is monotonous.

Lenin succeeded in grasping power in his own country, because with this background of universal misery and hopeless slave mentality he was able to organize into a disciplined group "a militant minority," whose desperation had driven them to passionate revolt. He could count on the fact that the great "lethargic majority" would not raise a finger in defense of the existing order. They had no fondness nor loyalty for it.

The success of his project for a universal "Dictatorship of the Proletariat" will depend on the mass psychology of other countries. He expects to be greeted as a savior by all whom he considers slaves. As a matter of fact he will be listened to only by those who consider themselves "slaves."

The problem resolves itself into a study of the prevalence and intensity of social unrest. The laboring masses of the civilized world are stirring. They are armed—or at least well taught in the use of arms. They have a new consciousness of power. Every one who is desperate, who has lost faith in the justice of our institutions, who is hopeless, is a menace. But those who feel themselves free men and citizens will be a source of democratic stability. They will try to change and perfect our civilization, but they will not try to destroy it.

To make the world safe for democracy, it is not sufficient to defeat autocracy. It is quite as necessary to eradicate slavery.

Chapter XVII
The Pendulum of the Revolution

It is obviously absurd to attempt to appraise to-day the effects of this upheaval in Russia. The crash of things overthrown will echo and re-echo through decades to come. A hundred years have now passed since what—before this mammoth convulsion in Russia—we used to call "The Great Revolution." It is rare nowadays to find a historian who does not view the work of Mirabeau, Danton, and even Robespierre with favor. Mirabeau was a libertine, who in the end betrayed the cause. Danton feathered his own nest out of the funds of the Ministry of War. And the "incorruptible Robespierre" was as blood-stained as any Bolshevist Commissaire of whom hysterical descriptions now affright us.

It is as safe a bet as one can make that historians in the year 2020, having weighed the evidence pro and con, will look upon the Russian Revolution and find it good.

Already we can note how gusts of freedom have blown away the stench of much decaying tyranny. The light has shone into many dark places. It is fatuous to think the results will not be felt outside of Russia. More likely than not the student of 2020 will find our keenest interests of the day—the war just ended, the peace as yet unachieved—insignificant compared to the mighty freeing heave and forward leap of humanity of this Greater Revolution. But such perspective we cannot hope for now. We are condemned to the nearer-sighted vision.

And I imagine that our historians, who write now so complacently of the French turmoil of a century ago, would have been more ruffled if they had had to live in the midst of the Terror. Someone has said that it is easier to see the hand of Providence in history than in current senatorial debates.

But somethings we can already see dimly. There have been other autocrats in our modern world; however, none but the House of Romanov dared to flaunt the title. And the House of Romanov is fallen. The united armies of Europe were able to put the Bourbons back on the throne of France, but even with their bayonets they were not able to keep them there. A Romanov restoration has even less chance.

An achievement of equal or greater significance in the field of economics, and comparable to this great event in the realm of politics, has already come out of the Revolution. The destruction of the old system of land tenure in Russia is complete. No one knows yet in detail on what plan the soil will be redistributed. The word they decide to use instead of "own" does not matter very much. The land is going to the people who till it. We cannot tell yet how it will work out, what unexpected transformations it will bring about. But the land now is in the possession of the hundred odd million peasants. The old landlords have less chance of recruiting an army abroad to reconquer their estates than the Romanovs have for the reconquering of their throne.

Most interesting—and most idle of all—is to speculate on the transformation which will result in Russian industry. I imagine that of greater effect than any of Lenin's decrees will be the fact that anyone who does not like his job in the city can escape now to the "free land."

The French Revolution, as we view it now through the perspective of these hundred years, falls readily into *"Les Etats Generaux"* "The Constituent Assembly," "La Convention" "The Directorate, the Consulate, the Empire." In some, the forces of destruction seemed to predominate. The Empire is generally classed as "Reaction," but much of the results of the Revolution were codified and rendered permanent by Napoleon. It is hard for us to-day to strike a balance between these different phases of the French Revolution. How much harder it must have been for the student of that day! This should render us cautious in our estimates of this contemporaneous Revolution in Russia.

But with that lesson in mind, we can school ourselves to think of this Revolution as a whole, which surely will have many phases, many contradictions, a tangle of cross-purposes. We can see for instance a sudden development of feminism, a despicable Anti-Semitic movement, the passionate desire of the Georgians; and a half score other nations to achieve their independence. Such things seem aside from the main issues of the Revolution, but they all have their effect; they are all participated in passionately by men and women of every race and class and party.

The Revolution in the end will be judged as a whole and Bolshevism is only one incident in the development, one phase of the process. We cannot tell whether the future historian will compare Lenin to Robespierre, Hebert, or Napoleon. But no one of these three men made the French Revolution, none of them ruined it. It was infinitely greater than any of them. I cannot see any close analogies between present events in Russia and the records I have read of the French Revolution. I would not know with which hero of that time to compare Lenin.

But it seems to me that one cycle is complete; that from one point of view, i.e., political organization, the Great Pendulum has swung from the tyranny of the Tsar through democracy—a point where the overwhelming majority supported the government and where those who governed sought to rule by democratic methods—to a new, but in many ways familiar, tyranny. More nearly I think than Napoleon ever came to copying the forms of the old monarchy, Lenin has revived the methods of the Tsar.

For three hundred years, the Romanovs had ruled in Russia. At no time was there any broad support for them among the masses. It is within the memory of those still living that the bulk of the population was relieved from personal slavery. The opposition to the regime has been growing constantly among the more fortunate classes.

Within recent years the discontent of the masses has developed visibly. The Tsar ruled, and proclaimed his right to rule, against the will of the majority of his subjects. He would have fallen long ago if his opponents could have united. But with a carefully recruited minority—his bureaucracy—he was able to defy the disorganized majority.

The regime fell abruptly in the spring of 1917, fell so easily that it was hard to understand how it had sustained itself so long in the face of such general detestation. There was then a period when the government—especially under the leadership of Kerensky—sought the democratic support of the people. An active effort was made to organize, even in the midst of the war, the free election of a Constitutional Assembly. This experiment in popular rule failed to be popular. Month by month, almost day by day, sections of the majority deserted. It could not carry the weight of the war, and at the same time organize the New Regime.

When it was tottering under the strain, it was attacked by "the active, militant minority" organized and led by Lenin. All the familiar old methods of the Tsarist regime were brought to life again. Once more there was a suppression of free press, the abolition of all liberties, arbitrary arrests, court-martial under the name of Revolutionary Tribunals—Terror. The pendulum had swung back.

But this is only from the purely political point of view. The economic revolution in regard to land still progresses. What is happening in industry is still uncertain. But even in the narrow field of political organization what a tremendous number of outgrown, lifeless things have been knocked down by the swing of the pendulum! It will swing again. How long Lenin and his minority can hold power is a matter to guess about. The Tsars with a smaller minority held their thrones for more than three hundred years. But the methods of Tsarism by which Lenin rules are outworn.

The Revolution in Russia has not completed its course—perhaps it is barely started. It has already laid the hoary ghost of hereditary absolutism. It has freed the land. Leninism is only one episode in the momentous process.

Book II
Siberia

Chapter XVIII
The Siberian Railroads

The whole life of Siberia is centered about the transportation system. The sparse population is grouped about the railway stations and river landings. A chart showing the density of population would coincide very closely with a map of trade routes.

One is continually reminded of our West. Not so very long ago Siberia was a vast waste, thinly peopled by roving tribes of nomads. I have met an old bureaucrat, whose first job in "the service" had been to carry dispatches back and forth between Vladivostok and St. Petersburg. The trip by "post horse" had taken five months, and the stories this old gentleman loved best to tell were like those of our pioneer grandfathers. A new life, a revolutionary change, came to Siberia with the railways. Perhaps some day, some Homer of Siberia will write an epic of the Iron Road and call it "The Life Bringer." I have even seen one fantastic poem which recalls the old Hebraic story of how the Great God took up a lump of clay, gave it breath and it became a man, and then the verses go on—their author evidently hoping for favor at court—to tell how the Great Tsar held Siberia in his hand, gave it a railroad, and it became a nation.

We take our railroads for granted and hardly notice them. In Siberia, so vast and undeveloped, its population snuggling so close to the Life-Giver, the importance of the railroads is always manifest. If they function smoothly, the people are prosperous. If they stop, misery comes immediately. Their political significance is as great and as obvious as their economic importance. Every fight between parties and factions centers on the railroads. They are the "objective" of every military campaign. Whoever controls them, governs Siberia. There are three main divisions in the railroad system:

I. The Trans-Siberian crosses the southern Urals from European Russia at Tchelyabinsk, passes through Omsk, Novo-Nikolaiev, Karasnoyarsk, Irkutsk, skirts Lake Baikal, and terminates at Chita. From that city two branches continue to the sea at Vladivostok.

II. A short branch line from Chita strikes the Chinese frontier at Manchuria Station and connects with the Chinese Eastern Railroad, which traverses northern Manchuria through Kharbin, and strikes the Russian frontier again at Podgranitza, a few hours from Vladivostok. This is the short route followed by the expresses.

III. Another circuitous branch makes a great loop from Chita along the Siberia side of the River Amur, through Blagovojensk to Khabarovsk, and then due south to Vladivostok. This is really a strategic or military railroad. It is much longer than the direct Chinese Eastern, but it is all the way in Russian territory.

The first two of these three systems—the main Trans-Siberian and the Amur loop line—were built and owned by the Russian Government. The Chinese Eastern Railroad was constructed by private enterprise. It is a striking example of international capital invested in a backward country, complicated by political and diplomatic motives. It is owned by the Russo-Asiatic Bank, which in its turn is owned by French investors. By diplomatic negotiations the Russian Government secured the concession from China. By the treaty a zone across Manchuria is leased to Russia. The situation is similar to our position in Panama. The technical sovereignty of the territory remains with China, but within the zone Russia exercises all the functions she would have by right—if she were sovereign.

For many years the Russian governor of the zone and the general manager of the railroad have been the same person—General Horvath. His powers have been practically unlimited. As long as he pleased the French investors by satisfactory dividends he was in every thing but name independent of the Tsar. Within the zone, he was an autocrat. He appointed his own judges, he commanded the Russian troops stationed there, and he had a private army, recruited from Chinese mercenaries, under the name of police. He was supreme—responsible only to the French directors of the Russo-Asiatic Bank. The Russian Government was too dependent on French capital to interfere with the exploitation of their railroad in Manchuria.

This railroad concession—of tremendous potential value—was a bone of contention between the nations. China, having let someone else bear the expense of building it, wanted the railroad. Japan looked at it hungrily. Her victorious wars against China and Russia had given her control of Korea, Port Arthur, and the "South Manchurian Railway," which connects up with the Chinese Eastern at Chan Chung. Many Japanese jingoes held that they needed this railroad to round out their "manifest destiny." France wanted to keep tight hold of the concession for the benefit of the investors.

It was the hope of reducing the intrigues which centered about the Chinese Eastern Railroad, which some years ago led our State Department to propose the "neutralization" of the Manchurian railroads. It would be hard to think up a suggestion which would rouse more opposition, rally more enemies, than this one. Those who at present own the concession and those who hope to oust them are equally opposed to "neutralization." Russia, China, and Japan regard the Chinese Eastern Railroad as a political pawn. To the French investors it is a financial speculation. Our State Department seems to have assumed that what everybody wanted was a railroad which gave equal opportunities to all and favoritism to none. But this was what nobody wanted.

None of our great transcontinental railroads could have been built if the business ethics of that day had been the same as we are accustomed to now. The Chinese Eastern was built at great expense, and the receipts from freight and passenger traffic have not begun to meet the interest charges on the capital. And such receipts—what we who are used to highly developed transportation systems would call "legitimate income"—will not make it a profitable investment until the country served is highly developed and densely populated. Its main receipts at present—what makes it a valuable concession—come from the monopolistic power it enjoys. By perfect freedom in the matter of discriminative and extortionate rates, it can hold up and milk every industry—mines, lumber, agriculture—along its route. It is these subsidiary—and from the view point of a settled community, illicit—profits which make the concession valuable.

There are only two ways to finance railroad building in undeveloped countries. One is construction by the State. Then during the period while, as a result of improved communications, the territory is being settled and developed the deficit between the great initial outlay and the slowly increasing earnings can be covered by taxation. The main line of the Trans-Siberian was built on this plan. The alternative is to offer private investors large enough profits to induce them to undertake the enterprise. The railroad will not earn such profits for many years. They must be arranged for by subsidiary developments. The Chinese Government was not rich enough to build this railroad on its own account. It wanted it built. It had to offer terms sufficiently generous to attract French capital. Very similar circumstances brought similar results in the case of the German financed Baghdad railroad through Turkish territory.

If you make the false assumption that the conditions in Manchuria are the same as in Massachusetts, Ohio, or Oregon, the terms of the concession are excessive. The franchises on which our early Western railroads were built seem unduly generous to us now. But they would not have been built at that time without the "land grants." When, as undoubtedly will happen, Manchuria has become highly developed, the concession will have become unjustifiably oppressive. But the French investors who risked their savings in the enterprise have not by any means received an excessive return on their capital as yet.

"Neutralization," i.e., the opening of the railroad on a basis of equal opportunity to all, the breaking of the monopolistic power to discriminate, would not only checkmate the political aspirations of the Far Eastern Powers, it would ruin the railroad financially. Its "legitimate earnings" do not as yet support it.

Just as the international politics of the Balkan Peninsula are very largely affected by the intrigues of non-Balkan Powers to control the Dardanelles, so all the politics of Siberia are influenced by the diplomacy "*des chemins de fer.*" The Chinese Eastern Railroad is the principal apple of discord.

Chapter XIX
The Czecho-Slovaks and the Allies

When I reached Siberia in September 1918, the military situation, which had been very confused, was beginning to clear up. The Czecho-Slovaks controlled the Trans-Siberian line from the Urals to near Irkutsk. They also held the port of Vladivostok. The Chinese Eastern was in the control of Horvath. And the eastern lip of the Trans-Siberian, about Chita was dominated by the anti-Bolshevist forces of the Cossack chieftain Semyonov.

The Soviet Army held the section of the Trans-Siberian from Irkutsk around Lake Baikal and nearly to Chita. Also large concentrations of Red Guards and liberated German and Austrian war prisoners were reported on the Amur River loop line.

On August 3, our State Department, followed immediately by the Japanese Foreign Office, issued a statement clearly limiting the function of our troops to two objectives: one, the guarding of the munition dumps and stopping their shipment to the Germans; and two, the protecting of the rear of the Czecho-Slovaks from attacks by the Bolsheviks and the liberated enemy war prisoners. The Japanese had landed large forces in Vladivostok and were sending a second expedition by train through Korea and Manchuria toward "the front" in the Lake Baikal district. American forces were just beginning to land in Vladivostok.

By the time I reached Siberia, the Japanese had already won their one victory and the legend about the menace of the German and Austrian war prisoners was exploded. The Bolsheviks had done their best to organize these prisoners into a formidable force. The poor devils, after long months in miserable prison camps, had been suddenly liberated and given their choice between vagrancy, which meant starvation, or warm clothes and good food in the Red Army. Of course they enlisted, and undoubtedly the Bolsheviks—as well as the allied diplomats—thought they would fight.

A few score miles north of Vladivostok, on the Amur loop line, the Japanese, with a few Czechs, encountered a formidably entrenched position and discovered that they were seriously outnumbered. They decided to wait till the American forces could come from Vladivostok. The Bolsheviks attacked before reinforcements could arrive. The Japanese, on the defensive, opened a heavy fire with their field artillery—which practically ended the war in the Extreme East. Since that salvo of artillery fire, the Japanese cavalry has been killing its horses in a vain effort to catch up with the enemy.

Khabarovsk and Blagovojensk, which had been reported to be heavily fortified Bolshevist strongholds, fell without a struggle. The Japanese captured large quantities of war material. Great numbers of the German and Austrian prisoners gave themselves up voluntarily and the entire Amur loop line came under allied control.

Western Siberia was in the hands of the Czechs. The allies held all the Extreme East. The central section about Irkutsk was still under Bolshevist control. It was necessary to drive them away from the railroad in order to open communications for the Czechs. The burden of this campaign was expected to fall on the Japanese. While they were concentrating an overwhelming force and large supplies, a small expedition of Czecho-Slovaks, under the dashing leadership of General Gaida, captured Irkutsk and the Lake Baikal section of the railroad. General Gaida's movement had been so rapid that the Bolsheviks had not even stopped long enough to touch the electric buttons and explode the carefully laid mines in the dozen odd tunnels of this section. They destroyed only one important bridge. The entire transportation system of Siberia was in allied control.

The Bolshevist military structure in Siberia had proven a house of cards. There were probably not more than 40,000 Czecho-Slovaks in the campaign. While they were still trying to leave Russia peaceably and, to prove their good faith, had given up their arms, till they had only one rifle to ten men, they were attacked by the Bolsheviks. Before they could begin to fight back, they had to wrest rifles and ammunition from their opponents. In spite of this handicap they had captured a territory as large as the United States.

There was at once a difference of opinion among the Allies as to the uses to be made of this easy victory.

The joint action between the Japanese and Americans worked pretty well. There was a tendency among the Japanese officers to argue that they had been sent there to fight the Bolsheviks and that if none of them appeared we ought to go out and hunt for them. General Graves, keeping to the spirit as well as the letter of his instructions, would not order any action against the Bolsheviks unless they threatened the ammunition dumps or attacked our allies.

But this was a minor divergence compared to that which developed between the American-Japanese combine and our other allies. They all, especially the French, were set on the idea of "re-establishing the Eastern Front," and they were able to persuade the Czechs to alter their plan of withdrawing from Russia.

President Wilson and his military advisers, in complete accord with the Japanese, had definitely decided against any large expedition to Russia. Our troops had been sent principally to assist the Czecho-Slovaks and other allied forces in withdrawing from Russia.

The Czecho-Slovaks themselves were uncertain. They were used to easy victory over the Bolshevist "Red Army" and believed that it was entirely practical to fight their way across European Russia till they met the Germans on their own frontiers.

THE CZECHO-SLOVAKS AND THE ALLIES   107

Many of them, including their most popular leader, General Gaida, were anxious to try it. They thought they would need very little help from the Allies and that mostly material. Also they were not at all averse to fighting the Bolsheviks. They were very thoroughly convinced that Lenin was actively supported by, and allied with, the Central Empires. Most of the prisoners they had captured in their Siberian campaign were Germans or Magyars. Until they got news that the Armistice was signed and the independence of their homeland recognized, their morale was admirable. And they were encouraged by irresponsible representatives of some of our allies to believe that Mr. Wilson had not meant what he said in the "Statement of August 3." They were encouraged to expect a serious allied attempt to "re-establish the Eastern Front." They were encouraged to stay, in the hope of fighting their way home across Russia.

The situation of the Czecho-Slovaks was tragic—and amusing. They were, with the exception of the American and Japanese troops in the Extreme East, the only effective force in Siberia. In their effort to fight their way out, they had captured this immense territory. It was rather difficult for them not to annex it. But they had no such wild ambition; all they wanted was to find someone to whom they could turn over this "white elephant."

This desire of theirs to get rid as soon as possible of the responsibility of running Siberia was the explanation of the half dozen diverse political regimes which sprang up after the Bolsheviks lost control. The prime necessity of the Czechs was to assure the regular operation of the railroad. But their small forces were strung out along the Volga from Kazan to Samara. They were spread out so thinly that they could not spare sufficient troops to govern all the large cities along the railroad—even if they had wanted to. And they did not want to mix up in Siberian politics. They adopted the only possible policy. Everywhere, as soon as they overthrew the Bolsheviks, they encouraged the organization of local governments. Themselves passionately democratic, in spite of their efforts toward neutrality, their influence was toward liberal institutions. But wherever they found reactionary elements in control—as, for instance, in Chita and Kharbin—they made terms with them, in exchange for guarantees of free use of the railroad. Even if they had thought it wise to attempt it, they did not have the forces to impose the form of government they liked. Their supreme need was to assure their communications by uninterrupted operation of the railroad.

Throughout Western and Central Siberia, as far east as Lake Baikal, Liberalism predominated. Town and rural councils were elected on the universal suffrage law issued by the Provisional Government of Kerensky. But the Czechs found the district of the Za-Baikal Cossacks—from the lake to Chita—in the hands of an adventurer named Semyonov. His regime could not be described as either reactionary or liberal. It was pure and simple banditism. Just as the robber barons of the Rhine used to fill their coffers by holding up river borne commerce, so Semyonov draws his income from holding up trains on the Trans-Siberian Railroad.

The Czechs found the zone of the Chinese Eastern Railroad in the control of General Horvath and they came to terms with him without any attempts to overthrow his reactionary government.

In Vladivostok, when they drove out the Bolsheviks, the remaining members of the former town council, which had been elected on the Kerensky law, assumed control, and they did not, as they should have done, at once call a new election. They preferred to hold the power themselves and the Czechs did not interfere with them.

So the Czecho-Slovaks, having turned over one section of the railroad after another to local Russian governing units, some reactionary, some piratical, some liberal, could withdraw from politics and, their communications assured, concentrate on their military campaign.

Their military situation was critical. They had held on to their extended line along the Volga in the expectation that there would be a concerted attempt by the Allies to "re-establish the Eastern Front." Their small forces could hold the scattered river towns only because of the very low fighting quality of the Red Army. But if they did not advance during the summer months all the way to Moscow, when winter stopped river navigation they would find it impossible to keep up communication and furnish supplies to their outposts. And they could not risk an advance unless assured of active support from us. General Gaida came back from the front to beg for speedy assistance. Those were days of gloom in Czech headquarters. Neither the Japanese nor the American authorities believed in any attempt to re-establish the Russian front. We could not give the aid which certain irresponsible agents of our allies had promised on our behalf.

We said to them in effect: "We came here to help you get out of Russia. The railroad is open. We cannot give you further military assistance. If you cannot advance and cannot hold your present line, the only thing to do is to retire."

They replied: "We cannot retire without delivering over to the Red Terror all these Volga cities. In all these territories we now hold, the population has organized local governments, municipal and rural. Under our protection they have come out openly against the Bolsheviks. If we retire all these people who have trusted us will be persecuted by the Reds. We know, because we have had to evacuate a few towns. We know what happened. We can't desert our friends to such a fate. "And we only need such a little help..." How they begged!

But in the end, they retired east of the Ural Mountains into Siberia. And Trotsky was able to announce a great victory. The way in which the population of this abandoned territory is welcoming the armies of Kolchak seems to indicate that the forecast of the Czechs as to what would happen when the triumphant Red Army advanced was well founded.

In the summer of 1918, in European Russia, I had found almost every party, except the Bolsheviks, passing formal resolutions requesting the Allies to send troops to aid them in the struggle against the German-aided Bolsheviks. But when the allied governments began to send troops to Siberia, almost all these varied sections of public opinion became embittered to find that "Armed Intervention" did not mean an unquestioning support of their party in its struggle for power.

This was illustrated first of all in the case of General Horvath. Kharbin, the principal city in the zone of the Chinese Eastern Railroad, was his capital. He had long ruled absolutely in this zone, with the aid of his Chinese mercenary troops, in the joint capacity of governor of the Tsar and general manager of the railroad. He was considerably more efficient than the general run of bureaucrats, but in other respects a typical supporter of the Old Regime. He was the hope of the extreme reaction. Kharbin had come to resemble what the Rhine cities must have been in the days of the French Revolution. It was crowded with "Emigres." All the old nobility, bitter enemies of the Revolution, who had been able to scrape together enough cash had fled the country. Scandinavia, as well as the European quarters of Chinese and Japanese cities was crowded with them. Kharbin, so near to the frontier, was an ideal spot for conspiracy. Horvath's little army had grown considerably through the accession of former officers of the Tsar's army, who had fled from the indignation of their soldiers. Kharbin was unanimous for "Armed Intervention" and hoped we would bring enough scaffolds to hang all the workingmen in Russia.

As soon as the news reached Kharbin that allied troops were landing in Vladivostok, that the Czechs had chased out the Bolsheviks, General Horvath announced himself supreme ruler of the Far East and started with some of his motley army to crown himself in the Cathedral at Vladivostok.

But the Allies refused to recognize his right to elect himself to this office. The remnants of the old town council, elected by universal suffrage in the Kerensky days, had taken charge of the city administration. The Allies, siding with the local government, rounded up and disarmed Horvath's "Army." The Reaction, which centered in Kharbin, was disillusioned about "Allied Intervention" and heartily sick of it.

The Bolsheviks of the Far East were equally disillusioned. They had been preaching for months that the only motive of allied intervention was the restoration of the autocracy. If this had been true every democratic group in Siberia would have joined them against the foreign friends of the Tsar. And so the Bolsheviks were disappointed—and very peevish—to find the troops of "Foreign Imperialists" acting, contrary to their prophecy, on the side of liberalism and democracy. For a while we were immensely popular with the Liberal groups. They thought that our defense of "local self-government" as against Horvath's personal ambitions, meant that we were always going to do exactly what they wanted. But they were soon disillusioned in their turn. They were not really very much interested in the war against Germany, but they did want us to help them re-conquer European Russia and drive out the Bolsheviks. When they found that we had no such intentions they also grew unfriendly.

Those who try to be neutral, whether in international or civil war, are sure to be unpopular among the belligerents. In general the desire of the Czechs and other allied troops to avoid mixing up in the local politics of Siberia worked out as a defense of the status quo. None of the allied commanders wanted rioting or insurrection in the vicinity of his troops. The people who started trouble were in the wrong. Sometimes this worked out fairly well, sometimes quite badly. But of course it was unpopular with those who were opposed to the status quo.

Chapter XX
The First Siberian Government

Of all the various local governments which had sprung up in the wake of the Czecho-Slovaks, the one at Omsk steadily demonstrated its superior political sagacity. The leading figure there was Vologodsky, whom his friends call "the Grand Old Man of Siberia." He is a staunch Liberal, not a party man, but enjoying the confidence of both the Socialists and the Constitutional Democrats.

He had been elected to the Constitutional Assembly from Siberia, and as soon as the Bolsheviks had lost power, he took the initiative in organizing a government at Omsk. He gathered around him a non-partisan group of well-known Siberians and gradually, patiently, skillfully they built up a governmental organization which continually won the adhesion of new sections. One local government unit after another gave its allegiance to the Omsk group. They called themselves "The Siberian Government," but it was not a "separatist movement." They hoped to be incorporated again in the Russian Republic as soon as the Germans had been driven out and an orderly regime had been established west of the Urals.

Certainly this Siberian Government could not have made its start except for the military victory of the Czecho-Slovaki forces over the Bolsheviks, but once they had the chance to organize they gradually won the recognition of the rest of Siberia. The local government of Irkutsk coalesced with them. Vladivostok and the maritime province followed suit. They won the nominal allegiance of all Siberia. Their decrees were recognized as binding, their orders were obeyed except in the domain of Semyonov and Horvath's zone across Manchuria. These two supreme rulers disliked the liberalism of the Omsk Government, they very much enjoyed their own independence and were much too strong to be coerced. They had to be placated. The adhesion they gave to the Central Government was mere lip service.

The Omsk Government had only been able to achieve this unification by a strictly non-partisan attitude and by the exercise of remarkable political tact. They had at first no force and no money, but the desire of Siberia for unity was great and local and sectional rivalries were gradually overcome. The main departments of government had been organized, and by the middle of September 1918, they had reached sufficient self-confidence to begin the collection of taxes and to call for mobilization of the younger men, who had not yet served in the army. They were able to raise and equip in the neighborhood of 100,000 men. Altogether the success of the

Siberian Government was the most hopeful effort at constructive politics which has been developed since the Revolution.

It was perhaps fortunate that the Siberian Government had at first no force at its disposal, and was therefore compelled to rely on the more democratic methods of persuasion. It is of course possible that, if they had consolidated their power, they might in time have become tyrannical, but there was no evidence of such development. Their main strength was their non-partisanship. While in general the political parties in Russia have been disruptive forces, refusing all compromise with those who advocate slightly different programs, and continually breaking up among themselves into smaller factions, the Siberian Government was marked by a real spirit of coalition. They were uniting the whole country on a program of local self-government and general liberalism, and successfully postponing all questions which were likely to relight the fires of partisanship until the Constitutional Assembly could be convened.

Their great weakness was their lack of funds, and the allied governments refused to recognize a separate government in Russia. There is little doubt in my mind that, if the Siberian Government had been recognized and granted loans, it would have lasted. A difference of opinion is possible as to whether or not "recognition" would have been a wise step, but I wish to emphasize the difficulties which any government must face at present in Russia without help from other nations. It cannot have sufficient funds to re-establish the country or even to pay the salaries of its employees. Commerce is so disorganized that the government can hope for very little from custom receipts. It will take any government several years of effective development before it can hope for any normal receipts from taxation. A "good" government has to face this problem just as much as a "bad" government. In fact the more reluctant it is to resort to tyrannical methods the worse off it is. Semyonov, for instance, finances himself by levying toll on the railroad. He has not stopped at train robbery; in one case, at least, he has looted a bank in Chita. The Siberian Government was strangled for lack of funds. It was too honest to steal. Any future government will find it very difficult to consolidate itself unless it is recognized and granted liberal loans.

The relations of this first Siberian Government to the Bolsheviks deserve a separate paragraph. It was carrying on an active war with the Soviet Government at Moscow. And it was prepared to defend itself against any organized Bolshevist revolt in Siberia. But it believed, and on the whole demonstrated, that the best way to circumvent the plans of Lenin was to offer the people a popular democratic government. The great mass of the people in Siberia—as in European Russia—will go to the other extreme rather than consent to a return to the old regime of the Tsar.

There are scattered throughout Siberia a number of convinced fanatic Bolsheviks who would prefer a dictatorship of the proletariat to democratic institutions. There are also a number of hidebound reactionaries who would prefer a return to the dictatorship of their small class to any form of majority rule. In an electoral contest between these two extremes, an overwhelming victory will be won by the Bolsheviks.

Vologodsky's policy was based on the conviction that there was a middle course of democratic liberalism between these two extremes and that the great majority would rally to such a program. In general, he was proved right by the event. In every case where the Bolsheviks were able to convince the electorate that it was a choice between them and the Old Regime, they won. But in every election where it appeared to be a choice between democracy and the reactionary or Bolshevist extreme, the liberal, democratic candidate won.

The reactionary politician will tell you that Siberia is honeycombed with Bolshevism. Wherever he has stood for election, he has driven the bulk of the voters into the Bolshevist camp. He will argue against the election of a Constitutional Assembly, because he knows his class will be outvoted. And, of course, in this matter he is in complete accord with the true Bolsheviks. Neither the old aristocracy nor the proletariat are sufficiently numerous to win in a general election.

The problem of the Liberals the world around is to smooth out the middle of the road so that no one is forced to choose between one gutter or the other. In Siberia, the liberal democrats of the first Omsk Government proved that, wherever they had had the chance to organize local self-government and give the people an object lesson in free institutions, they had no reason to fear the verdict of universal suffrage. They could count on a majority.

Whenever Vologodsky and his friends found the Bolsheviks in arms, they fought them with arms. But in Siberia they fought them with arguments, and in such cities as Irkutsk, where they had been able to organize a popular government, they succeeded in winning to their side large numbers who had formerly supported the Bolsheviks.

However, this first Siberian Government hardly lasted beyond the embryonic stage. It was never able to exercise full authority in the district of the Za-Baikal Cossacks, nor in the zone of the Chinese Eastern Railroad and Semyonov's unspeakable tyrannies and the reactionary intrigues of Horvath constantly poured oil on the smoldering ashes of Bolshevism.

Chapter XXI
The Socialist Revolutionaries and the Directorate

A new element in the political situation was introduced by the appearance of what came to be called "The Samara Group." More than two-thirds of the delegates elected to the Constitutional Assembly—the elections took place at the same time as the Bolshevist insurrection which overthrew Kerensky—belonged to the Socialist Revolutionary Party. After the assembly was summarily dispersed by Lenin, these delegates continually attempted to preserve their organization. There was, for instance, a secret convention held by them in Tambov a few months after the dissolution, where they organized, expelled from their ranks a few members who were suspected of sympathy with the Bolsheviks and, among other things, issued a manifesto requesting the allied governments to send troops to Russia. They were all fugitives from Bolshevist "justice," and in disguise and under false names, just as they had fought the Tsar, and outwitted his police in the old days, they scattered over the country agitating among the peasants against the Lenin dictatorship. When the Czecho-Slovaks captured Samara a large number of these Socialist Revolutionists, members of the Constitutional Assembly, gathered there and organized a small government of their own, which they claimed represented the majority of the Constitutional Assembly and was the legal inheritor of that institution—the last which had been chosen by the free universal suffrage of the Russian people. They issued an appeal to all the anti-Bolshevist factions in Russia to attend a conference in the city of Ufa to discuss the formation of an All-Russian Government.

Delegates came to Ufa from a number of the local governments which had sprung up on the outskirts of European Russia under the protection of anti-Bolshevist forces. Rather to my surprise the Siberian Government also sent a delegation. I did not think that they would consent to subordinate themselves and the government which they had actually organized, and which was growing stronger every day, to this vague idea of an All-Russian Government. I could not see that the Samara Group had anything to offer except the phrase "All Russia" and a very sketchy legal claim to power based on their election to the Constitutional Assembly. As a matter of fact months had passed since their election and few if any of them dared to revisit openly the constituency which had chosen them. But an element, the force of which I had not realized, dominated the Ufa conference. The Siberian Government had been definitely informed that the Allies would not recognize any separatist government, but that they would be friendily disposed toward an "All-Russian" Government. The end of the war was in sight and all efforts were turned toward the Peace Conference. Allied diplomacy needed an individual delegation representing Russia. The palace of Versailles is large, but not large enough to have accommodated diplomatic missions from all those who claimed to be supreme rulers of Russia. The Siberian Government was at the end of its resources financially. And to an extent hard for the foreigner to realize, the Russians have an immense *amour propre* in this matter. They wanted a representation at the Peace Conference, and so all factions were willing to surrender immediate advantages in order to have a single power which would be recognized by the Allies. The Ufa conference turned into a feast of unity. The Siberian Government practically abdicated. An "All-Russian Directorate" was formed, consisting of three members of the Samara Group, Vologodsky, and one other member of the Siberian Government. The directorate at once went to Omsk, and took over all the existing machinery, which had been so patiently built up by the Siberians.

The basis of the compromise was fundamentally unsound. The Samara Group brought little or nothing to the combination and received a three to two majority in the new government. All the resources at its disposal were the work of the Siberians. This was bad enough, but much worse was the fact that the Samara Group was dominated by party considerations and at once departed from the non-partisan idea on which the success of the Siberian Government had been built. It was at once evident that the Socialist Revolutionary Party believed that the spoils belonged to the victor. Efficient administrators who had built up the various departments for the Siberian Government were discharged and replaced by people whose only qualification was that they were loyal members of the Socialist Revolutionary Party. Within the directorate itself, party lines were drawn sharply. The three Socialist Revolutionary members began to meet privately as a party caucus to decide on decrees without consulting their Siberian colleagues. The "All-Russian" phase of their government was only a pious wish. The only actual sovereignty they exercised was in Siberia, through the instrumentality of the organization created by Vologodsky and his friends. But they constantly ignored the wishes of the Siberians, and issued decrees which had been accepted in private by their majority of three.

Perhaps the worst count against the Socialist Revolutionary members of the directorate is that they at once opened war on the local governing bodies—town councils and rural Zemstvos. They had their eyes set on the new Constitutional Assembly and were "preparing the elections." Many of the rival parties were represented in the Zemstvos and town councils and the Socialist Revolutionists were bent on controlling all the machinery of elections.

There was a further cause of discontent in the fact that the Socialist Revolutionary Party was committed to the abolition of the old system of landed estates and the division of the soil among the peasantry. Many of the officers whom the Siberian

Government had drawn into their organization to drill their new army came from the landlord class, and were bitterly opposed to the Socialist Revolutionary program.

There were also two dissentient factions of the Socialist Revolutionary Party. One was under the leadership of Marie Spirodonova, and for a short time had frankly sided with the Bolsheviks; and the other, under the discredited leader, Tchernov, was supposed to be flirting with the enemy. The dismissal of certain army officers, supposed to be "unsound politically," by the directorate disorganized the army in the midst of a campaign and added to the discontent of the officer class. In short, the directorate, by its extreme partisanship, had discontented all sections of Siberian society, except the members of the Socialist Revolutionary Party. It had thrown confusion into the ranks of the liberals, who were trying to build up local self-government, by relighting the fires of party disputes. It had stirred into a blaze the smouldering conflict between liberalism and reaction. Having divided the forces of democracy, it was stupidly inexpedient to force a fight with the aristocrats.

Chapter XXII
The Cossack Conspiracy

This growing distrust of the directorate came to a head in what was popularly called "The Cossack Conspiracy." The Cossack troops are not commanded by Cossacks, but they are "Crack Regiments" and their officers in general have been men of great wealth and of great pull. Semyonov, the ataman of the Za-Baikal Cossacks, was the only real Cossack in this group. He was very bitter against the efforts of the directorate to reduce him to order. The discontented found a refuge in his headquarters. And finally a group of officers obtained control of a regiment in Omsk and arrested the three Socialist Revolutionary members of the directorate and held them prisoners for some days.

The two remaining members of the directorate, Vologodsky and his Siberian colleague, called a meeting of the Council of Ministers. They declared 'the country in danger" and decided that, under the circumstances, a dictatorship was necessary. Admiral Kolchak, the Minister of Marine (which did not exist), was the only military man among them.

There is an absolute contradiction in opinion in Siberia as to Kolchak's responsibilities in this matter. The adherents of the deposed "directors" affirm that Kolchak was the head of the whole Cossack Conspiracy, that he had been nursing his ambitions for months and made his strike at the first opportunity.

On the other hand the adherents of Vologodsky maintain that Kolchak knew nothing of the Cossack Conspiracy; that when it broke out the two other members of the directorate and the Council of Ministers were completely surprised and very much dismayed; that there was the gravest danger that the "Cossacks" intended to make Semyonov or some other extreme reactionary dictator, in which case a new outbreak of civil war in Siberia would have been inevitable; that they felt the only possible hope was to put into power someone who had been identified with the first Siberian Government and could hope for the support of all those who had been loyal to it and had very recently become dissatisfied with the directorate; and that Kolchak had only accepted the position with great reluctance and after a vehement pressure on the part of Vologodsky and his Liberal friends.

Practically the first act of Admiral Kolchak was to arrest the Cossack officers implicated in the conspiracy. They gave themselves up willingly and demanded an immediate public trial. They admitted all their acts and made their defense on the ground of patriotic motive. The trial caused a great deal of interest and excitement. It was a foregone conclusion that if the new dictator punished them, he would lose the support of a large section of the army officers and that if he released them he would with equal certainty lose the support of the Socialist Revolutionaries.

At the trial the accused officers were able to introduce a great deal of evidence which, while it did not mitigate against the charge of armed conspiracy against the government which they had sworn to support, thoroughly discredited the three deposed directors in the minds of a very large section of the community. The charges made by the officers that these men were personally dishonest or that they were in negotiation with the Bolsheviks were not in any way substantiated. But their accusation that the Socialist Revolutionary directors had been inspired by a disastrous partisanship was fully proven. It was not so much a "trial" as a "political debate." It was hard to tell whether the officers were on trial for their lives or the arrested directors were being impeached.

The trial resulted in an all-round Scotch verdict: the offending officers were acquitted and the three Socialist Revolutionary directors were exiled.

I was not present at these proceedings at Omsk. But I was able to watch the effects on public opinion at the very opposite end of Siberia, in our office at Vladivostok. The first telegraphic news was very meager, simply that the Socialist Revolutionary directors were under arrest. Then came Kolchak's manifesto as dictator, and the announcement that the conspirators were on trial. All the Russian employees in the office at once took sides. Everyone except the Chinese boy, who scrubbed the floor, stopped work to discuss the news. The partisans of a "strong government" were jubilant, the "good old days" were coming back. They said it was an outrage to court-martial these brave officers who had saved the country from traitors. The three Socialist Revolutionaries on our staff took up cudgels for the deposed "directors," and were quite certain that the monarchy would be proclaimed in a few days. The liberals were depressed and uncertain. Even after they heard that Vologodsky was premier, they did not know whether he approved of the new order or had accepted office under duress. The truth of the matter was that at Vladivostok we did not have any facts on which to base a judgment.

The stream of visitors to our office—newspaper editors, merchants, school-teachers, officers—judged the matter entirely on the basis of their past allegiances. At that time I was in daily conference with members of the town council and provincial Zemstvo. They had been very bitter against the directorate because of its interference with "local government," but they were just as bitterly opposed to reaction. On the whole it was a gloomy time in Vladivostok. Relying on the "order" which was maintained by the allied troops, the counter-revolutionary forces had come out in the open. Their glee at the downfall of the directorate was oppressive. They expected great things from Kolchak.

The Zemstvo leaders were at first inclined to expect the worst. But they reserved judgment. It was some time before the "local governments" of the Extreme East gave their allegiance to the Kolchak regime.

Gradually more detailed news began to reach Vladivostok of the very tense situation which had preceded the coup d'etat. At last people began to arrive who had been in Omsk during the exciting week. The restoration of the Monarchy—feared by the Liberals, hoped for by the Reactionaries—did not come off. Gradually a feeling spread that there must be something to be said on both sides. And this movement of public opinion was rather helped by a statement issued by the exiled "directors" as soon as they had crossed the frontier into China. It was a verbose and very weak document, carefully avoiding any reference to the specific charges which had been brought against them. It excited very little sympathy for them.

The common fear of the first moment, which I shared with all my Liberal and Socialist friends, that Kolchak stood for rampant reaction gradually changed to uncertainty. Only one of the Socialist Revolutionaries in the office stuck grimly to his partisan guns. The others, while still loyal to the ideals of their party, admitted, somewhat reluctantly, that their three representatives in the directorate had by their narrow fanaticism brought Siberia to the verge of a new civil war and that the Kolchak expedient had at least postponed it.

It was perhaps the attitude of the extremely reactionary papers which did most to reconcile liberal opinion to the New Regime. At the first news of the Cossack coup d'etat they had been lyrical with joy. But their enthusiasm for Kolchak soon cooled. Their chagrin at the turn of events soon became apparent. Horvath and Semyonov—the recognized leaders of their party—were not, they said, being treated 'fairly."

The attitude of the Bolshevist leaders was similar. They were disappointed with the way things developed. Their one chance lay in dissensions among the "bourgeoisie." Nothing would have pleased them better than a war between the Socialist Revolutionaries and the friends of Vologodsky. Civic peace was the last thing they wanted. The gradual rallying of educated public opinion in Vladivostok to the support, or at least toleration, of the Kolchak dictatorship was remarkable, for there—as I will show later—we saw his regime at the worst.

Chapter XXIII
Kolchak

The personality of Admiral Kolchak is an enigma. The most diverse reports are given by people who know him intimately.

Before the war, he seems to have been an honest, hard-working sailor, the one Russian admiral who had the confidence of the British authorities. In general the Russian Navy was rotten with corruption and favoritism. In this foggy atmosphere, Kolchak seems to have stood out, clear cut, straightforward, efficient.

Just as the French were helping to reorganize the Russian army, after its defeat in Manchuria, the British were trying to rebuild the navy, which had been smashed by the Japanese. Kolchak was the man they liked to deal with.

It is perhaps of more importance to note that he had some degree of personal popularity among the sailors; at least he was not so hated as many of his colleagues. When the Black Sea Fleet, which he commanded, revolted, the sailors killed a great many of their officers, but they rowed Admiral Kolchak ashore in a small boat, uninjured.

He was himself a decided Anglophile and was supposed, although his position in the navy made it inexpedient for him to take any outspoken political position, to be in sympathy with the Constitutional Democratic Party of Professor Milyoukov; that is, to advocate a limited monarchy somewhat on the model of British institutions.

What he thinks to-day, or what are his ambitions, I find it impossible to determine. Some of his Liberal supporters, who are in constant contact with him, tell me that, as a result of the Revolution, he has moved toward the Left and is convinced that there is no chance of a monarchical restoration in Russia—no matter how 'limited"—and that he is now prepared to support loyally a democratic republic. On the other hand some of his reactionary friends have told me that he is pledged to them, as soon as his troops reach Moscow, to offer the throne to a grand duke.

At least he is a very astute politician. His supporters are about equally divided between the Right and the Left. As a rule his military forces are in control of the former, and the civil government throughout the vast territory of Siberia is in control of the latter. If he came out for an openly reactionary program, he would lose his liberal support. If he definitely committed himself to the Left, there would be danger of a new "Cossack Conspiracy." He has successfully performed the difficult feat of walking a tight rope. Up to the present he has kept the two very jealous factions from fighting. How long he can continue to avoid taking sides is, of course, uncertain.

All of his supporters are convinced that it is the supreme duty of the Siberian Government to push the war against the Bolsheviks in European Russia. This is just as true of the Socialists and Liberals as of the Reactionaries. This state of war is a regrettable influence, which handicapped the first Siberian Government and the directorate just as much as it does Kolchak. As long as he accepts this interpretation of his duty, he cannot afford to take any action likely to offend the corps of army officers, and many of them are reactionary. It is unfair to hold him personally to account for this situation, which was not of his creating and which weighed as heavily on his Liberal and Socialist predecessors as it does on him.

But after all, the personality of Admiral Kolchak does not matter much these days, when we no longer believe in "The Great Man Theory." The significant struggle is not between conflicting sides of his character, but between the political forces of progress and reaction.

The Liberals are weakened by factional fights and petty personal ambitions; but this is every bit as true of their opponents. And the Siberian Liberals are faced by a problem which has come very vividly in the last few years to all the Liberals of the world. How to concentrate on the conduct of a war and at the same time preserve civil liberties?

The development of democracy in Siberia is retarded by the war against the Bolsheviks, in the same way that Kerensky's attempt to democratize the old empire was smothered by the baneful influence of war with Germany.

Chapter XXIV
Civil War

If I were asked to state in what way American opinion in general differed most strikingly from my own impressions of Siberia, I would say without hesitation that it seemed to underestimate the bitterness of the civil war.

If a man from Mars had visited this country a year ago he would have found it difficult to understand why we were so wrought up against Germany. During 1914 and '15, most Americans were rather vexed at the European nations for hating each other so. And to-day few of the people I meet since my return from Siberia, few of the writers whose editorials I read, seem to realize that the bitterest of all kinds of war—civil war—is raging in Russia.

It is not like our war of the sixties. Siberia is not trying to secede from Russia, nor Russia from Siberia. Many Siberian Bolsheviks, who have managed to step across the line, are fighting in the ranks of Lenin's army, while a large proportion of Kolchak's supporters—in the civil government and military organization—are refugees from European Russia. The bitterness against the Bolsheviks in Siberia is perhaps exaggerated. Perhaps we and our allies hated the Germans to an unreasonable extent. But in one case, as in the other, there is no gain in denying or underestimating the bitterness of this hatred.

Siberian life, as I have said, is more than usually dependent on the railroad. For a few months the proletariat—the organized workers of the railroad and the few industrial cities—exercised a dictatorship. By a series of bitter strikes they paralyzed the country. They opened the gates of the war prisons and recruited their principal armed force from the Austrian and German prisoners. It was a force entirely adequate for the work of terrorizing an unarmed population. Bolshevism never became as centralized nor as well organized in Siberia as it did in European Russia. In some localities it was more moderate and sane; in others more ruthless and rabid. But it was Bolshevism which introduced war into Siberia. Before their advent, the people had tried to settle their differences by argument. The Bolsheviks drew the sword.

I happened to get a number of detailed reports about the "Siege" of Blagovojensk. Among them was one from an American YMCA worker. In this city, where there is only a small number of industrial workers, the population rallied to the defense of the town council which they had elected and resolved to resist the dictatorship of the proletariat. They easily drove off the first and second and third expedition the

Bolsheviks sent against them. But at last the Red Army brought up artillery and organized a regular investment. The only way to bring food into the city was by boat across the Amur River from Manchuria. However the river route was exposed to a cross-fire from the Bolshevist batteries, which were manned by well-trained German artillerists. The passage was impossible except on moonless, cloudy nights. At last the Bolsheviks brought up some "star shells" and made this doubly hazardous.

The defenders had no artillery except one battery they had captured in a sortie. But they had no ammunition for it. They could not reply to the regular shelling of the city. In spite of being immensely outnumbered they repelled every attack and held out several months.

It was famine which finally forced them to surrender. The Chinese merchants across the river would sell food only for gold and silver and jewels. It was not the danger of the river crossing under well-directed artillery fire which forced surrender but lack of currency. It was as gallant and high-hearted a defense as the history of siege warfare offers. The reign of terror which followed the entry of the Bolsheviks was as terrible.

Very similar resistance was put up in other parts of Siberia—it was only chance which gave me fuller reports of this case. The "Siberiaks" are a frontier people, much less inclined to docile submission than the people of the Motherland. Now people who lived through the siege of Blagovojensk and their like are not disposed to "treat" with the Bolsheviks. They refuse to consider them "honorable opponents." They insist that they are "traitors" who overthrew the Revolution with the aid of Germany, and who kept themselves in power by the help of German and Magyar war prisoners, and whose brief period of power was marked by fiendish barbarism.

Semyonov and other anti-Bolshevist leaders have committed unspeakable atrocities against the workers, indiscriminate vengeance which has fallen heavily on the innocent. There is no excuse for such horrors. But they are somewhat explained—although not mitigated—by the fact that the Bolsheviks set the example in ruthlessness. If it is true, as all Liberals claim, that stupid repression incites violent revolt, it is equally true that stupid "Terror" from below incites violent reaction from above. The Bolsheviks can not claim to have used gentler methods of warfare.

The presence of many refugees from European Russia is also an important element in the Siberian situation. The old aristocracy are mostly in the extreme east, where they have joined up with Horvath and Semyonov. The cities of Central and Western Siberia are crowded with refugees. Omsk, the political center, had a prewar population of about 200,000 and to-day numbers close to 600,000. In the ministries of the Siberian Government you will find very many prominent Kadets and Socialists from European Russia. This element is even more bitter against the Bolsheviks than the Siberiaks. They have been driven from their homes. Some of their relatives and dearest friends are still in danger.

There was one man from Petrograd, who had become an active worker in the Zemstvo of the Vladivostok province, who came often to see me. In the days of the

Old Regime and the Provisional Government he had held a position in the Petrograd branch of the Co-operative Bank. One of his brothers, a volunteer officer, had been killed by his men in the mutiny at Tarnopol. Just on the eve of the Bolshevist uprising, he had been sent down to Moscow on some affair of the bank, and was there during the insurrection. The directors of the bank had given him a mission to Siberia, to explain their policy toward the new government to their branch houses there. He succeeded in getting into long distance telephonic communication with his wife in Petrograd, and told her to come with the children by the northern route, through Vologda to join him at Omsk. That was the last he had heard from her. It was very hard to get him to take an attitude of "sweet reasonableness" toward the Bolsheviks.

To the Siberiak who had lived through such events as the siege of Blagovojensk, the nightmare is over. But for these refugees from Russia, unable to communicate with their friends and loved ones at home, the horror of the situation is as yet unrelieved.

The struggle between the forces of Kolchak and those of Lenin is not a simple class war, as some of our American Socialists believe. All strata of society—from the old aristocracy to the factory workers and peasants—are represented in the anti-Bolshevist forces.

Historical analogies are apt to be misleading, but the Siberian attitude toward the civil war constantly reminded me of the opposition to the First Napoleon in France—fanatical Bourbonists there joined hands with fiery Jacobins; the peasants of the Vendee, with pictures of Christ on their banners, led by their village priests and the atheistical and communist followers of Hebert, worked together to pull down the usurper. It is a similar opposition which Lenin has created.

Many supporters of the Old Regime are siding with Kolchak. The "rich" peasants are in arms to protect the small farms from confiscation. But the Bolsheviks have not nearly as much to fear from these "reactionary" elements of the opposition as from the altogether more formidable forces which are rallying to the idea of government based on the consent of the majority. The democratic opposition of this type is more threatening in numbers and in morale.

Aside from the Nationalistic Armies—such as the Finns and the Letts—there are three considerable forces in the field against the Bolsheviks. In the north is the Socialistic Government of Tchaikovsky, in the southeast the organization of Denikin, and most important of all is the Siberian Army of Kolchak, the Mugwump.

All these diverse groups are so bitter that the mere suggestion of a conference with the Bolsheviks at Prince's Island[1] threw them into a rage. All, from their different points of view—reactionary, "Middle of the Road," opportunist Liberalism, Socialism—believe that the regime of Lenin is utterly iniquitous. The Church, although its influence is surprisingly small, has excommunicated him. They are all

---

[1] Prince's Island, Prinkipo, in the Sea of Marmora, the proposed site of negotiations among the Russian parties, hosted by the Allies at the end of World War I. The White forces refused to attend., although the Bolsheviks signaled their willingness.

convinced that the only conceivable end of the civil war is his destruction. And, as the people are recovering from the weariness of the World War, the confusion of the Revolution, as the issue becomes clearer, they are mustering in ever growing strength. The leaders of these anti-Bolshevist forces say that we could shorten the campaign greatly if we gave them practical help. But—with or without our aid—they are going to fight it out to the end.

Chapter XXV
Kolchak's Regime

My personal observations of Siberia under Kolchak's rule were confined to the extreme east, the Vladivostok area. I saw it at its worst. And at first my estimate of the new government was very hostile. But the situation in this district had been bad from the start—long before Kolchak had any responsibility in the matter. Along the zone of the Chinese Eastern Railroad, the frankly reactionary Horvath was ruling after the manner of the Old Regime. Kharbin, his headquarters, had become the center of counter-revolutionary intrigue. He was so strongly established that neither the Liberal Government of Vologodsky nor the Socialist Directorate had dared to interfere. The district of the Za-Baikal Cossacks was in the control of Semyonov and his regime was an orgy of banditism, but he also was strong enough to laugh at orders from Omsk. The command of the whole military district was held by General Ivanov-Rinov, whose peculiar position will be described later. And Vladivostok and its suburbs was the concentration camp of the Allied Expeditionary Forces.

The mere presence of large bodies of foreign troops inevitably had a determining influence on politics. When the Czecho-Slovaks overthrew the Bolshevist Government of the city in the summer of 1918, the old town council, which had been elected under the Kerensky regime, came out of hiding and took over the city government.

The allied command, while endeavoring not to interfere in internal politics, took the attitude that they would prevent any armed disturbances. The first time they put this decision in operation was when they disarmed the troops of General Horvath, who wished to establish himself as supreme ruler. This act prevented any further disorder. There was no chance of a violent overturn of the town council by any faction, as all the opposition knew that first of all they would have to conquer the large Japanese and American forces concentrated about the city.

This system, while it prevented "disorder," did not work very well in Vladivostok. The personnel of the town council which we found ourselves supporting was not strong nor even honest. There was a dual power, which made it possible for them to dodge all responsibility. When they did something the populace did not like, they hinted vaguely that the move had been dictated to them by the allied command and whenever any reforms were demanded by the people, the town council would pretend that the Allies would not like the change. There would probably have been better—and more popular—government in Vladivostok, if the allied forces had definitely assumed responsibility.

The first Omsk Government had been embarrassed by the support of one of the most efficient generals of the Old Regime, Ivanov-Rinov. In the early days he had been of great assistance. He was able to carry with him a large number of the officers of the old army, for he had great prestige in military circles. During the war against Germany, he had distinguished himself as a fighting general of marked ability and dash. However he was the worst type of reactionary and an inveterate intriguer. I think that the Siberian Government wanted to get rid of him, and because of his popularity among the officers feared to dismiss him. They sent him out to the extreme east as military commander. The directorate did not dare to disturb him, and Kolchak, when he became dictator, confirmed him in the position of military governor of this district. It was already evident that it had been an extremely bad appointment. But bad as Ivanov-Rinov had proved himself to be, Kolchak could not have disgraced him without sending a large force to deal with him. And Kolchak's one *raison d'être* was to prevent a new civil war. Ivanov-Rinov had used the opportunity given him by Vologodsky and the Directorate to entrench himself. Besides the soldiers directly under his command, he had won the support of Horvath and Semyonov. It was an unscrupulous—and strong—reactionary triumvirate. He certainly would have resisted an order to lay down his command. Kolchak was too weak—just as his predecessors had been—to attack him.

Ivanov-Rinov was the type of "old guard" reactionary. His idea of military discipline was the "knout" and frequent executions. The only way he could think of to combat Bolshevism was to hang all workingmen. His tyranny was not only brutal and bloody, it was utterly inefficient. He, more effectively than any agitator, converted the population to Bolshevism. When new classes were called to the colors to strengthen the army for an offensive on the Ural front, the mobilization went through with very few disorders in Western Siberia, where the local governments were Liberal. But in the extreme east conscription was bitterly resisted. Ivanov-Rinov probably had to kill two peasants for every one he forced into his ranks.

With the possible exception of the territory around Chita, ruled by the Cossack bandit Semyonov, the Vladivostok area, under Ivanov-Rinov, was the blackest spot in the domain which Kolchak claimed to govern. And Kolchak, like his Liberal and Socialist predecessors, must share the blame for tolerating these hideous conditions.

In sharpest contrast to my personal observations in this unhappy district were the reports which came to me from the Americans of our organization in Western Siberia, as was also the steady stream of news that the Co-operative Societies, Zemstvos, Liberal and Socialist groups of Central and Western Siberia were rallying to the support of Kolchak. The only possible explanation is that different districts have had very different fortune.

When the "Cossack Conspiracy" overthrew the Directorate, practically all of Siberia west of Lake Baikal was well organized on a liberal basis of democratic self-government. The cities had their town councils and the rural districts their Zemstvos, elected on the Kerensky universal suffrage law. And everywhere that the Russians have had free opportunity to develop such institutions they have shown marked ability in local government. All reports that I have received indicate that Irkutsk today is better governed than any city has ever been in all Russian history.

It is true that Kolchak confined in office certain exceedingly reactionary governors, that instead of fighting with such bandits as Semyonov he came to terms with them and tried to bring them into cooperation with him against the Bolsheviks, but it is equally true that when he found a democratic local government existing, he did nothing to interfere with it.

Thus, as in very many elements of this excessively complex Russian problem, we get flatly contradictory reports. The person whose field of observation has been Vladivostok and the Extreme East, reports nothing but horrors about the Kolchak government. On the other hand, people coming from the country west of Irkutsk and from the principal cities of that district, affirm that the liberal elements are in control under Kolchak and that their power is growing and being consolidated in all the civil affairs of the government. Still a third line of testimony comes from those who have been with the army at the front. There they find that almost all the High Command, having supreme jurisdiction in the military zones, are drawn from the old aristocracy and only in exceptional cases have any sympathy for liberal progress.

Various allied influences have fostered each of these diverse phases of Siberian politics. There has been just as sad disunity among the foreigners as among the local inhabitants.

The officers of the British and French military missions at Omsk have generally had the soldier's viewpoint and have worked for a "strong government" capable of supporting the army at the front. Their influence has varied with their personalities. Most of them have confined themselves—as they should—to their military duties. Some have mixed in politics. General Knox, who is a Tory in British politics, has remained a Tory in Russia, naturally finding his friends among, and giving his support to, the hopeless wrecks of the old aristocracy. His "pressure" has been at least counterbalanced by the steady democratic influence of the Czech leaders. Some of the Japanese, who believe that the best fish are to be caught in troubled waters, have given aid and comfort to Semyonov and other Cossack bandits. On the other hand "official" Japan has supported the liberal movement. American influence has been consistently on the side of the local self-governments.

The purely local forces in Siberia seem fairly evenly balanced. If there were no foreign interference, it would probably be a long fight before any one group could put its rivals out of business. As the foreign interference has been impartially divided between the forces of progress and reaction, it has not had much influence. But if the foreign governments could unite on a Siberian policy, they could swing the balance either way they chose.

Kolchak not only has to walk a tight rope as between the political parties of Siberia but also to trim a middle course between the conflicting suggestions of his foreign advisers. He needs recognition and foreign loans. On one side he is told that the way to get them is to push his campaign against Soviet Russia, to compromise or postpone every issue of local politics, and concentrate every pound of energy on the civil war. On the other hand, he is told that to gain the foreign support he needs he must develop civic liberties and fight the reaction in the interior. As the foreign governments do not know their own mind in this matter, as their advice is conflicting, their influence is reduced to a minimum. If they would unite in support of democratic liberalism, they would have decisive force. Kolchak would bid heavily for their support by accepting their program—or he would quickly give place to someone who would.

Chapter XXVI
Efforts to Help Russia

During the months I was there, the efforts of America and the allied nations to help the Russians were on the whole dismal failures. I have no doubt of the sincerity of this desire to give aid. From the moment the Bolsheviks realized their failure to stop the war by their separate negotiations at Brest-Litovsk, they began to prophesy "Peace at the expense of Russia." According to their theory, the capitalists of the world had a beautiful opportunity to quit fighting among themselves and recoup all their losses by dividing up Russia. Their papers gave this alleged plan in detail. Germany was to "get" the Balkans, Poland, the Baltic provinces, and a trade monopoly in Central Russia. Arkhangel was to go to Britain, Crimea and Odessa to France, America was to annex Kamchatka, and economic privileges in Siberia were to be shared with the Japanese.

The only foundation to this proposal was that Germany would have liked it and made it clear to her enemies that she would treat on this basis. If the United States and the associated powers had been as iniquitous as the Bolsheviks believed, this was an easy exit from the war. But the Allies fought on. Some private individuals in the Entente nations, a few officials, were so incensed at Russia's deflection that they did not care what happened to her. But public opinion in the allied countries would have repudiated any "peace at the expense of Russia." They applauded sincerely Mr. Wilson's announcement that we would "stand by Russia." But it was dishearteningly hard to discover the best way to do it—harder still to get any agreement as to the best way.

Our experience with the railroads is typical. We are particularly proud of our ability in this line. When we came into the war, it was well known that the Russian transportation system was in a terrible state. Russia had plenty of man power, but not enough equipment. Our allies and private munition makers had piled up equipment at Murmansk, Arkhangel, and Vladivostok, but the railroads were inadequate to carry it to the front. This seemed a problem we could help to solve.

At the request of the Provisional Government we sent a large and efficient "Railroad Mission" to Russia, under the leadership of John F. Stevens, of Panama Canal fame. But they very quickly discovered that the rehabilitation of the railroads was hardly within their competence. They were the best America could produce in technical efficiency and experience. But the technical phase of the problem was the smallest difficulty of all. It was primarily a political problem. There were diplomatic complications and there was a very disturbed and uncertain labor situation. However, with much patience and with the co-operation of Kerensky, the political wrinkles were being ironed out. A hostile Minister of Ways of Communication was replaced by one who was friendly. A plan to put Stevens and his men to work was arrived at a few days before the Bolsheviks ousted Kerensky.

Attempts to put the plan through under Bolshevist control failed—some of Stevens' men were for a while in prison—and they withdrew to Japan to await a new opportunity.

When the Czecho-Slovaki had freed Siberia, it seemed that the opportunity had come. But now the principal obstacle was diplomacy—"*la diplomatie des chemins de fer.*" The tangle of conflicting interests involved in the Chinese Eastern Railroad held things back. At last, due very largely to the patient and able efforts of Roland S. Morris, our ambassador to Japan, this situation was cleared up. In January 1919, an interallied Commission to control the Siberian Railroad was created. A Russian was appointed chairman, and the technical management was confided to Stevens.

However a new delay arose. Stevens and his men had already been waiting nearly two years. This time the trouble was financial. The Trans-Siberian had always been run at a loss. And since the Revolution the State had not been able to collect taxes enough to make up the deficit. Besides the deterioration of rolling stock and equipment, there were nearly 60,000,000 roubles owing to the employees on back pay. According to the diplomatic agreement, the reorganization was to be financed by a pro rata assessment on the signatory powers. The other governments waited for us to put up our quota. But after the accord had been signed, our State Department discovered that it could not advance the amount to which it had pledged us. There was no legislation by which our government could lend money, except to recognized governments which had been associated with us in the war against Germany. If Kolchak had been recognized, we could have met our obligation in this matter easily. The Secretary of the Treasury could have written out a check. But in the absence of a recognized government with which to deal, the only way to finance the project was by special congressional appropriation. Meanwhile Mr. Stevens was expected to reorganize a bankrupt railroad, with no money at his disposal.

There is no one thing in which America could so obviously and glowingly help Russia as in rehabilitating her railroads. This must be the first step in re-establishing her economic life. The technical problem is, granted large financial advances, easily solvable. The difficulty is political.

In sharp contrast, there is the work of our railroad engineers in France. There they could get to work. There they found a stable government to deal with There nobody suspected them of trying to steal the railroads they rebuilt.

The unstable political conditions of Russia, the intense bitterness of the civil war, which breeds suspicion that every disinterested act is intended to aid the enemy, makes it very difficult to find a way to help the Russians.

To the same general cause may be credited the failure of the project of economic and commercial relief for Siberia. The people are engaged in a civil war and that means that "politics" come first. Efforts to ignore the political controversy, which interests them so immediately and passionately, enrage the Russians. Even the most humane endeavors, if they are based on ignoring that these people are "fighting mad," are foredoomed to failure.

With the best will in the world, our Administration organized, under the War Trade Board, a government-controlled corporation to re-establish normal trade relations with Siberia. War conditions made obvious difficulties at this end, but they were successfully overcome. A committee was formed of the chiefs of the Shipping Board, the Metal Control and the War Trade Board. At a time when tonnage was excessively scarce and we were moving our largest monthly number of troops to Europe, Mr. Hurley found some freight ships to allot to the Russian trade. Mr. Baruch could release metal for the manufacture of goods needed in Siberia. And Mr. McCormick lifted the embargo on export for Russia and could control prices to prevent any excess profiteering at our end. The only condition which we made was that the Russians at their end, in order to get American export licenses, should furnish assurances that goods they imported should be used in bona-fide commerce and not be cornered for speculative purposes.

In order to get around the difficulty of the exchange rate on the rouble—so unfavorable to the Russians—every effort was made to organize direct barter, to allow Russian merchants to pay for their imports, by exporting to us the raw materials we could use.

All forms of commercial enterprise had been immensely disarranged by the revolutionary ferment, but the Co-operative Societies had weathered the storms much better than the ordinary commercial firms. It was obvious that such manufactured goods as we could export from America could best be distributed by the Co-operatives. I had several conferences with officials of the Administration during the weeks I was in Washington in the summer of 1918, and they had every disposition to deal with the Co-operatives.

The War Trade Board chose for their representative in Vladivostok Mr. Heid, who had long been in Russia as representative of the International Harvester Company. His principal customers in the past had been the Co-operative Societies. He was also disposed to work with them. And as the Co-operative Movement is based on the elimination of private profit, it was a natural assumption that they would be pleased at our attempt to prevent profiteering in this case.

However, when Mr. Heid attempted to enter into pure and simple trade relations with Co-operative Societies, he at once discovered that he had to meet not only an economic but also a political condition—and this in spite of the fact that the Co-operatives claim to keep out of politics. It is undoubtedly true that the majority of the members have kept to this faith and have stuck closely to their economic interests. But since the Bolshevist Insurrection this is no longer true of their leaders.

There are half a dozen rival Co-operative organizations in Siberia. They were nominally united in the Central Co-operative Bank in Moscow, they all sent delegates to the National Congresses, but each has its individual corporate interests. Some were primarily interested in buying for their members, some in marketing the produce of their local branches. And there was acute competition between the boards of directors of the different organizations. Each is of course anxious to increase its membership. In some cases the directors had, in the hope of prospering under official patronage, recognized the Kolchak Government. In other cases the directors, partisan friends of the Socialist Revolutionary members of the ill-fated Directorate, were opposing the de facto government. There was no united Co-operative Movement to deal with, and to discriminate between the factions was to favor the one side against the other in the internal politics of Siberia.

The obvious solution seemed to be to offer exactly equal terms to all Co-operative Societies, irrespective of their political leanings. In this way we could avoid taking sides. The trouble was that they all wanted us to take sides. The first proposals which they submitted to the representative of our War Trade Board were, when analyzed, bids for an absolute monopoly of all imports and exports. If anyone of the Co-operative Societies had been able to get such terms from the American Government, it could have eliminated its rivals and could have forced everybody in Siberia to join its organization or go without a market in which to buy or sell. It would have had an equal leverage on the consumers of our products and the producers who wished to sell to us. To have accepted such proposals would have been to confer on some group a power which was much more political than economic. In general the Co-operatives preferred not to trade with us at all, rather than to trade on equal terms with their rivals.

But even if this difficulty could have been overcome, our grandiose project of assistance in quickly re-establishing the economic life of Siberia would have been reduced to a small area around Vladivostok. The railroad was too disorganized to carry any large stream of commerce into the interior or to bring out raw material to pay for the import. The development of normal trade relations must also wait till something like a stable government is established. Until some government gathers enough momentum to suppress such banditism as that of Semyonov there is little hope of normal business. There was a large section of the railroad between Chita and Irkutsk where every train, unless it paid a ransom, was officially robbed.

Almost all efforts by the various American organizations to help Russia were similarly handicapped by "political" considerations. We were trying to be neutral. And no neutral is ever popular among belligerents. Whenever our government announced its determination not to help one faction of Russians against the others, there was a howl of disapproval from all factions, each thinking that if we had any sense of honor we would help them. Even the Red Cross and the YMCA found their opportunity for service limited by this point of view. The Siberians are engaged in a civil war. They believe that it is a "moral issue" and that neutrality is a disgrace.

Chapter XXVII
Psychological Difficulties

There was another element in the failure of these attempts at economic relief which was a sore strain on our patience and which will impede every similar attempt in the same direction. It is a difficult matter to analyze and state fairly. It comes partly from the Russians' long tradition of corrupt practice in politics and business, partly from their habit of "bargaining"—never expecting that the first price is the real price—partly from a lack of experience and disbelief in disinterested service, and partly from a naive exaggeration of their own importance.

One day, while the War Trade Board was trying in vain to make a start at giving effective economic assistance to Siberia, three representatives of one of the Co-operative groups called at my house. They said that they had come to talk over with me the proposals of the War Trade Board. I tried to shunt them off to Mr. Heid. I explained that he was the only person authorized to deal with them in the matter, that they were wasting their time and mine, as I had no knowledge of the situation except from a few friendly and informal talks with Mr. Heid. They said that was just what they wanted—a little friendly and informal discussion—before they went to him with a definite proposal.

This is very typical of Russian methods. They like to go at things indirectly, to sound out a man's friends, talk over their projects "confidentially" with one of his associates, before they come to grips with him. They expect these things which they have told his friends "in strict confidence" to be at once reported to him. They call this "preparing the ground."

This is an established custom in Russian transactions. From our American point of view, it seems a great waste of time. If a Russian decides to buy a piano for his wife, he looks up a "friend" of the piano dealer and talks it all over with him first. When I was trying to buy a large quantity of paper in Moscow for our work, the paper dealers, before they came to see me themselves, sent some of their friends to discuss the matter. People who wanted passports for America were continually coming to see me about it, because I was a "friend" of the consul. They felt the need of a "preliminary presentation of the case," before they went to the proper authority.

The first proposal of these three men from the Co-operative Societies was plain graft. They said they had a deal ready which would be very profitable to American commercial interests, and they wanted suggestions as to how to word their proposal so that Mr. Heid could get his share of the profits. I said that I imagined that Mr. Heid was fairly well off, anyhow, that he certainly was getting an adequate salary from his job and did not need the money. I was very sure that if they offered him a bribe he would reject their offer without further consideration. (I discovered later that my assurances on this subject had not satisfied them and that they sounded out another American official on the bribability of Mr. Heid.)

They then began to expatiate on the immense profits American capital could make if it went into an alliance with them. I presume that they knew what they were talking about and believed what they said. Nobody disputes the great natural wealth of Siberia and that the Co-operatives control a large part of it. But I tried to make them understand what war conditions were in America. Granted that there was a great market for wire nails in Siberia, American nail manufacturers were busy on war contracts, a year or two behind on the orders of the home market. There was a great demand for farm tractors in Siberia, but Mr. Ford was making submarine chasers and the other tractor factories were making "tanks." The people who used to turn out agricultural machinery were producing machine guns and Liberty Motor parts.

Labor was being deflected from the normal processes which might furnish the goods they needed into the shipyards. Fuel and metals were being rationed away from the factories they were interested in to war industries. All the economic life of America was being tied up by the embargo and the restrictions of the War Trade Board. "Normal Commerce" had gone out of business for the duration of the war.

"The government has created this organization," I said, "out of friendly desire to help Russia. To make a way for you through all these war-time entanglements. It doesn't matter what high profits you offer the individual manufacturer in America, he can't accept the deal without the sanction of the War Trade Board. He can't get the fuel or raw material, he can't get freight cars, he can't get an "export license," he can't get shipping space. But if, on the other hand, you go to Mr. Heid with a bona-fide proposal which will meet Russia's economic needs, furnish her with manufactured goods cheaply, help to stabilize the foreign exchange, facilitate the marketing of her products, you don't need to offer excessive profits. Heid will put it through for you. The War Trade Board at home will get you what you need, issue the necessary licenses and carefully fix the price so you can't be cheated. This is a friendly scheme, a war-time emergency organization. It offers you not only the best terms you could hope for, but the only way you can get goods."

But this was altogether too good to sound true to them. It brought them to their great point, the cimax of the argument, which they wanted me to pass on to Mr. Heid. They drew the circle of their chairs a little nearer and the spokesman became even more confidential. They had had a very tempting proposal from Japan. Of course they would much prefer to deal with Americans. They were full of fear of the "Japanese commercial invasion." Among other evils it would shut out American trade. If the Japanese got control they would "close the door" in our faces. They hated the idea. But after all, in our American phrase, business is business, and the Japanese were offering to furnish them with everything they needed very much cheaper than we.

I jumped up and congratulated them. "Fine," I said; "that will relieve my government of a great worry. They have been struggling with the war-time restriction to open a way to commerce with you because they thought you needed our assistance. It will be lots simpler if you can get what you need in Japan. That will save no end of ships. You explain to Mr. Heid that you don't need American goods, that you can get your market in Japan and he'll cable home. It will be a great relief to Washington."

"But," they protested, "you'll lose the Siberian market."

There was a map of the world on my wall and I pointed to all the countries which were clamoring for our output. China, South America, devastated Europe. "Before 1914," I said, "our factories were busy keeping up with our home market. And now for five years an ever increasing number of factories have been diverted to war products. The home market is undersupplied and wages and buying power have gone up. At home a manufacturer, if the War Trade Board allows him to sell in the open market, can get good prices and money for his products. He can't manufacture fast enough, and if he does want a foreign market a great many of them are better than Russia. Don't think you will make us mad by trading with Japan. We haven't any surplus to sell you. We are offering you some out of our shortage."

They went away disgruntled, but unconvinced. They held out to the end for their extreme terms, perfectly sure that we were so hungry for "the Siberian market" that we would end by meeting them.

It would be unfair and impatient to jump at the conclusion that the Russian mind cannot comprehend "honest proposals." The Russian people have had very little experience in them. In their dealings with each other they do not "put all their cards on the table." They are in the habit of dickering over their bargains. There are only one or two "fixed price" stores in all the country, and the Russians do not like them. They are suspicious not only of foreigners but of each other. They are always looking for the hidden motive, the "real reason" back of any offer. The American Red Cross in Siberia did its utmost to keep out of politics, but most Russians regarded it with sneering suspicion. It was the same with the YMCA. Any suggestion that these enterprises represented a spirit of disinterested service was laughed at as cheap hypocrisy. They were the advertising end of the campaign of American capitalists to capture Siberian trade. This frame of mind was typified in the sullen distrust which Stevens and his corps of railroad men had to meet. How those men wished that they had been sent to France instead of Russia! They were a representative body of Americans. Some of them perhaps were dissatisfied with the jobs they had thrown up to join this expedition to Russia, and hoped to find more lucrative positions in Siberia. But just like their friends who went to France, most of them had made a real sacrifice to serve their country in the great crisis of war. Many of them were deeply thrilled by the news of the Revolution and wanted a chance to aid in the democratic reconstruction of Russia. I have never seen any more admirable doggedness than the way they rallied after the first disillusion, when they found that instead of being welcome they were generally suspected of trying to steal the railway. They stuck it out—and are sticking it out—in an effort to prove such suspicions unfounded.

Psychiatrists might explain this Russian suspiciousness as a form of the "mania of persecution"; it has its counterpart in an "illusion of grandeur."

When the Bolsheviks concluded their separate peace at Brest-Litovsk, all Russians thought that Germany had won the war. They did not think that America could furnish a counterbalancing force. They did not believe that victory was possible to any combination which did not include them. It was a ghastly wound to their *amour propre* to Bolsheviks, Socialists, Liberals, and Conservatives alike, that we had the presumption to go on fighting and could win without them.

This overestimation of their importance in the world is especially marked in matters of commerce and industry. Almost all Russian railroads have been bad investments. When the natural resources of the country are developed the railroads will begin to be financially profitable. But at present and for a good many years to come, the annual deficit must be met by taxation. And yet it is very hard to get a Russian to believe that, if some foreign railroad men had free capital, they could find better investment elsewhere. It is the same with gold mines, lumber concessions, or the commercial market.

There is, for instance, a great demand in Russia for nails. A merchant in Irkutsk gets at our consulate an old prewar catalogue and finds a keg of nails listed at five dollars, according to the normal exchange rate a trifle less than ten roubles. Today the American manufacturer can get ten dollars for that keg of nails in the home market. And the rouble has fallen to the point where the Siberian merchant has to pay out at least one hundred roubles to buy a draft for ten dollars. Instead of retailing the nails for fifteen roubles, he must raise his price 1,000 percent, and charge 150. The traffic will not bear such a jump. And yet the Russian merchants are convinced that their market must be more attractive to foreign commerce than any other. They expect all the other nations to bid wildly against each other for the privilege of trading with them.

I have not given this long list of discouragements as an argument against continuing our efforts "to help Russia." We must stick to it—as our railroad men have so admirably done. Just in so far as we understand the causes of past failure, we are more likely to succeed in the future.

Almost every one we have sent out to Russia—in the Red Cross, YMCA, diplomatic, economic, railroad, and military missions, in the organization for which I was responsible—have gone with high hopes of a real chance to serve. They have all been met by a cold douche of suspicion. The weaker ones have crumpled up and come home—or been sent home.

And there is another reason for analyzing at such length the failure of our efforts to help re-establish the normal economic life of Siberia. Those who sympathize with the Bolshevist regime are raising an outcry against the embargo on trade with Soviet Russia. Trade union congresses here and in the allied countries are discussing resolutions of protest against the embargo. An embargo on private trade with Russia is rather like a law which imposes the death penalty on suicides. Those whose idea of "helping Russia" is summed up in the slogan "hands off" are totally uninformed. The way to help Russia is to "stand by." No mere negative removal of prohibitions against trade will help, either in Siberia or European Russia. What is needed is a positive constructive program of assistance. Private initiative will not be adequate. If the people of America, of England and France, wish to help Russia they will have to spur their governments on to concerted action. Governmental finance will be necessary to stabilize Russian exchange. Ships will have to be subsidized to make the otherwise unprofitable route to Russian ports. Some governmental control will be necessary to divert manufactured goods from more stable markets to Russia. Some State guaranty must be found before bankers will handle any more Russian loans. The policy of "Hands off Russia" means that that distracted country would have to pay more for a loan than a turbulent Central American republic. A policy of "not doing" will not help anyone.

Before closing this paragraph, I wish to return to this intangible difficulty of "Russian Psychology." It is utterly impossible to give any adequate treatment of the subject. I have dwelt above on its most unlovely side—this ready distrust and suspicion.

Almost all who have been in Russia return with a very real friendship for the people. From my own observations, I would say that Americans, more than other foreigners, are quickly captivated by the peculiar charm of Russian life. There is a lovable and very appealing character not only among the more fortunate class, but especially among the simple folk. There is a rectitude of heart about most Russians which more than compensates for certain peculiarities of intellect, which seem faults to us. And anyone who has been brought up to that love of freedom, that faith in the brave chances of tomorrow, which is our American heritage, cannot fail to be moved by the tremendous aspirations of Russia for a freer and better future. So many things which we take easily for granted these people are fighting and dying for. We come home valuing more than we did the things we have inherited and for which they—with a self-abnegation never demanded of us—are striving.

I do not think that the Russians are in any wise less honest than we, less capable of frank and friendly relations. Their experience has been very different. And it is just in these matters of commerce and politics, where their experience—the background on which they see the problems—differs most profoundly from ours.

When we try to do business or to enter into political relations with them we strike these differences with brutal force. And this has been as large an element as any other—perhaps the biggest of all—in our failures to help them.

We have passed through the rawest business individualism. Take for instance the "Boosting Campaign" of any of our energetic cities. In the local Chamber of Commerce, which fosters it, there are hardware dealers and grocers, wholesalers and retailers, manufacturers and real-estate brokers, bankers and professional men. Each undoubtedly keeps one eye on his own ledger, is especially careful of his own interests, but all realize that general prosperity will increase their individual profits. Rivals, according to the theory of pure individualism, work together for the growth and well-being of the city in which they are collectively interested. There is no parallel to this in Russian business life.

It is not superior morals which makes most American business men believe in the "Open Door" in foreign trade. Reasoning from their own experience, they believe it is better business. If there are equal trade opportunities for all in China, Asia Minor, Central Africa, those countries will become more prosperous. "Opportunity" is not a fixed quantity from which rivals must be excluded. It is better business to increase prosperity and expand opportunity. There is no limit to it. There is room for everybody.

But an American business man, who wants to develop the prosperity of Russia, is at once met by the suspicion that he wants to monopolize it. Just to the extent that his own impulses are enlightened and generous he feels himself rebuffed and insulted by the Russians. If our Railroad Mission had wanted to steal the Trans-Siberian Railroad they might have succeeded in "doing business." Anyhow their feelings would not have been hurt. As a matter of fact they had no such sinister plan and so they felt themselves insulted.

In the same way it has been easier for men to succeed in Russia, whether their aim was high or low, by bribery and corruption than with us to-day. Our ideas of what is dishonorable are very largely dependent on the opinion of our neighbors. Near where I lived in Kharbin there was an impressively palatial home being built by an employee of the Chinese Eastern Railroad whose salary was about five hundred dollars a month. His position allowed him to control cars. You could not transport goods without "consulting" him. Every one knew the nature of his graft—it was perfectly open. But there was no social condemnation of it. Now it angers an American railroad man, who has come out in a burst of patriotism, to have people offer him bribes. But their act is just as natural as his anger. They are accustomed to doing it.

Among the educated Russians, the conservatives as well as the radicals, the crudest form of Marx's materialism has taken a strong hold. It is the fashionable Russian philosophy of the day to believe that the only powerful motives in society are the hopes of immediate material gain. If they cannot see how your activity is swelling your bank account, they think there is something mysterious and especially sinister about it.

While they rather boast of their own dreamy, impractical idealism, they are inclined to think that it is a distinctly Russian trait and that all foreigners are, by definition, gross materialists. Most of the people they have met in their own experience who have amassed large fortunes are gross materialists, greedy and heartless, exploiters of other people's misery. America is reputed to be very rich, so it logically follows, according to theory, that we are the very types of profit-mad capitalists.

This "psychological" resistance which has defeated some of our attempts to help and has hindered all of them, is something which will be overcome only slowly. There is no one thing, no "official statement," no single act, which will suddenly clear up these hindrances. Winning the real friendship of Russia is a long-term affair—as difficult as it is eminently worth while. Some errors in our own policy might be rectified quickly, but this intangible suspicion with which all our efforts have been met will be overcome only slowly.

There are of course among the Russians many glowing exceptions to the type of mind described above. But I think that most of the men we have sent to Russia on diplomatic, economic, or humanitarian missions would agree that this habit of indirect, corrupt methods, this suspicion of sordid motives in others, was the most difficult obstacle they had to overcome.

Chapter XXVIII
Intervention

I have frequently referred to the anomalous situation created by the presence of our troops in Russia at a time when our government declared its determination not to intervene in local politics. In unsettled times the bare presence of an organized military force is, inevitably, a political fact. The situation was as complicated—and sometimes as inconsistent—as the bitterest critics of the present Administration claim. But there were good things as well as bad mixed in the complication. In Vladivostok I was able to see how the presence of allied troops thwarted the ambitions of Horvath and tempered the tyranny of Ivanov-Rinov. In the Arkhangel district, where our troops were more numerous than those of our allies, we supported a Socialist government, whose leaders would probably have been jailed under our Espionage Law at home.

Complicated as the situation was, I can not see how it could have been simplified unless the Allies had been able to reach a complete accord on a Russian policy.

The presence of allied troops in Russia antedated the Bolshevist regime. After considerable hesitation and uncertainty and against the passionate advice of some, the decision was reached to withdraw these troops. Many of them actually sailed from Arkhangel and Vladivostok and were incorporated in the armies on the Western Front. But this policy of withdrawing our troops from Russia was continually interfered with by the Bolsheviks and at last checkmated by their attack on the Czecho-Slovaks. "Intervention," in the sense of armed conflict between the Allies and the Bolsheviks, had begun.

At almost the same time, and in all probability in accordance with the same policy, there was an anti-Japanese riot in Vladivostok, and marines were landed there from the Japanese and British warships in the harbor. The question was no longer "Shall we intervene?" but "How can we make the existing intervention fruitful?" Two currents of opinion among the Allies at once became apparent. One side advocated "Increasing Intervention," the other "Decreasing Intervention." The two extremes were defended respectively by the French and the Americans.

The French presented three main arguments.

I. Military. It was necessary to divide the German forces by simultaneous attacks on both her fronts. A joint American and Japanese expedition of a few hundred thousand men could cross Siberia with little opposition, organize a front along the Volga, join up with an Anglo-French Expedition from Arkhangel and the anti-Bolshevist forces in South Russia, and either advance rapidly across Russia to the German frontier or force Hindenburg to dispatch a large army to stop them. The allied forces sent from here would be, the French maintained, augmented by such Irredentist troops as the Czecho-Slovaki and large numbers of Russians loyal to the Entente. They figured that, with such recruits, every man we sent from home would tie up at least three German soldiers, while they could hardly hope to occupy more than one enemy on the Western Front.

II. Economic. There were the immense munition dumps at the ports. They were certainly our property, as Russia had repudiated all obligation to pay for them. And they were certainly being turned over to the Germans as fast as the rickety railroad system allowed. Of perhaps greatest import was the mass of food supplies and raw material in Russia so desperately needed by the Germans. Allied troops in Russia, even if they did not score great military achievements, could interfere with the German schemes of revictualing.

III. Sentimental. The position of our friends in Russia was desperate and we had an obligation of honor to come to their assistance against the joint menace of Germany and the Bolsheviks. Scattered about Russia there were units of Irredentist prisoners—Armenians, Czechs, Italians, Romanians, Serbs—whom we had helped to organize. If they fell into the hands of their former masters, German, Austrian, or Turkish, they would be hanged as traitors. They were all fighting for their lives. The smaller units had already been wiped out. But some of them had fought their way through the Austrian-German-Bolshevist "Red Army" and had united along the Volga. We were bound to attempt a rescue. And there were large numbers of the Russians who were suffering through their loyalty to us. Many scattered about in hiding, some organized in military units in the Don.

Most important in the tense game of international politics at that moment were the Czecho-Slovaki. We had joined in recognition of their national aspiration for independence. We were counting largely on their aid in the overthrow of Austria. We could not afford to discourage them by deserting their soldiers in Russia.

The attitude of the American authorities was to hold the intervention down to the lowest possible dimensions. The attempts to divide the German forces in the manner the French proposed meant certainly to divide our own. Our General Staff was emphatically opposed to any attempt to re-establish the Eastern Front. And for political reasons our government was reluctant to sanction any increase of "intervention."

But we were a party to the Supreme War Council at Versailles, we had contributed largely to its development into a unity of command with power to enforce its orders. Our arguments prevailed in regard to the matter of sending large forces to re-establish the Eastern Front. But our delegates there either believed in the advisability of sending small expeditions to guard the munition dumps and rescue the Czechs or they were unable to convince their colleagues that it was inadvisable. The Supreme War Council decided on the expeditions to North Russia and Siberia.

The United States could of course have broken with her associates and have refused to send any troops to Russia. But such an action, in spite of its obviously disastrous effect on the conduct of the war against Germany, would not in any way have stopped "intervention." We could have smashed the Supreme War Council by refusing to accept its decisions, but we could not have prevented the other nations from doing what they thought was necessary.

Even the most ardent advocates of non-intervention would hardly propose expanding the Monroe Doctrine to include Russia. We were not in the mood to drive the British out of their naval base at Murmansk, nor to send an ultimatum to the Japanese. We also were fighting the German submarines. We also have landed marines in various ports to protect our citizens from mob violence in times of disorder.

"Intervention"—the presence of allied troops in Russia—was already a fact. The only question which faced the Administration at Washington was how to make American participation in the intervention as beneficent as possible.

Distasteful as service in Russia has been to the officers and men of our Expeditionary Forces, I do not believe that any unbiased observer who believed in the righteousness of the war against Germany would question the fact that their presence there has been a moderating and liberalizing influence, a force which prevented a great deal which threatened to be worse.

But the matter cannot be dropped here. It is a very superficial view of the case to think of "intervention" as limited only to armed forces. Our Red Cross has intervened very beneficently in Siberia in its campaign against the spreading of typhus. Our railroad men are intervening with admirable determination to rebuild the system of transportation. And unarmed foreign intervention often takes a more sinister turn. The International Debt Control in Turkey is an example. The bankers of Europe did not have troops at their command in Constantinople, but by their intrigues they were able to intervene greatly—and generally disastrously—in the domestic politics of the Sultan.

When the last allied soldier has been withdrawn from Russia, "intervention" will not have ceased. Their governments will continue to send diplomatic agents and salesmen to Russia. The diplomats will continue "to bring pressure to bear" on internal politics in behalf of their national interests. The traders will use what influence they can muster for their private interests. Technically we have avoided "armed intervention" in Mexico. But Mexico has been torn by foreign intrigue for a generation.

"Intervention" by one means or another is part of our modern international life. Nations can hold it in check only when they are themselves strongly organized. The French and British do not, for instance, lose sleep over our intervention in their politics; they are strong enough to stop it if it becomes obnoxious. Weak nations cannot resist intervention. And there will be intervention in Russia, by France and Germany, by Japan and Britain, by America, as long as her internal dissensions keep her weak.

When their period of convulsion is over and the Russians have achieved a stable government, they will not have to worry about "intervention."

However, allied intervention in Russia has been incoherent and very much less effective than it might have been. The unity of action which the nations associated against Germany finally reached in military matters was never achieved—as the long-drawn-out Conference of Paris prove—in the diplomatic field. The discord among the Allies was especially baneful in Siberia.

There has been in our press a good deal of comment on friction between the Japanese and American forces. It is certainly true that our officers have not always been in complete agreement with the Japanese High Command.

But it is my own impression that the Foreign Office at Tokyo has shown a more sincere desire to co-operate with Washington than have some representatives of our other associates. And at least some of the sand which has caused friction between Washington and Tokyo has been tossed into the machine by our other allies who were not enthusiastic over the idea of American-Japanese co-operation in the Far East.

There is no Foreign Office in the world which has complete control over its agents. The control becomes weaker as the scene of action is further removed from the capital. It is necessary to grant large discretionary power to a diplomat on a distant mission, where communications are limited and slow. It is not possible to blame on the home government all the friction and hard feelings which spring up among their representatives at the other end of the earth. The premiers of the Entente nations may have been under the illusion that there was cordial co-operation in Siberia. There was no such illusion among those on the spot.

Sometimes the rivalry between representatives of the various allies was picayune and amusing, as when they stole each other's railroad cars. It was an altogether more serious matter when the French and English promised the Czecho-Slovaks, in spite of the formal statement of our Government, American and Japanese support on the Eastern Front.

The signing of peace is certain to simplify the problems in Russia and Siberia greatly. One of two things will happen. Either the League of Nations will prove strong enough to unify the efforts to help Russia, or, the war being over, each nation will be able to go forward frankly according to its own policy, without fear of weakening the alliance against Germany. Either there will be agreements on an international policy or no nation will be forced to give up its ideals for fear of offending its allies.

Book III
What's to Be Done?

Chapter XXIX
Some Elements of the Problem

It is very encouraging on coming home to feel how keen and widespread is America's interest in Russia. The impression is strong that most of our people are heartily in accord with President Wilson's policy of "standing by Russia." Public opinion is interested. Russia is still a "heading story." Even Trans-Atlantic flights do not entirely crowd it off the "front page." Meetings where Russia is discussed are always packed. There is evidently a general and very real desire to understand what is going on over there and an earnest wish "to help."

There is profound sagacity in this attitude. Anyone who believes that the world, as well as his home town, should be made safe for democracy, must be interested in the Russian struggle. The Great War had for us two objectives—the concrete job of smashing the military machine which threatened our liberties and the less tangible task of overcoming the habit of mind which had created the menace. It was only a very superficial view which regarded these two goals of our striving as identical. We have crushed the armies of the reaction in the Central Empires, but we have not yet defeated its spirit there—nor at home. The latter is the more important business and it promises to be the longer campaign. The founders of our republic believed that it would require eternal vigilance.

Now that the war is over it is no longer necessary nor even admissible to think of this struggle between the forces of the dismal past and hopeful future in terms of "nationalism." The friends of democratic progress can no longer symbolize the enemy in the person of the German War Lord. There are those who sympathize with and support the ideas he stood for in every nation—in even the tiniest village. In the countries most devoted to the ideals of liberty, the necessity of the war has drawn many of such a sinister turn of mind into positions of importance and power. The reaction is more threatening to-day in all the Entente countries than it was in 1914. The struggle now is international—Pan-Liberalism vs. Pan-Chauvinism.

If the spirit of autocracy and imperialism revives and "wins to power anywhere— in Germany, among the new little nations, in the Far East, in Russia—it will be necessary for us to mobilize once more and fight it all out again. If peace is to be permanent, Russia also must be made safe for democracy.

The problem there is the same—although, of course, the details differ—as the one we are familiar with at home. The "politicians" are only standard bearers. The "parties" are only spear heads—significant, unless there is behind them a real force of popular aspirations. The discussions of, or the actual drawing up of an ideally perfect Utopian Constitution, fitted for a race of demi-gods, will not help very much. There are a vast deal of more important problems. Schools must be built, wheels made to turn, crops to grow. The name which is given to the man on top—Director, Dictator, President, Chief of the Executive Power, or General Manager—is not so important as the organization from below. If life in the villages is free, there is no danger of a Tsar. If life in the villages is prosperous, the "Government' will soon recover from bankruptcy. If the village schools are good, we can have confidence that Russian Foreign Policy will be enlightened.

Such problems—just like those at home—require a statesmanship which, while never losing sight of the Vision ahead, holds close account of present realities, however unpleasant. Above all the task of constructing the New Russia—the fit partner for a League of Honor—will require patience. It demands a broad spirit of tolerance. Anyone who loses faith when progress seems too slow, anyone who is cocksure and irascible when things do not "go right," will be a poor friend of Russia. History is not rich in the biographies of men who could have solved such problems overnight. There will be much hesitating and uncertainty, much staggering and stuttering—occasional fainting fits—before Russia gets her stride.

There is considerable noisy shouting in favor of a "hands-off-Russia" policy. But the general sentiment in America, as near as I can gauge it, is that we should "stand by." However, on the question of how we should "help Russia," councils are desperately divided. There is no general accord on any "constructive program." Much of the discussion in our newspapers is extremely partisan on one side or the other, much of it seems "inspired." That our reactionary papers should sneer at the Revolution is not to be wondered at. But to one coming from Russia, our liberal press seems just as uncomprehending and ill-informed. Only as everyone who knows anything about Russia has recorded his observations, can we hope for a generally well-informed public opinion to back up a workable program.

The contradiction in evidence is not surprising—Russia is so appallingly vast. There is such a bewildering myriad of interesting trees to distract attention from the forest. Anyone who professes to know all about Russia, who is sure of just what we ought to do, is absurd. The situation develops so rapidly, continually bringing to the surface new and hitherto ignored problems, revealing unexpected complications, uncovering latent aspirations, engendering new forces, that any set program, hard and fast in its details, is ridiculous. There is nothing static about Russia; it is all tremendously dynamic.

So I have no detailed program to offer. But in the bewildering complexity of problems there are some elements on which I have found my own observations in very general agreement with those of my Russian friends and American and allied associates. They will have to be given consideration in the evolving of any proposals to help Russia.

First of all any plans of reconstruction must accept the fact that there has been a tremendous and fundamental agrarian revolution. Underneath all the quibbles and quarrels of the political factions, there has been in progress the complete and utter destruction of the old system of land tenure. This revolution is incomplete, as no definite solution has yet been found for the problem of redistributing of the land. But the old landlord class has been dispossessed. Their legal papers, their "deeds of ownership," are as worthless as the parchments of the *ancienne noblesse* of France.

If the Russian aristocracy had heeded the warnings—and God knows there were enough warnings—they might, by timely concessions, have saved something for themselves out of the wreckage. Ten years ago there was much discussion of "buying them out." There was a period before our Civil War when the Abolitionists were willing to argue about compensating the "owners" for the liberation of the slaves. But in one case as in the other, the "vested interests" preferred to hold on to their "rights" desperately—until at last they were wrested from them by might. They allowed the time for compromise to pass. And so in Russia "private property in land"—at least in regard to large estates—has gone the way of "chattel slavery."

Anyone who proposes to re-establish the landlords in their ancient "rights" is a wild-eyed Utopian. The Germans tried to do it in the Ukraine. And they found to their grief that it cannot be done without the reconquest of Russia, village by village. And the peasant soldiers, when they went home from the army, took their rifles with them. A Russian village to-day is hardly self-respecting unless it has a machine gun and some strips of ammunition. The Bolsheviks have failed in their effort to impose their will on the villages. More shots have been fired in their war against the peasants than in their "foreign wars."

The force which the Russian aristocracy could muster for such a campaign is negligible. They are weaker to-day than a year ago when the peasants chased them away with sticks and stones. They cannot hope to reconquer their estates themselves and certainly no democratic nation is going to lend them troops for such a purpose. No government of the Entente nations, even if it desired to do so, could hold its citizen soldiers to such a sorry task.

While the reinstatement of the old land owners is as impractical as it is undesirable, the "Land Problem" is still acute in Russia. No way has yet been worked out to distribute the land to the people who till it—individual ownership of small holdings or some of the proposed forms of collective ownership—which will satisfy the peasants' sense of equity and give them the impetus to work which comes from a feeling of stability and security. To-day the peasants are much more occupied in staking out claims—and defending them from invasion—than they are in raising crops. They are uncertain who will enjoy the harvest. They have no incentive to plant more than what they need themselves and can defend. There is no market for any surplus they might produce and Bolshevist "food raiders" from the starving cities are abroad in the land.

So Russia, normally a great exporter of foodstuffs, is not growing enough to feed her own population. Until a new system of land tenure is stabilized and the peasants know that they will enjoy the harvest on which they labor, there will be no relief from this condition. They will continue to plant only what they need for their own food and what they can hope to defend. But just in proportion as they win confidence in the New Regime and begin once more their normal production—and there is no reason why it should not be greatly increased—the price of bread will go down for the workers of Moscow, Vienna, Rome, Paris, and Berlin.

This agrarian revolution, affecting at least 80 percent of the population, is the great economic accomplishment of the Russian Revolution. And to an extent as yet impossible to measure, it will affect the city workers—by wiping out a great deal of unsound industry.

At the first rumor of land distribution there began an informal demobilization of the army. The soldiers deserted in large numbers and hurried home to share in the division. To an almost equal degree there was a similar demobilization of industry. The factory workers were just as anxious to share in the land distribution as the soldiers. Those who succeed in getting land will be very slow to return to the miserable squalor of the industrial slums. Any expansion of opportunity in agriculture will deplete the labor market, automatically force up wages, and greatly ameliorate the condition of the workers. The agrarian revolution will free Russia from the curse of "cheap labor."

Few things are certain in politics, but a democratic regime in Russia will be dominated by the peasants, and it seems inevitable that they will demand the removal of the high tariff on the manufactured goods they require. There is very little of Russia's mushroom industry which can survive a shortage of cheap labor and a reduction in protective tariff.

An illustration, typical of a great deal of Russian industry, is furnished by the International Harvester Company. There was a large and growing demand in Russia for agricultural machinery. The American firm had perfected its product at home, but after the Witte high tariff project went into effect, it was more profitable to erect factories inside of Russia, and so avoid custom duties and at the same time take advantage of cheap labor. If there is a considerable rise in wages and decrease in tariff schedules, it will in all probability be more profitable for them once more to manufacture for the Russian market at home. It was only on the basis of high tariff and cheap labor that the Russian cotton factories could compete with England and Germany. This was true of a whole series of Russian industries.

The overwhelming peasant majority will probably insist on State aid to agriculture rather than to industry. The peasant democracy of Bulgaria offers a possible analogy. The profits of agriculture, instead of being skimmed off by the landlord class to be spent in luxuries at home and abroad, will stay with the peasant to be invested on the farm, in manure, in livestock, in wagons and harvesters, in better homes. Not until Russia's farms are fully capitalized is she likely to turn her attention seriously to manufacturing again. She will sell her surplus foodstuffs and import the cheap industrial products of her neighbors.

There will be only two groups in Russia opposed to this course of development. The Captains of Industry, who were beginning to form an important element in politics, and the Social Democrats, whose hope of power rests on the growth of an industrial proletariat. But even if these two elements combined they would form a numerically insignificant and impotent minority.

Any project "to help Russia" which ignores this fundamental agrarian revolution is foredoomed to failure. The first duty of any new government, and of all outsiders who wish to assist in the regeneration of Russia, is to find some solution to the problem of redistributing the land. If internal peace is desired the principle of "usufruct" must be accepted, i.e., that the land belongs to those who use it. To enforce any other principle means a bitter village war. Agricultural productivity on which not only the prosperity of the nation but also the very life of the people depends, can only be revived by giving to the tillers of the soil the conviction that they will reap and enjoy the harvests which they sow. Whether or not they shall actually "own" the land is a somewhat academic question. The important thing is to give them a certainty that they shall own the crops they raise. This point could be met by either "individual ownership of small holdings" or by one or another of the schemes for collective ownership. Soil condition and local customs differ so greatly, that I am skeptical of any proposal for a uniform system of land tenure. A large degree of decentralization to meet the varying conditions of the vast Russian territories is desirable. The majority of educated Russians are in favor of some form of nationalization of the land. Large sections of the peasantry—but how large is uncertain—would also prefer to do away with private property in land.

Whatever form of land tenure the Russians decide upon, it seems obvious that they should arrange to derive a large part, if not all, of the State income from the land. "Private Property" having been at least temporarily outlawed, the land reverts to the nation. It is their greatest asset. It matters very little whether the people who are given the land to till should pay for the privilege in "rent" or "taxes."

The State, which is bankrupt now, has here a large source of income. Another outstanding element of the Russian situation is the contrast between National and Local Politics, the conflict between Centralization and Decentralization. The people show marked ability in handling the problems of local self-government. Their political inexperience—so often commented upon by foreigners and sometimes sneered at—is noticeable only in their attempts to organize a "Central Government." Plato said that "The Republic" was sure to fall prey to a tyrant if it grew to such a size that the citizens could no longer know each other personally. While we have disproved this pessimistic dictum by the great development of means of communication, undreamed of by the Greek philosopher, it finds much substantiating evidence in modern Russia.

In the National Congresses and All-Russian Conferences this lack of political *savoir-faire* is noticeable, but when dealing with people and problems within their horizon the Russians get along very well. This is remarkably true of the peasants. They have managed their village affairs by democratic community rule from time immemorial and in spite of serfdom and endless oppression have shown just as much sagacity as the ordinary New England town meeting. In 1906 I had the opportunity to study closely the peasant deputies in the first Duma. They were sometimes amusing but always impressive. Few of them could read or write. Their ideas about foreign politics were naive. They did not believe that the world is round—all the land they had ever seen looked flat. They were not in the habit of writing or receiving letters and were only vaguely interested in reforms of the postal system. Most of the affairs of State, about which the Constitutional Democrats and various brands of Socialists made eloquent orations, were entirely beyond their comprehension. But they knew exactly what their villages wanted. They were uneducated, but very wise. There were a great many things which a statesman is supposed to talk about that they had never heard of. But there were also a great many things which the ordinary politician ignores—about the real problems of humble life—which they knew with a profound experience.

This distinction between information and wisdom, which was noticeable a dozen years ago, has been made even more clear by recent events. A surprisingly large number of local organizations have sprung up spontaneously all over Russia during the course of the Revolution: Soviets, Land Committees, County Councils, Town Governments, and so long as they stuck to their neighborhood functions they have have done amazingly well.

The Revolution destroyed the old bureaucracy in a week. To build up the machinery of a new government was slow work. The politicians in Petrograd were too busy with "affairs of state," with the problems of the war, and their petty partisan disputes, to give adequate attention to organizing the country.

A detailed account reached me of what happened in one sleepy provincial town a day's journey south of Moscow. The news of the Revolution which the good citizens received was no fuller nor more accurate than what we read in our American newspapers. Nobody in Petrograd had time to think of them. No instructions came from the new ministry of Prince Lvov. The Tsar's governor, who was generally hated, posted up a few bulletins which came by official wire and then ran away. The police also disappeared. For a few days there was no government at all. A gang of hooligans started looting and some citizens got together and organized a Defense Committee and a Volunteer Militia. The Kadets—lawyers, doctors, teachers, and the like—took the initiative in getting things started, but at once the workers in a samovar factory and the munition plant organized a Soviet. Very soon the peasants from the countryside began sending in deputations to find out what they were to do.

Unable to get precise news from the capital, they sent a delegation to Petrograd. There was a Kadet from the amateur Town Council, a leader of the Soviet, and a young Socialist Revolutionary doctor, an employee of the Zemstvo, who was chosen by the peasants. In a few weeks they brought back a joint report. And things went very smoothly in their town for several months. There were geographical organizations—rural and urban—on the basis of universal suffrage. Special interests created their own organizations. There was a Committee on Trade and Industry—what we would call a "Chamber of Commerce." The workers had their Soviet. The peasants organized a Union about their Land Committee. The Officers' Club took over the management of war activities. Even the landlords organized. Everybody knew everybody else. All were familiar with the problems they had to discuss. And civic peace was maintained—as long as they stuck to their local affairs.

The same sort of thing happened all over Russia. Without any instructions or directions from above, the people organized to take care of their local needs at once adequately and peaceably. Trouble started when the "Central Government" began to interfere, or when issues involving the "Central Authority" arose. The effort in America to separate local and national politics—to arrange for municipal elections in different years from presidential campaigns—shows the same problem here.

It is hard for us to realize the degree of "centralization" in Russia under the Old Regime. If, for instance, it was desirable to raise the wages of a janitor in a public school in Odessa, it was necessary to get authorization from the Ministry of Education in Petrograd. When the Czecho-Slovaks upset the Bolsheviks in Vladivostok, the remaining members of the Town Council, elected under the Kerensky regime, came out of hiding and reassumed control. For many months they were cut off from communication with the rest of the country and so were thrown on their own resources. Later the railroad was opened up and Vladivostok gave its adhesion to the Siberian Government at Omsk. The Central Government at once sent out a delegate named Zimmerman to govern Vladivostok, to "bring it into line," to reduce it to uniformity. But the Town Council had enjoyed the power it had been exercising and did not want to surrender any of it. A series of conflicts arose between the Central Government, represented by Zimmerman, and the Town Council which paralyzed all governmental activity for several weeks.

Zimmerman was an earnest, intelligent man—very much shocked at the reluctance of Vladivostok to submit to centralization. Mr. Morris, our ambassador to

Japan, was then in the city and Zimmerman went to him with his troubles. "What," he asked, "is the relation in America between the local governments and the representatives of the Central Authority?" He was immensely surprised when Mr. Morris told him that the only Federal employee whom the ordinary American ever sees is the postman.

Instead of sending representatives to the capital from the local government units, as is our custom, the Russians are habituated to the idea that the Central Authority must send representatives out to the local governments to keep them in order. So they are inclined to put vastly more responsibility on their Central Government than we are willing to trust to ours.

Just as the Russians have shown marked ability in handling their local affairs on a democratic basis, they have so far failed to meet the problems of a Central Government. But failure in this matter is, of course, only a relative term. No country can claim to have solved the problem satisfactorily. There is constant discussion in France and the British Empire on "Reconstruction." New experiments in constitutional organization are to be expected in both cases. And in America the old controversy between "State Rights" and "Federal Authority" is unsettled. There are many reasons why it is especially hard for the Russians to create a satisfactory Central Government.

First, undoubtedly, is that such problems are highly technical and demand education, rather than native wit or wisdom. The people in Russia, who have been trained for such work, the only ones familiar with the problem, had made their careers under the Old Regime, corrupt, reactionary bureaucrats of the Tsar. There was not much "Big Business," constantly educating young men in large administrative undertakings. There was no highly developed, active middle class, which could be drawn on for the work of government. There had been no free political life to develop a hierarchy of ward politicians. State governors, congressmen. The human material for a Central Government has not been trained.

The extreme "centralization" of the old Tsarist regime has had a blighting effect. Those who are trying to reform and decentralize the government of France tell the story of one of their Ministers of Education who boasted during one of his speeches that at that very moment—11:35 a.m.—every boy in France between the ages of fifteen and sixteen was studying the chapter in the history text-book about Cardinal Richelieu. A similar mania for uniformity is common in Russia and immensely increases the difficulty of attempts at Central Government. The diversities of humanity can be reduced to such barrack-room uniformity only by force.

This weakness is particularly noticeable in the proposed solutions of the land problem. It seems obvious to an American that the conditions vary immensely from district to district. In the northern provinces, forestry and hemp growing predominate over food-producing agriculture. A system of land tenure which admirably meets the needs of Arkhangel Province would surely be unsuited to the fertile, wheat-growing "black soil" belt or to the beet sugar districts of the Ukraine or hillside vineyards of the Caucasus. Yet nine-tenths of the bitter controversies which have split up the revolutionary parties have assumed that there must be one perfect and uniform land law for all Russia.

Another impediment to the development of a stable Central Government in Russia has been the extreme and puerile partisanship of the educated classes. The way in which the Socialist Revolutionary members of the "All-Russian Directorate" broke up the structure of the Siberian Government, in the hope of assuring the victory of their party at the next election, was typical.

We are cursed with partisanship in America—as the senatorial debates on the League of Nations show—but it is worse in Russia. With us the evil of partisan motives among our professional politicians is somewhat tempered by the fact that public opinion controls in the end. While as a rule the educated Russians—whether they are Bolsheviks. Socialists, Liberals, or Reactionaries—do not appeal to the democratic verdict of the majority. Lenin is far from being the only intellectual snob in Russia who is unwilling to trust the masses, who despises the "lethargic" majority.

The Russian people seem to me unusually tolerant, but the small educated class on top hardly knows what the word means. When a difference of opinion arises among them, it does not occur to either side to argue it out publicly and let the majority decide. They are all afraid that the majority—the stupid, illiterate Dark People—might go wrong and side with their opponents. The Bolsheviks are not the only ones who are cocksure, absolutely convinced that they—better than anyone else—know what is best for the people.

So nearly always when one group wins control of the Central Government, they neglect the practical business of governing to "consolidate" their partisan power, to prepare for elections and suppress seditious "unorthodox" ideas. Far too much time and energy is wasted in Russia on political heresy trials.

The hope for the future lies in the development of local self-government. We could expect today the election of Provincial Assemblies, which would compare favorably with our State Legislatures, from the personnel already trained in the problems of peasant communities, town and county councils. The voters would know, at least by name, the men they voted for. They could follow and to some extent control the acts of their representatives. A decade or so of provincial politics would produce men trained and equipped for national and international affairs.

In 1912, I remember, there were many friends of Mr. Wilson who feared he could not be elected because he was not well enough known. Many of his opponents used this as an argument against him. He was not a "National Figure." A good record in New Jersey for a couple of years was not supposed to be enough. There is no individual in Russia who is anywhere near as widely known as Wilson was to us in 1912.

Local and provincial self-government must be fostered not only to allow the training of a new generation for larger political spheres, but also in order that the electorate may become acquainted with them.

Any outside effort to help Russia to her feet must be based on an understanding of this difference in the problems of local and central governments.

A problem which every government the world around has to face is the organization of Police Power. The element of coercion is present in every community. There are two extreme types and most governments lie somewhere between them. At one extreme is the pure type of tyranny, where an individual or a small oligarchy hire a Pretorian Guard to enforce their will on a subject people. This used to be the common form of government. It persisted into our day in the Russia of the Romanov autocracy. The other extreme is best illustrated in the Vigilance Committee of our frontier days. There the citizens came together spontaneously to enforce the will of the whole of the community in one definite matter—generally it consisted in running down some particular "Bad Man." Its essence is that the Police Power is supported by public opinion and is exercised in behalf of the community.

Most modern governments have arrived at some compromise between these two extremes. In all large communities there are so many Bad Men, so much temptation to anti-social action by individuals, that it has proven worth while to develop the voluntary, spontaneous, and occasional Vigilance Committee into a mercenary, organized, permanent Police Department. The division of labor in creating a special Police Force allows most citizens to go about their business in peace, but yet in most modern countries an obligation still rests on the private citizen to co-operate in the prevention of crime.

In every civilized community there is a struggle for the control of the Police Power. The ideal is that it should always be the servant of all the people. There is an ever present danger that it may become the servant of some special class or vested interest. The degree in which the democratic will of the community controls the Police Power varies greatly from place to place.

The Anarchists insist that all governmental coercion is evil. But everyone else, although they may protest against individual abuses of Police Power—which are always too frequent—accept the idea in principle. The democratic ideal is to assume that the organization and policy of the Police is always readily controlled by the will of the majority.

This problem is particularly acute in Russia. The old "Force" of the Tsar's Government suddenly collapsed. Since then no government, except that of Lenin, has been able to organize a working Police Power. The others have had to rely on persuasion. Kerensky could not "force" the army to fight nor the citizens to submit to his decrees. He had to argue with them. And that to a large degree has been true of all the attempts to create a government in Siberia.

This lack of Police Power has not been an unmixed curse. Certainly, the more a government can rely on persuasion, the less it has to resort to force, the better and more democratic it is. The control of force is always a temptation to tyranny. Vologodsky's first Siberian Government at Omsk was an interesting experiment in a government with very little power trying to consolidate itself by deserving the respect and winning the consent of the governed. However, it has not been an unmixed blessing. The nonpartisan, liberal ministry of Vologodsky, the Socialist Revolutionary Directorate, and Kolchak's mugwump Dictatorship have all suffered in public esteem at home and abroad, because they could not muster sufficient force to reduce the bandit, Semyonov, to order.

There is no "organized major force" in Russia. The best, as well as the worst, government it is possible to imagine will be faced by this same problem. The nation is broken up into a myriad of hostile groups. No one of them—not even the Bolsheviks—has been able to conquer all the rest. The conditions are ripe for minority dictatorship, one minority after another.

Power is dispersed. Arms are plentiful. When the soldiers demobilized they took their weapons with them. There will be continued disorders in Russia until some government arises capable of organizing so strong a Police Power that no discontented minorities will challenge it flippantly.

Those of us who wish to "stand by" Russia must use what influence we have toward getting this "organized major force"—which will surely arise sooner or later, even if it has to wait for some unborn Napoleon or Genghis Khan—into the democratic control of the majority.

Another point which anyone who hopes to "help Russia" must bear in mind is the bitterness of civil war. Many of our efforts to bring assistance to the Russians have already come to grief through having ignored this state of mind.

It has been my luck ever since 1914 to be a target for the shafts of sarcastic incomprehensions which belligerents always let fly at neutrals. During the years before we entered the war I was mostly in Europe. After having had a hard time trying to justify the neutrality of my government in the face of what the people among whom I lived very passionately believed to be "Moral Issues," I was sent—in 1917—to Russia. Once more I found myself in the midst of a war toward which my government had adopted an attitude of neutrality—this time a civil war. The Russians whom I knew best, from both sides of the barricades, were profoundly convinced that a "moral issue" was involved in their strife—a moral issue so obvious that no honest person could be "neutral."

I had begun to think that I understood—although I did not sympathize—with this bitterness, but I was completely surprised at the effect which the proposal for a conference of all Russian factions at Princes Island had on public opinion in Siberia. I did not know that such a move was contemplated, but when I read the dispatch I thought all anti-Bolshevist parties in Russia would welcome the chance to bring the regime of Lenin before the bar of the democratic conscience of the world. They could have turned the conference into a Great High Court of Justice—beside which any trial of the Kaiser would seem unimpressive. An opportunity was offered them to authenticate the accusations they were making against Lenin and his associates. They were all appealing for outside assistance in their struggle with Bolshevism. Here was their chance to state their case to all the world. I thought they would jump at it.

They certainly jumped—but in the opposite direction. I had underestimated the bitterness of their belligerency. They wanted to execute Lenin, not try him. The attitude of the Bolsheviks was, in the reverse sense, just the same. They were willing to come to Princes Island if the verdict were given to them in advance, if they were accepted as the rightful government and all their adversaries declared outlaw rebels. Each side, out of the bitter experience of civil war, has prejudged the case. They do not want any judgment from outside. Both sides are so vehemently convinced of the justice of their cause that they resent any suggestion of compromise with injustice. They do not want us to arbitrate—they want assistance in their Holy Crusade against iniquity. Whichever side we may prefer, it is just as well to realize that as far as bitterness is concerned there is no choice between them.

A serious handicap which will weigh down heavily on any attempt to establish "good government" in Russia is the fact that very few of the people have any idea what the phrase means. The more fortunate classes have traveled widely and so have come in indirect contact with the idea. But the mass of the people have experienced only two forms of government, that of the Tsar and that of Lenin—both tyrannical and inefficient.

Taxes have always been extortions. In our American propaganda we tried to spread the idea that under a good government taxes are an investment, that the citizen should know, has not only the right but also the duty to insist on knowing, how every cent of the tax fund is expended and just what returns he gets for his money. When the Armistice stopped our work, we were planning a motion picture, "How Uncle Sam Earns his Pay." The first reel was to show how Uncle Sam collects his wages, how each American citizen contributes his share through taxation to the immense income of the government; and then several reels to show how the money goes back to the community through the work of the Departments of Agriculture and Interior. How the Coast and Geodetic Survey is of service to our sailors, how the government protects the health of the people, how children are cared for and educated on the public funds—all the thousand and one activities of the State, in which the citizen recognizes the dividends accruing on his investment in taxes. This motion picture was only an unachieved project, but we did a great deal on the same line in our printed propaganda. It was a brand-new idea to most Russians. It had not occurred to many of them that a government borrows the taxes from the people and that a good government should repay with interest.

Few people can have a concrete picture of anything which has not been part of their actual experience. So far the Revolution has been busy destroying what was old and pernicious, but now as it turns to the task of constructing a new order it suffers from the lack of experience. The people do not know what—as citizens—they should expect and demand of their government.

Very closely allied to this lack of a clear-cut ideal of what a democratic government should be like is the general subject of illiteracy. We take for granted the speed with which we can communicate through our general ability to read and write. If the Premier or President of our Western Democracies delivers an important speech, it reaches and is read by all his fellow citizens within a few hours. We are in danger of forgetting that this miracle of our civilization cannot be performed in Russia. The telegraph might take the word of some great event to every railroad station in Russia and yet it would be months and months before the news spread to a majority of Russian villages. Some of them are probably still praying for "our Holy Sovereign" the Tsar, not because of royalist sentiments, but simply because they have not heard of his abdication.

We are so used to the general ability to read and write that we forget the tremendous importance it has as a force of social cohesion. It is not only that every one in America to-day can read long arguments for or against the League of Nations and that so public opinion will crystallize more rapidly than if we had to rely solely on word of mouth. It is even more important that we have been accustomed to read about the same subjects simultaneously for several generations. In the days when only a favored few could read, government by public opinion was unthinkable. The democratization of the art of reading is the most stupendous political development of the last century. Compare, for instance, Aristotle and a modern editorial writer. More people read the thoughts of the latter within twenty-four hours than ever saw one of the precious manuscripts of the former during his entire lifetime. Compare the centuries it took before the first missionary brought the story of Christ to Britain and the speed with which the ideas of Darwin spread through our Western World. All our methods of government, all the aspirations and practical achievements of democracy, are based on the development of the printing press.

There is a thin layer on the top of Russian society—a cream which could be skimmed off without disturbing the depths below—which reads as easily as we do. But the majority of those who are classed in the census as "literate" have to spell out each long word in the newspapers letter by letter and as often as not guess at its meaning.

No matter what democratic name is given to any government in Russia, it will be for years to come a government of illiterates. This has little influence in the conduct of local affairs, but in all national and international issues involving principles or events beyond the horizon of their own experience, the electorate will be uninformed and ignorant.

SOME ELEMENTS OF THE PROBLEM

Any new government which does not devote the largest part of its budget to public education will be working on the roof of the democratic structure and not on its foundations. It would also be ignoring the most clear cut and outspoken aspirations of the nation. The "Dark People" realize their darkness and plead for light. The demand for freer educational opportunities in Russia is universal. This was the one subject on which we could always interest people in our American propaganda. They wanted to know all about our public schools. It was the one subject which entirely transcended partisanship. Professional politicians were as much interested as school-teachers and the peasants more than either. Any new government which hopes for widespread popular support must put a comprehensive program of public education in the forefront of its platform.

Of more immediate urgency—if of less fundamental importance—is the re-establishment of commerce and industry. This is a matter for experts, but even the layman can see the two basic problems of transportation and finance. All the well-intentioned efforts to help in the economic rehabilitation of Russia have so far come to grief on these rocks.

A direct exchange of produce is conceivable without money, but even such rudimentary barter cannot exist unless the commodities can be brought together. The War Trade Board office in Vladivostok could not find in that port enough goods for export to pay for one fair-sized cargo of imports. The American Government was prepared to deliver the much-needed manufactured goods on the dock, but, in spite of all the accumulation of raw material in the interior, there was none on the spot.

One of the greatest difficulties I had to face in European Russia was the procuring of print paper. The price was very little dependent on the cost of production. It was determined by transportation charges. I was for some weeks in negotiations with a large plant not fifty miles north of Moscow on the Yaroslav Railroad. The management, which had always been progressive, had accepted the New Regime and had, in cordial co-operation with the employees' "Shop Committee," maintained full production. But they were being forced to close through inability to transport their output. In the month of April, 1918, they were only able to get eight freight cars. Their normal output was ten carloads a week. Their warehouses were bursting. And week by week the deterioration of the transport system by rail and river routes has intensified.

When in the early weeks of 1919 a diplomatic accord was finally reached and an Inter-Allied Railroad Commission, with Mr. Stevens as its technical head, was created, the Trans-Siberian Railroad was sixty million roubles back on its payroll.

So the rehabilitation of the railways—like most other projected reforms—runs into the problem of finance. It will need an Alexander Hamilton, some wizard of finance, to work out a new basis for finding money for the needs of the State and some new basis for "credit transactions" between traders.

The abolition of the vodka monopoly cut a great hole, almost one-third, in the Russian Budget. Since 1914 there has been practically no commercial importation, with a corresponding drop in custom receipts. The regular collection of taxes came to a stop with the Revolution. Metal currency has disappeared. Paper money was over-issued—reluctantly under former governments, blithely under the Bolsheviks. The depreciation of the rouble in the International Exchange is tragic.

Disheartening as the situation is, it is not hopeless. The natural wealth of Russia is beyond computing. Her mines have hardly been explored. The Caucasus Oil Field is one of the richest in the world. As yet there has been only surface scratching in her deposits of coal and metals and precious stones. In spite of the wasteful use of her forests for fuel, their wealth has hardly been touched. There is enough fallow, unbroken land to raise her food production tenfold. And greatest of all her "undeveloped resources" are the minds of her people. No one can set a limit to the increase in production which would result from general education. And an entirely new source of State income has been created by the reversion of all property rights in land to the nation. In some way it must be doled out again to those who use it. No matter what system of land tenure is decided upon, Russia's treasury will surely benefit by sales, rent, or taxes.

But grain will not come to harvest on the richest soil, nor will coin come from any Eldorado, without labor. Neither taxes nor rent can be collected from the unemployed. If the statesmen of the new Russia can get the vast population back to productive work, the country will recover its solvency with surprising quickness.

The Russians will have to solve the labor problem among themselves. But if they are to make rapid recovery in their economic affairs, they will need to borrow much capital from abroad. Those who are planning the organization of government in Russia must face this problem. If they are to put under exploitation the vast natural wealth of their domain, if they are to undertake seriously the development of general education, they cannot rely immediately on the normal income of the State, they must secure large foreign loans. It will be necessary for them to win the approbation of the governments and peoples of other countries, as well as of their own electorate.

Therefore it behooves those who wish "to help Russia" to think out and formulate as clearly as possible the kind of government we would care to support in Russia, the terms on which a new government in Russia could win our approbation and our aid.

There is still another phase of this complex Russian situation which must be considered by all those who would "help" intelligently. The Russians would call it "the liquidation of the Revolution," i.e., the casting up of the account of debits and credits to see if the capital is intact, and a dividend can be declared. We would be tempted to call it "getting back to normal life" but to them it means "getting forward" to a condition of orderly progress they have never known.

So many opponents of progress have made a fetish of the word "Order," that in France the phrase *"gens d'ordre"* is synonymous with Reactionaries. But even the most eager Revolutionist believes in "Disorder" only as a transition stage to some "New Order." Russia has been in covert or open revolution for several generations. This means that the best brains of the nation's youth have been withdrawn from normal enterprise and expended in a holy crusade for Liberty. Young men and women who ordinarily should have contributed to the work of civilization as doctors, engineers, scientists, artists, teachers, have by the infamy of the old order been driven into conspiracy and open revolt. A corresponding number of older men who might have been employed at something socially useful have been kept busy hunting down these young people, spying out their plans for decreasing the misery of life, and holding the very cream of the nation in the prisons of Siberia. It is an incalculable—but very heavy—tax which disorder has laid on Russia.

On a vast scale in Russia there has been long continuation of such waste. One of the revolutionists, Gershuni, when on trial for a political assassination, said to his judges: "History will forgive me for my crime. But it will never forgive you for having driven us, who abhor bloodshed, to murder."

Some foreigners, especially Americans, have criticized the Russia of to-day for its lack of constructive brains in business, in engineering, in politics. The explanation is as simple as it is tragic. All young Russians of education and any ardor of soul have voluntarily given up the professions which we call constructive and have dedicated their lives to the war against autocracy. The bones of those who should have been the "constructive leaders" of the new Russia have been eaten by quicklime at the foot of innumerable gallows.

The more coming governments in Russia can found their structure on Justice—political and social—the fewer young people of constructive ability will they have to imprison and execute. All higher considerations aside, viewed only from the ledger point of view of dollars and cents, no nation can afford to be at war with the best of its citizens. Such political disorder as has been endemic so long in Russia is appallingly expensive. The establishment of order—an order in which all those who love justice will eagerly co-operate—must be contrived if any new Government in Russia wishes to rule over a prosperous nation.

Chapter XXX
"Hands Off" or "Stand By"

In the preceding chapter, I have tried to sketch briefly some of the elements of the problems which must be faced by any new government in Russia, and which should be given serious attention by any foreigners who wish "to help Russia." As I write, the Peace Conference at Paris has not announced any definite policy toward Russia. It may do so before this gets to press or disagreement may drag on for months. But it is possible now, without attempting to prejudge its decisions, to indicate the two extreme proposals it is considering. All the probabilities are in favor of some compromise on middle ground between these improbable extremes.

On one hand is the proposal of "Withdrawal from Russia." There are important groups in all the Entente countries who have taken for their slogan: "Hands off Russia." But I think those who are most vehement in this sense would be the first to insist that there would be nothing gained unless the "withdrawal" was complete.

There would be very little accomplished if only one or two nations acted in this matter—if Czecho-Slovakia or Japan or France or America called home their troops and the forces of the other Allies remained. Those who regard any "intervention" as a crime would be glad to see their own nation freed from what they consider "the shame" of the present situation. There are many in America who take this attitude passionately. Our troops in Russia would undoubtedly be glad to come home; it is not a pleasant field for service. But their withdrawal—if the Allies were left—would not materially help Russia. It would be regretted by very considerable sections of Russian opinion. The degree of regret and the kind of people who would regret it most differs from district to district. Where the American troops have been predominant among the Allies in the Arkhangel district, a Socialist Government has sprung up, and been maintained by us. Some of its leaders have been so radical that our immigration authorities would probably deny them admission to the United States. But it seemed to be what the people wanted and our representatives prevented a reactionary *coup d'etat* on the lines of the "Cossack Conspiracy" which upset the All-Russian Directorate at Omsk. In Siberia, where our troops have been numerous but not predominant, they have been a moderating force and their presence has been a check on the sanguinary reprisals of such reactionary leaders as the bandit, Semyonov, and the military governor, Ivanov-Rinov. The territories occupied by our troops have been cities of refuge for those who are oppressed. No one in Vladivostok would regret the withdrawal of American troops more than the Bolsheviks.

An agreement among all the Allies to withdraw all their troops would be difficult to arrive at and if it were reached the probable results would be the break-up of Russia into a number of territorial governments, some Bolsheviks, some Liberal, some Reactionary. Each one of them would have civil war within its own borders and all would be engaged in external wars to defend or enlarge their frontiers. There is no reason to believe that any one group is strong enough to conquer and dominate the rest. There would be certain gains in such a break-up. If it were long continued and sufficiently bloody, it would definitely kill the idea of extreme centralization which has been very pernicious. It would allow small and more easily manageable groups to develop a "national consciousness." It would Balkanize Russia. But there would be losses more immediate and appalling than any gains.

Most Russians of all factions would deeply regret the dismemberment of their country. It would not bring "Peace." Such a condition of chaos would invite foreign interference once more. Few nations have been so patient in such circumstances as we have been in regard to Mexico. We could not throw the protection of a Monroe Doctrine about Russia. An attempt to put in practice the "hands off Russia" policy might easily lead to a more disastrous "Intervention."

The other extreme proposal is "International Government." Enlightened Russians would resent being given the status of an African colony by the application of the mandatory system. But many of them are convinced that for the moment, with such a bewildering tangle of difficulties to overcome, there is very little hope of any Russian group successfully organizing a Central Government without help from abroad. Each faction, with the usual partisanship, would welcome international action which recognized its leaders as the legitimate government, which helped them keep together the territory of the old Empire, solved for them the difficult problems of transportation and finance, and kept "order" for them while they put the rival factions out of business.

A few Russian politicians are sufficiently broad-minded to realize that if the allied governments recognize any partisan group they would encounter the drastic opposition of all the other factions. Such Russians are striving for a coalition of all parties on a non-partisan basis. The program of this group could be summed up in the one sentence, "We must develop the local self-government bodies—Zemstvos and Town Councils—before we can hope for a stable, democratic central power."

This is so obvious that many Russians will say that they are indifferent about the form of the central authority, provided free development is assured to local government units. Some believe that an international commission—in its nature free from the blighting influence of internal partisanship—would for a period stop the absorption of the best brains of Russia in the factional squabbles of national politics and allow a concentration on the administrative problem of local affairs.

Neither of these two extreme solutions is in any way probable. In these days of immensely complicated international relations "withdrawal" is hardly more than an empty word. Even if all the men who wear the uniforms of the Allies were recalled, that would not end foreign interference in Russian affairs. Trade relations—above all finance—would still have an influence. The citizens of other nations have too great an interest in the development of Russia to permit their governments to ignore them. And on the other hand, the other nations are so exhausted by the strain of the great war that they would be reluctant—even if it were thought advisable—to assume such new responsibilities as the organization and maintenance of an international government for Russia.

There is every reason to expect a compromise between these two extremes. Some group of Russians—at least pretending to be democratic and non-partisan—will probably be recognized as an All-Russian Government and given effective assistance.

There is a very strong sentiment among all Russian factions for the preservation of the frontiers of the old empire. This is counteracted by the equally strong sentiment of several frontier groups of non-Russians for national independence. A loose federation, granting the largest autonomy to distinct racial groups, would probably come nearest to satisfying the greatest number. The desire for the preservation of territorial integrity under one sovereignty is very widespread.

In general the Foreign Offices of other countries would prefer to see one reconstituted Russian State, instead of a hodgepodge of small units. This is partly mere inertia and respect for tradition—there always has been one Russia. The older members of the Society of Nations are already rather appalled by the clamor of the new and inexperienced members. Diplomacy would not be simplified by the creation of half a dozen more governments. But there are many more cogent arguments for a united Russia than the preferences of the diplomats. It would, for instance, immensely simplify the economic rehabilitation of the country. While the war was still in progress the American Government took a firm stand against breaking up Russia by encouraging "separatist movements." I have seen no indication of a change of policy. It may, I think, be safely assumed that the tendency of the allied nations, while trying to safeguard the interests of the formerly subjugated nations, will be to preserve the frontiers of Russia as they existed in 1914. While some of the frontier nations like Poland, and Finland, will be encouraged to realize their "national aspirations," the influence of foreign diplomacy will be on the whole toward a united Russia.

There are to-day four "governments" actually exercising a large sovereignty in some parts of Russia. The Bolshevist Council of the People's Commissaires in Moscow; the northern government under Tchaikovsky; General Denikin's military regime in the southeast and the dictatorship of Kolchak in Siberia. They all face the same financial difficulties. The income from the customs has stopped with the collapse of commerce. Their receipts from taxation are negligible.

We are likely to get a false picture of the nature of the civil war in progress. Our minds are filled with the circumstances of the great campaign against Germany. The civil war in Russia resembles the greater war only in its bitterness.

Many more reports have come to me from Kolchak's army than from those of Denikin or Tchaikovsky, but I believe the conditions are practically the same on all fronts. In Siberia it is more a debate than a battle. It is rather like the wars of which Homer sang. The heroes deliver orations before they hurl their spears.

Kolchak is operating on a front so long that it would have required several million men to hold it in France or Flanders. He has perhaps a hundred thousand men. The Bolshevist forces are drawn out as thin. A quarter of a million soldiers on both sides would be a large estimate of the forces engaged on the Siberian Front between the Ural Mountains and the River Volga. But this is a fairly densely populated district. There are at least ten million peasants in the territory Kolchak has "reconquered," and a large part of them are armed. Under such circumstances propaganda is more important than artillery. If Kolchak wrote "Reaction" across his banners, if he openly pledged himself to the re-establishment of the landlords in their former estates, a large part of his own army—themselves peasants—would at once desert, and his scattered detachments would be overwhelmed by the inhabitants. Kolchak's advance will be at once halted if the Bolshevist agitators can succeed in making the people think he is reactionary. On the other hand, if Kolchak's spies in the ranks of the Red Army or behind it can persuade the people that he is a liberator from the tyranny of the Bolsheviks, his advance will be rapid. If we read in the papers that the Siberian Army has occupied or has lost the province of Perm, it means that the peasant population—immensely outnumbering the combined armies—has taken an active preference for one side or the other.

Something in the nature of a democratic election is in progress. Public opinion in the disputed territory on the relative merits of the two sides in the civil wars controls the fluctuations of the "front." It is very largely a war of propaganda.

Actual fights are rare. More commonly a propaganda victory results in an outpost suddenly changing sides. If one of Kolchak's officers is especially brutal, his command immediately turns Bolshevik. The great advance of the Siberian Army indicates that on the whole such wholesale desertions more commonly happen from the Bolshevist side, and that a great part of the present population of this district sees more chance of realizing their aspirations under Kolchak than under Lenin. General Denikin's forces in Southeast Russia are operating in even more densely populated territory. So far as the anti-Bolshevist forces make themselves unpopular in the territory they occupy their advance will be slowed up. If they advance rapidly it shows that the people are tired of Bolshevism. No amount of money which the Allies might grant to Kolchak or Denikin would make it possible for their small armies to conquer the hundred million peasants, if, as certain advocates of Bolshevism here claim, they are enthusiastic and fanatical supporters of Lenin.

This situation is clearly understood in Siberia. There is no hope of a purely military victory over the Bolsheviks if their army is loyal and the immense civilian population in the field of operations sympathizes with them. Political considerations are more important than gunpowder. This exercises a steady pressure toward liberalism on the anti-Bolshevist forces. The only available officers were trained under the Old Regime and trained leadership is necessary. But whenever an officer becomes patently reactionary he begins to "lose battles." Ivanov-Rinov is probably the ablest general in Siberia. But if he were put in command, the Bolsheviks would win all along the line. So he is transferred to the extreme east—as far as possible from the Front.

The press dispatches of June and July indicate that Trotsky has weakened his front in the south to concentrate against the Siberian Army. But the Red forces could not have advanced so successfully, no matter how heavily reenforced, unless there was serious dissatisfaction with the Kolchak Government within his army and behind it. It will be a sharp lesson to the Siberians of the danger of allowing the reactionary element to predominate even locally at the front. Some more generals, who have too strong a political following to be dismissed in disgrace, will probably be transferred to posts where they can do less damage. The Siberian Army will not begin again to advance until its own morale is strengthened and the civilian population quieted by the removal of the more stupidly reactionary officers. Those who are too dense to learn the lesson from these painful reverses will have to be retired. The more intelligent of the officers will drop the old manner and try to win the confidence of the civilian population and the loyalty of their men. No reactionary policy seems to have any chance of success. The same conditions face Denikin in South Russia. If his striking victories make him overconfident and tyrannical toward the local population, his advance will stop suddenly. The main element in the fight between Bolshevism and its opponents is the political struggle to win the support of the nation.

The great mass of the peasants are not much interested in the Central Government. They are but little concerned over the respective merits of Lenin, Kolchak, Denikin, or Tchaikovsky. They care not at all about who is the ruler in Moscow. They are wholly occupied with their local problems and judge the combatants by events in their own neighborhood. They will fight anyone who tries to take the land away from them or force them into military service.

The armed forces are evenly matched. If the allied governments agreed to recognize and support any group, they could render it quickly predominant but they could not render it stable unless they influenced it to a program which would rally popular support. A policy of reaction, any insane attempt to put the landlords back on their estates, a failure to accept the results of the Revolution in economics and politics, will give the country back to Bolshevism. Unless the allied governments insist on very definite guarantees in this matter any effort on their part to bring order out of chaos in Russia will be worse than wasted.

Of the four candidates for "recognition" it is least likely that the Allies will deal with Lenin. He is outspokenly hostile. Quite aside from the dispute as to his relations with Germany, he has always been venomous and vehement in his denunciations of the Allies. He does not believe in the ideals of democracy and does not consider himself bound by any agreements he may find it expedient to make. The other three at least profess cordiality. But neither Tchaikovsky, Denikin, nor Kolchak have a fair chance of stabilizing their regime without formal recognition, generous and continued moral and financial support.

In the end the man who pays the piper calls the tune, so it does not seem to me very important which person is chosen for recognition. If it is decided to recognize some Russian Government—and that seems to be the trend—the important thing is the condition under which such recognition and support are granted.

In all probability the Russian situation will, for many years to come, resemble the prewar regime in Egypt. The laws and decrees bore the signatures of the Egyptian Khedive and his native ministers, but they were originated and edited by the British. Some outside agency representing a League of Nations, or some group of nations which has shown its ability and desire to give effective aid, will indirectly control much of the policy of the Russian Government until such a time as the Russians themselves, recovered from the exhaustion of the Great War and the upheaval of the Revolution, regain the internal strength which history shows to be the only effective protection from foreign interference.

Those who would "help Russia" must strive to make this temporarily inevitable, foreign influence in Russian development as beneficent and democratic as possible. The conditions on which outside support is given to Russia are of supreme importance.

It is possible that the League of Nations will speedily develop sufficient power to be the dominant "outside influence" in Russia. We may see it sending a High Commissioner to advise and within certain limits control the actions of the new Russian Government. This would be the simplest and most clear-cut arrangement. But the greatest danger that faces the young League is that it may be tempted to assume responsibilities beyond its strength. It will probably be several years or decades before it acquires enough prestige for such a task. In the immediate future we will more probably see the various nations sending ambassadors to Russia. They will be relieved from the necessity of joint action with their colleagues—an ideal imposed upon them by the war—and each will be free to follow the interests of his own nation.

The American ambassador to the newly recognized Russian Government will be in an especially favored position. Russia is in pressing need of loans and we have more money to lend than the other nations. Russia is in great need of our manufactured goods and of a market for her raw material. She needs our machine tools and machinery, she needs the technical help of our engineers. She will want the service of much of our merchant marine. The American Embassy ought to be the center of diplomatic gravity in the New Russia.

We can imagine an American ambassador arriving in the capital of New Russia and presenting his credentials to the new executive—whom we must also imagine. And we can hope that our representative is well chosen, a man of strength and practical experience, a forward-looking man, typifying the democratic aspirations of our people, big enough, withal, to realize that there is room in the world for every generous effort, that no nation has a monopoly of good intentions, that just as our business experience has shown us that we can sell more goods in an open market than in one we have closed to our rivals, so in the market of wares of good-fellowship, the more competitors we have the better. In short, let us hope for a man tall enough to look above and beyond the jealousies and intrigues of ordinary diplomatic practice.

After the exchange of set speeches and formal courtesies, we can imagine him returning to his embassy and settling down to a period of waiting. The Russian Foreign Office would be expecting him to call for more informal discussion and he would wait patiently till he was summoned. The Russians are born bargainers and suspicious of strangers. Many of our efforts to help them in the past have come to grief through ignoring this. When we have made some frank and direct offer, the Russian authorities have stayed awake nights trying to figure out what extortionate concession we wanted in exchange. Our efforts to rehabilitate their railroads were delayed by such suspicion. The efforts of the War Trade Board to start again the wheels of commerce faded out in the same way.

The first question in any deal is, what party needs the other's commodities most. Does A need B's automobile more than B needs A's money? We are in a very strong bargaining position toward Russia, now that the war is over and her utility as an ally against Germany is no longer in question. American commerce is today offered many more opportunities than it can accept. There are more applicants for such excess capital as we have to loan than we can possibly satisfy. If left wholly to private initiative and the accustomed search for profit, American enterprise will not turn toward Russia. This fact does not seem to be realized by the public at home; it certainly is not in Russia. In Vladivostok I have seen half a dozen agents of great American interests arrive—encouraged by our government—in high hopes of reaping a rich harvest in the depleted Russian market. There was one who kept his smile for a month before he left for China. The others took the next boat home or at best stuck it out a couple of weeks. The American merchant can sell his goods elsewhere on much surer and much shorter credit. The American engineer can get a better salary and a more stable labor force in other countries. And the American banker, unless he is rich enough to wait a long time for the return of his money to risk a big gamble, turns in disgust to safer fields. If our government decides on a policy of "Hands off Russia," it means that Russia will be boycotted by all but the wildest speculators. Most capitalists are timid, and they have too many opportunities elsewhere to be tempted to plunge on the Russian risk.

We do not need anything from Russia. Therefore it would be well for this imaginary ambassador to wait till he is sent for. When the new government asked—as it surely would—for some specific help, he could state his position without danger of being charged with officiousness or meddling.

"Recognition" is merely a formal affair; it does not imply any great cordiality. The United States exchanged diplomatic representatives with the Tsar, but there was very little friendship. So our ambassador could explain that if the new government desired cordial help from America it would be necessary for it to show an intention to govern in a spirit congenial to our own. A government in Russia which attempted to re-establish the old order, which suppressed popular liberties and stained itself with vengeful cruelty against the opposition could not hope for widespread Sympathy in America. Such a government could expect no friendly financial aid if it needed loans. It would have to come to the open market and outbid all other applicants for credit. On the other hand a government which was obviously winning the consent of the governed, endeavoring to build up local self-government and the ideal of majority rule, would be sure of enthusiastic popular support in America. It would be very expensive for a Russian government suspected of reactionary intentions to float a loan in Wall Street. It would be easy to secure wide popular subscription on most favorable terms to build little red schoolhouses all over Russia.

The conditions of American recognition and support of any government in Russia will be very much more important than the personnel of that government.

Chapter XXXI
Educational Co-operation

The question of "official recognition" is an affair of the government. Many of the elements which will determine action are not within our knowledge nor subject to our influence.

There is, however, one immediate concrete thing which we all—in our capacity of private citizens—can do "to help Russia." The greatest need of her people is for increased opportunities for education and these we can furnish free from all partisan bias. We can help them in their great task of public education without trying to judge between their political factions.

The organization of the necessary campaign against illiteracy is a stupendous affair, which must be arranged by the Russians themselves. It is hardly possible for us to help in teaching a language which we do not understand. Russia has good teachers for such work, plenty of them, but they have no adequate equipment.

When reading about the work our American people have done for devasted France and Belgium, I have often wished that a committee might be organized to build a model schoolhouse in Moscow or Petrograd, a string of smaller schoolhouses for the rural communities. It would give them an idea of what a free people can do for the children.

A famous French surgeon told me that the greatest service which America had done for the wounded French soldiers had been not the generous war charities, but the organization of the American Hospital in Neuilly years before the war. It had been built very largely for the selfish interest of the rich expatriated American Colony of Paris.

But it had exhibited to the French doctors the American system of hospital organization and of graduated trained nurses. French nursing had always been done by Sisters of Charity—well intentioned but untrained. The existence there near Paris of an American Hospital organized on our lines had profoundly and beneficially affected French practice long before 1914.

I would like to see an American School unit put up in one of the great cities of Russia a normal college, training young teachers by actual practice in a great modern city school building, with all its affiliated branches—diet kitchen, cooking school, medical examination rooms, gymnasium, auditorium, and outdoor playground.

Once such a unit was built it could be turned over to the municipality with endowment for its upkeep. They would be quick to grasp its meaning and how to manage it. There are no such school outfits in Russia to-day. We could so easily give them an ideal to build to. I like to think of a motto from the great Frenchman, Danton, carved over the portal: *"Apres le pain, l'education est le premier besoin du peuple."* We could make it a sermon in stone on the text: "Education, the road to Democracy."

But the need is as great and more accessible to our immediate help in higher education. In the years before the Great War, the Russian universities, while admirable, were inadequate. A very large percentage of educated Russians had been forced to complete their technical training abroad. Doctors, agricultural experts, teachers, civil and electrical engineers, chemists, men and women of every profession went to foreign universities to supplement the education they could get at home.

Since 1914 very many of those who had gained a technical education have been killed at the front. During the war, study in foreign schools was impossible and the universities at home practically closed. The young men who should have been training for the professions have been soldiers. And so to-day Russia is shorter than ever in trained technicians. The need for opportunities for study is crying.

Before the war most young Russians who went abroad to study naturally went to Germany. The universities there had a world-wide prestige, they were close at hand, the cost of living for students was low. Such Russians as disliked the German Kultur and preferred to study in Switzerland or France had to pay about 25 percent extra to indulge their preference. The cost of travelling to America and of living here in our universities was prohibitive.

The very week in which the Bolsheviks signed their peace at Brest-Litovsk, the newspapers announced that the German Government would offer special facilities to Russian students. The embassy, opened by Von Mirbach in Moscow, organized a special bureau to attend to the applications for passports to study in Germany. As usual the Germans were very much on the job. They offered a large number of scholarship purses to encourage poor students to come to their schools. They hope, and are taking active measures, to train and mold the mind of educated Russians even more in the future than they have done in the past.

Here is an immense opportunity for America. If we wish for friendly relations with the New Russia, if we wish to popularize our ideals of government there, there is no better means than the encouragement of Russian students in our institutions of learning. In no way could we do more "to help Russia" than by the establishment of a great scholarship endowment which would attract Russian students to America to complete their technical training. The allotments would have to be sufficiently generous to cover the differences in cost between coming here and going to Germany. But no money could be better spent.

INDEX

advertising, nationalization of, by Bolsheviks as a device for controlling the press 88–89
agrarian programs of political parties in Russia 44–49. *See also* Land.
agrarian revolution in Russia, viewed as a fundamental fact and the greatest economic accomplishment of the revolution 100
Allies, policy and approach 82–91
All-Russian Congress of Co-operative Societies 29–31
All-Russian Directorate 117–19.
America, United States, representatives in Russia 84–91

Bloody Sunday 76–77
Bolsheviks 67–72
Breshkovskaia, Katherine 49
Brest-Litovsk, Peace of 53–54, 92
British representatives in Russia 83–91
Buchanan, Sir George, British ambassador 85

Civil War in Russia 120–21
Cooperative Movement in Russia 29–31
Cossack conspiracy 117–19
Czecho-Slovaks 105–10

Denikin 92, 164–65
diplomacy of Allies in Russia 82–91
Duma, Imperial 41, 48

education, as a means of helping Russia 170–72

Gapon, Father Georgi 76–77

"Hands-Off Russia" policy vs. "stand by Russia" policy 162–69

Heid, representative of War Trade Board in Vladivostok 132–33
Horvath, General, Russian governor and general manager of Chinese Eastern Railroad 102–03, 105, 108–09, 126

Intervention, Allied 142–45

Japan, help of and intervention by 73, 106, 131, 142–45

Kerensky, Alexander 55–59
Kolchak, Admiral 120–29
Kornilov, General Lavr 56

land, problem of, main issue in Russia 44–49
Lenin, Vladimir 8–11, 83–97
Lockhart, Bruce. British representative to Bolshevik government 83
Lvov, Prince, Provisional Government 25–28, 35

Marx, Karl 8–9
Miliukov, Paul, leader of Constitutional Democrats 35
mir system in Russia 45–49
Mirbach, Count von, German ambassador in Moscow 79–81

Nieselle, General, head of French Military mission in Russia 83–85

Omsk, first Siberian government 111–13; All Russian Directorate 114–16

peace as burning issue 50–54
press, Bolshevik methods of control 65–66
Princes Island Conference (Prinkipo) 124
Provisional Government 23–26

psychological difficulties in dealing with
    Russians 135–41

Questionnaire for the Bourgeoisie 181

"Railroad Mission" by US to Russia 130–31
Red Cross in Russia 84–85, 138
Reed, John 84
Russian psychology 135–41

Siberia, military situation and governments
    101–29
Siberian Railroads 101–04
Socialist Revolutionaries 41
Soviet 32–37
Spirodonova, Marie, leader of SR Party 48
Stevens, John F. head of US RR Mission to
    Russia 130–31
Stolypin, Petr, land reform 69

Tchernov, leader in SR party 48
Ten Days that Shook the World 84

Vologodsky 111–13, 117, 126

zemstvos 27–31

www.ingramcontent.com/pod-product-compliance
Lightning Source LLC
Chambersburg PA
CBHW032026230426
43671CB00005B/210